Strategic Marketing and the Future of Consumer Behaviour

Strategic Marketing and the Future of Consumer Behaviour

Introducing the Virtual Guardian Angel

Theo B.C. Poiesz

Professor of Economic Psychology and Professor of Health Care Marketing, TiasNimbas Business School, Tilburg University, the Netherlands

W. Fred van Raaij

Professor of Economic Psychology, Department of Social Sciences, Tilburg University, the Netherlands

Edward Elgar
Cheltenham, UK • Northampton, MA, USA

Published by
Edward Elgar Publishing Limited
The Lypiatts
15 Lansdown Road
Cheltenham
Glos GL50 2JA
UK

Edward Elgar Publishing, Inc.
William Pratt House
9 Dewey Court
Northampton
Massachusetts 01060
USA

Reprinted 2008

A catalogue record for this book
is available from the British Library

Library of Congress Cataloguing in Publication Data
Strategic marketing and the future of consumer behavior : introducing the virtual guardian angel / edited by Theo B.C. Poiesz, W. Fred van Raaij.
    p. cm.
  Includes bibliographical references and index.
  1. Marketing–Management. 2. Marketing–Forecasting. 3. Consumer behavior–Forecasting. 4. Strategic planning. I. Poiesz, Theo. II. Raaij, W. Fred van.
  HF5415.13.S8776 2007
  658.8'02–dc22

                                                        2007038602

ISBN 978 1 84376 772 5

Printed and bound in Great Britain by the MPG Books Group

Contents

Figures

Tables

Preface

We started this book a number of years ago through a genuine curiosity about future consumer behaviour. Impressed by the speed and impact of many market developments, we assumed that consumer behaviour will be seriously affected by these developments in the years to come, and that this will have important strategic implications for the market supply side.

Thus we were stimulated to predict the future; an ambitious and risky adventure. We needed this book to legitimize the approach taken. No prediction can be guaranteed to be correct and neither can this one. In order to stay on the safe side, we talked to literally hundreds of marketeers and strategists. Their comments have sharpened our thinking, adapted our viewpoints, and encouraged us to continue. The vast majority of them supported our viewpoint. Several marketeers doubted or disagreed with our vision, and some agreed with the general idea but disagreed with the time period that it would need to materialize.

The first version of this book was written in Dutch. In 2003 the book received the Marketing Literature Award of the Platform of Innovation Management. This led to many invitations to present our viewpoints and to consult organizations in the adoption of the strategic direction specified in this book. There are now various initiatives in many markets, including non-profit markets such as health care, which do signal that the view presented here has potential value.

We understand that this does not allow us become overconfident. Therefore, we present this book as a 'grand' but not unlikely hypothesis on the future, combining three trends on client relationships, product bundling and sophistication, and the applications of information and communication technology. The combination of these three trends leads us to a largely uncharted future with opportunities and threats for businesses and consumers.

We hope that this book may provide an agenda for discussion on future scenarios. And who knows, the book may even help to shape the future.

Theo Poiesz and Fred van Raaij
Tilburg, the Netherlands

1. Predicting the Future

Predicting is difficult, especially when it concerns the future
(Wim Kan, Dutch cabaret performer)

SUMMARY

Modern saturated markets are becoming increasingly more complex, with more (international) competition, fully developed products, the Internet and SMS as new marketing channels, and new instruments such as customer databases. How can marketers still create distinctive value for their products and services in these crowded markets? Consumer needs are often too volatile and too uncertain to serve as a solid base for product development. In this book, we attempt to look five years ahead with a scenario method to indicate developments in consumer behaviour, while taking into account new strategic marketing opportunities and requirements.

INTRODUCTION

In the past, the seller and the buyer met each other at a pre-arranged place and time, for instance at the cattle or butter market. Here, product presentations, negotiations and transactions took place. For both parties the situation was familiar and rather predictable and the roles of both parties were clear. Market structures and processes were simple and clearly arranged. Marketing as such did not exist and did not need to exist. Commercial activities were limited to sales techniques and even these were transparent: 'Buy Johnson cooking pots!' or 'Visit the circus performance in town!' as the signs of two sellers proclaimed. The purpose of the communication (which was predominantly personal) was to indicate that the product or the service was available, that it had excellent quality and, moreover, was surprisingly cheap, whether this was true or not. Other marketing instruments had not yet been developed. The producer typically was also the seller. Products were manufactured primarily to fulfil the basic needs of consumers. Basic needs led to basic products. Competition was still limited, because supply and demand matched rather closely. The price was determined by the costs, the profit, the seller's persuasiveness, and whatever consumers were capable of paying and willing to pay. The distribution was limited to the meeting point – the market place. If a seller's supply exceeded demand at a particular market place, the number of market places was simply increased in order to sell the surplus. The hawker was the marketer *avant la lettre*. Instruments such as branding and direct mail were still unknown; wire- and cable-based techniques awaited invention; auditory and visual communication were restricted by human sensory systems; the mere prediction of future techniques such as radio and television probably would have led to the fire stack, and techniques such as SMS and the Internet were way beyond imagination.

MORE COMPLEX MARKETS

It was a long time ago that the face-to-face meeting at the market place was the rule rather than the exception. Since that time, the market has developed into a metaphor. The market itself, the market supply, and the market demand have become increasingly complex. The interaction between supply and demand created structures and processes of almost unparalleled complexity. Which consumer or final customer these days is still able to understand how the supply side of the market is organized? Complicated chains of specialized suppliers have developed in which almost no individual suppliers are capable of providing the desired end product on their own. Suppliers function in value chains in which the partners are mutually dependent and compete with parties in other chains (or even the same chain).

At the supply side of the market, several parties have acquired different roles: producers, wholesalers, industrial buyers, retailers, intermediaries, mediators, brokers, matchmakers, regulators, inspectors, employers, employees, marketers and, of course, managers. Each of these parties has their own place, role and function within the total market process and is here, more or less, indispensable. Each party is positioned at a particular location within a particular value chain and provides their own explicit value to the product. The parties and their roles are not always neatly separated from each other. They may show overlap and may sometimes even be completely integrated. One supplier may service a variety of different, even competitive chains. The same customer may enter into transactions with different suppliers. A party may be both supplier and customer within the same chain. And suppliers and customers may even be found within the same organization, business unit, or department ('internal marketing').

Market structures that once were established and gradually developed into their present form, are now rapidly changing. Due to market developments, the function of certain links in the chain may become weak or obsolete, which raises the question of whether their function can be taken over by other links in the chain. This is an interesting issue, for the fewer the links, the lower the costs, the lower the final price to the end user, and the more attractive the total proposition to the final customer. The issue is also interesting as it points to the possibility of internal competition within the chain. For example, the Dell computer company skips the retail channel (disintermediation). For the purpose of improving efficiency and lowering costs, the supply side may be integrated backward or forward within the chain. Links within the chain merge, shortening the chain. A market party takes over the function that was originally performed by another party. In order to increase value, a chain may hook up with another chain and may even form networks of mutually supporting parties. Market relationships are formed by collaboration and competition. And even these may be combined. Collaboration does not exclude some internal competition, and competitors may to some extent collaborate (for example, Sony and Philips) to support their mutual interests – for example to set international standards. Airlines tend to join forces in international alliances. In doing so, they collaborate and compete at the same time. There is collaboration within branches (airlines, automobile importers) and there is collaboration across the boundaries of the branches (export organizations).

So, different types of structures, processes and movements may be observed within and between chains. Tasks and functions that once appeared to be an essential part of a particular organization may suddenly become the subject of discussion and may be outsourced or sold. A department that initially was a legitimate cost centre may be required to become a self-supporting unit, may have to change into a profit centre, may be 'put in the store window' – available for the highest bidder, or may be closed – to be replaced by an external party with a better offer. The result is that growth and stagnation, creation and dissolution coexist in the market and give it the qualities of a living organism. However, this in itself does not guarantee a continuous improvement of market performance. The market is an arena in which a diffuse power game is played at different levels with ever-changing players, playing fields, playing rules, referees and spectators. The game varies in transparency so that even the fittest may not survive. Players attempt to survive by using their scarce resources of labour, capital and knowledge. The party that uses these resources to produce the greatest added value as experienced by the customer, is most likely to survive. This raises the question of which conditions best support the creation of added value. This question will be addressed in different ways in this book.

The market – or the collection of market segments – is not only turning out to be exceedingly complex, but also extremely volatile. The market is like a living and especially lively (active or hyperactive) organism. Compare this with the original concept that we started with: the market as a stable and well-organized place where predictable transactions occurred and where the parties clearly knew their own roles and functions.

SEARCH FOR ADDED VALUE

Due to the fact that market supply increases much faster than market demand, competition is becoming more and more critical for suppliers. In principle, competition may occur in a market with the aid of two instruments: added value (product differentiation) and price. Treacy and Wiersema (1995) distinguish a third strategy: customer intimacy, adapting products and services to customers' needs and desires. This third strategy is one that is central in this book as well. Here, marketing does not aim for a standard-quality product or service (a commodity) at a low price, but for a product or service with a high, distinctive quality at a high price. Added value is the critical notion here. It means that the customer perceives or experiences more value as compared to some reference point. The reference point may be, for example, an expectation with regard to a product, or an experience with a competing product. The supplier chooses a position on the continuum and protects the product's position against the activities of competitors.

Due to the hyperactivity displayed in many markets, the number of free market positions is being reduced dramatically. Niches are becoming increasingly smaller and more difficult to find. Some established positions are like impregnable bastions. For many products a free entrance to the market no longer exists, although it should be noted that the Internet and direct marketing lowered the market entrance threshold for some. Whoever still wants to determine their own way in the market needs to have abundant resources. The amount of resources should be sufficient to make more commercial 'noise' (that is advertising) than the competitor or to buy the market party that stands in the way.

A limited number of parties are able to follow a price strategy due to the large scale by which the fixed costs can be divided over many product units. Other parties – the majority – have to rely on strategies that focus on creating added value for which the customer is willing to pay a higher price.

Market segments exist for both strategies. In principle neither strategy is superior to the other. Yet this book focuses on added value as the core concept of marketing. We want to see marketing as a continuous search for new or improved products and services by strategies such as customization and differentiation. In principle, marketing is focused on growth through added value rather than growth through price cuts. Price competition is a symptom of high market maturity. Mature markets are characterized by a relative lack of innovation. Ultimately, progress is dependent on the increase of value, not on the decrease in price.

Price-based competition is often considered a second best strategy (even though cost control can be an art in itself). After all, if producers cannot make their mark through added value, they are forced to rely on a low-price strategy. In an increasingly complex and evermore volatile market, we feel that the question of added value is more intriguing than the question of how sales can be increased through price cuts. So if suppliers cannot add value, they condemn themselves to price-based competition. Added value is a continuous challenge as it tends to suffer from inflation. Once achieved, a differential advantage may have a short life because customers get accustomed to the added value and may even take it for granted. The mail-order company that could deliver goods to the customer within 24 hours had a clearly noticeable added value at first, though this 24-hour delivery time has now become the standard for mail-order companies and is no longer considered to be a surplus value. Added value and continuous innovation go hand in hand. Similar to a satellite that remains outside the gravitational pull of the earth by maintaining sufficient speed, a product needs to innovate continuously in order to stay away from the threat of 'commoditization'.

First, added value needs to be created; then, it needs to be communicated. Just one of the two activities is insufficient. An innovation that is not communicated to the target audience will perish due to obscurity. Communication about a so-called innovation ('NEW!') without really presenting any form of added value lacks credibility and may lead to a damaged reputation for the supplier.

In short, added value in the absence of marketing is unthinkable, and without added value, products are easily perceived as being too expensive. For this reason it is not surprising that marketing has become increasingly important over the past decades. This observation does not only apply to the so-called profit organizations, but also – increasingly – to non-profit (or not-for-profit) organizations such as hospitals, universities and charity organizations. Two developments are worth noting here. The first is that non-profit organizations are starting to discover the value of marketing insights. The second is that a number of traditional non-profit organizations are becoming more and more self-supporting by the reduction of external (government?) support. The free market forces them to understand that it is essential to claim and defend a position vis-à-vis the competition. Therefore, this book is not only for the traditional marketing-oriented commercial companies, but also for all organizations and institutions that, for their survival, depend upon the ability to provide added value to their customers. In their book 'Redefining Health Care', Porter and Teisberg (2006) emphasize the need to compete on added value in the health care sector.

The tremendous competitive pressure has resulted in growing attention to the development of marketing and in the professionalization of the marketing function of companies and institutions. Organizations that fall behind with their marketing activities risk entering the dreaded sphere of 'commoditization' and price competition. Due to these market and marketing developments, not only have the number of marketing instruments expanded significantly, but also the number of choice options within these instruments.

Added Value in a Complex, Volatile Market

The main goal of market organizations is to create and retain customers. The end user or final consumer is the rationale for the existence of all parties in the value chain and is the point of convergence for all processes related to production and marketing. All decisions and movements in a market are ultimately intended to optimize the supply for the end user. Even the role of a customer, who is located higher in the value chain and therefore also functions as a supplier himself (for example customers of semi-manufactured articles, dealers and intermediaries) is subordinate to the role of the end user. In essence, the choice made by the consumer from the total supply of goods and services may be compared with the vote of the citizen in the political process. With a purchasing decision, consumers cast a vote: 'I believe in you!' Consumers vote with their euros, pounds and dollars. At the most basic level, this suggests an important distinction between various types of 'voters'. Some consumers choose a certain product or brand based on a strong conviction; some consumers choose more or less arbitrarily; some consumers select the brand with the lowest price; some consumers accidentally do not choose a particular product or brand; and some consumers even deliberately vote against a certain product or brand. This distinction alone suggests that the pursuit of added value requires a much finer segmentation than the rough distinction between purchasers, potential purchasers and non-purchasers. Companies should know whether consumers perceive added value and whether they interpret the added value as intended by the suppliers.

Are customers in a complex and volatile market capable of determining the added value of a product? Or does the principle of the dominance of added value only apply in a market with perfect competition, in which consumers are fully aware of the total supply, the prices, and the differences between the various products in terms of their added value?

It is clear that in a market that is complex and non-transparent, and in which product differentiation obscures the comparability of products and services, customers are unlikely to develop a clear picture of the supply. This allows some suppliers to ask a higher price than would be possible in a fully transparent market, or to present less value for the set price. In principle, the Internet might be able to increase the transparency of the market and to clarify the differences between the price–quality relationships. The Internet might lead to price erosion (Bertrand competition) for those products that do not offer a clear added value. Here the question is to what extent the Internet is actually capable of informing the consumer so that an accurate assessment of (added) value differences can be made.

PERSPECTIVE OF THE CONSUMER

The critical role played by the consumer makes it necessary for suppliers to consider the developments in markets and marketing from the perspective of the consumer. The consumer is the central party around which the market revolves. From the professional perspective of the supplier, the market may often be fairly well surveyed, and developments may also be reasonably monitored. However, the consumer does not feel the need to fathom complicated market structures, market processes and rapidly occurring developments in the market. As the market is structured differently for each product, consumers do not desire to have an overall and accurate view on the functioning of the total market. Since developments occur in such rapid succession it is not worthwhile for consumers to be continuously updated.

It is not an exaggeration to state that from the perspective of the consumer, the market is chaotic and non-transparent. Usually, consumers do not have an overview of what is going on in the market, nor do they have a full overview of the supply. They are not able to characterize the products correctly in terms of added value, and they are not able to distinguish all marketing activities in terms of the relevant supplier and product. Added value is often the intention of the marketer, yet, considering the above, may be very difficult to realize at the level where it counts most. May added value still be created at the consumer level – where it really (only?) matters? This is a difficult but also important question, since added value which cannot be made noticeable, visible or understandable to the consumer cannot have the effects as desired and expected by the supplier.

This creates a curious paradox. On the one hand, marketing is needed to support the added value. On the other hand, marketing kills the perception of added value. Marketing has reached a point where it suffers under its own activities. The more massively, frequently and intensively marketing activities are applied in order to generate and communicate added value for individual products, the less transparent the market becomes, and the more difficult it is for marketing to convince consumers of added value. More and more, marketing has become its own competitor.

Marketing and Consumers

The supply side of the market swarms with attempts to intimidate consumers, to inform them, to persuade them, to deceive them and to guide them. The countless products, services, varieties, types, brands, stores, messages, promotions, discounts, packaging materials, media, sponsored events, bonus programmes, savings stamps, affiliation systems (airline bonus miles) and customer loyalty cards make the simple consumer dizzy. At the aggregate level (regarding combined markets and products), marketing is a massive and confusing phenomenon.

The supply side overwhelms its beloved consumers through an excess of commercial activities. While individual suppliers are focused on creating an even more intensive approach towards consumers, their activities at the aggregate level seem to create a boomerang effect. There is overload of information and overload of products, services and brands. Too many alternatives lead to decision delay, inertia and less satisfaction with the selected product or service (Schwartz, 2004). Consumers become increasingly alienated from the market, are no longer aware of the existence of many products and services, and are no longer able to assess accurately the value of many other products and services. Added value, as the core concept of marketing, is gradually but definitely becoming an illusion. Marketing is making itself impossible, and this is a euphemism.

NEEDS AS THE BASIS FOR MARKETING?

Let us return to square one. One of the traditional marketing principles is the idea that the market supply should be optimally synchronized with the interests and needs of consumers. This sounds like a cliché. After all, has it not always been the purpose and intention of suppliers to meet the needs and wants of the consumer? Ask what the consumer wants and try to deliver this in the best way possible. Against the backdrop of the market and the marketing changes described earlier, this cliché acquires a special meaning. The starting point is that the supply side should adjust itself to the demand side and not vice versa. However, this assumes that the needs and wants of consumers may be identified. Or that consumers are capable of knowing and formulating their own needs, wants, desires and wishes. Yet a number of problems exist with these concepts, which may be subsumed under the concept of 'need':

1. In the present, the technological progress in the market occurs more rapidly than consumers are capable of following, and the competitive pressure requires a continuous focus on added value in relation to the existing supply. In this time, consumer needs have a tendency to lag behind actual developments. This means that needs are bad counsellors in marketing policy making. The logical sequence – demand or need first, then supply – is slowly reversed. Supply creates needs. But this is not always the case. Suppliers need to invest before they know the match with consumer needs, which implies the risk that there is no match and that scarce resources are spent in vain on research, development, production and marketing. To reduce this risk, suppliers may study consumer problems or negative consumption experiences in order to anticipate what consumers might find useful ('need') in the future, though it basically means that needs and demand follow the supply and do not, or hardly ever, provide direction to product development.

2. Another problem is that needs tend to be unstable, which also happens to be generally true for many consumer ambitions, desires, wants, wishes and preferences. Consumers demonstrate an odd phenomenon called 'habituation'. This means that a need, after having been satisfied, expands into an even larger need or to a need at a higher level, until that need has also been satisfied and, again, adjusts itself in an upward direction. A satisfied customer is a temporary phenomenon at best. The underlying mechanism is called the preference drift or the 'hedonic treadmill' (see, for example, Van Praag, 1971). In their own need treadmill, consumers run around from satisfaction to habituation. Habituation is followed by a new need, and need fulfilment is followed by habituation, and so on. The cycle repeats itself, albeit at an increasingly higher level. The hedonic treadmill is both a curse and a blessing for suppliers. It is a curse because it makes consumer needs difficult to define and elusive, but it is a blessing because it means that market demand is a never-ending story. Demand cannot be satisfied indefinitely. The supplier's work is never done.

3. A final problem related to the need concept is that if the supply actually does match the need of a consumer segment, this will still not guarantee success. The reason is that it is difficult to meet two conditions for acceptance of a new market supply. The first condition is that the demand side should be aware of the very existence of the new product or the new service. The second is that the consumer should be

9

able to recognize the relative value of this new product or service compared with the existing products. If both conditions are not met, market success may be elusive even though there is an optimal match with the need in an objective sense. Even a perfect product may not sell itself.

The various problems with the need concept could be a reason to remove it from the list of relevant marketing concepts altogether. The need concept is still used by suppliers, but in an asymmetrical fashion. If a product has been successful, then it is claimed – in hindsight – that a 'need' was fulfilled. At the same time, this 'need' cannot be used to determine – beforehand – whether a product will be a success or not.

To summarize, we can state that in recent years developments have occurred so rapidly that it is not clear how well market supply is (still) synchronized with market demand. It is also increasingly unclear which role marketing plays in this regard. The question concerning the significance of marketing has become increasingly important over the past few years. Given the current developments, the answer will determine the rationale for marketing in the years to come. Originally, marketing was the answer to market saturation, but now marketing itself seems to be approaching a saturation point. Marketing is suffocating under its own weight.

A PROVISIONAL CONCLUSION

While most companies view and present themselves as customer-oriented, in reality they may still be very product-oriented. Companies may not focus on added value for the consumer, but on added value in relation to the competitor (who, by the way, lost sight of the consumer as well). The result is that products may fail to match the way consumers function (either physically, mentally or psychologically). Contemporary products show a tendency to outgrow the consumer. With increasingly elaborate but unclear functions, these products seem intended to lead their lives independently of that of the consumer. Due to the technology push products show a tendency to become so sophisticated that proper usage would require, almost literally, taking a training course. Laptops, palmtops, mobile phones, software programs, car accessories, and video and audio equipment have extensive manuals and functions that are seldom used. Consumers do not have the time for these instructions, and therefore, they restrict themselves to using only a few of the available functions. The same applies to fast-moving consumer goods, which are 'supported' by such an abundance of product information that as a result consumers are kept from being informed. We assume that there is a curvilinear (inverted U-shaped) relationship between the number of functions of a product and the number of functions that are actually being used – its functionality. Stated differently, we assume that a curvilinear relationship exists between the assumed added value and the actual added value for the customer. See Figure 1.1.

Number of used functions

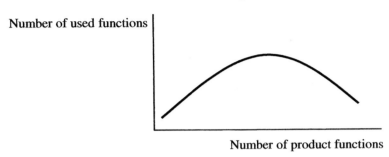

Number of product functions

*Figure 1.1 Relationship between the number of available product
functions and the number of used functions*

ANTICIPATING THE FUTURE

It does not seem legitimate to assume that the market problems will spontaneously be alleviated or even disappear over time. On the contrary, it seems fair to suggest that the problems will become more manifest in the coming years. We must therefore consider the question of how marketing will develop in the near future. The answer to this is important for suppliers who need to design a strategy. The answer is also relevant for the strategic position of marketing itself.

We will address the question by considering the supply side and the demand side separately, with the understanding that supply and demand form the two sides of the same coin. They are inextricably tied to each other and each owes the other its very existence. This means that developments on the one side are immediately noticeable on the other side. But it needs to be emphasized that the demand side is the ultimate criterion. It is the customer or end user who, ultimately, assesses and decides on the purchases and who evaluates the (added) value being provided. For this reason, the consumer is not only the point of convergence for marketing activities, but is also the focus of the analysis presented in this book. What will the market look like in the next few years? What will change? What are the consequences for marketing? And what does this mean for future consumers?

THE TASK OF THIS BOOK

A prediction of future consumer behaviour is like an equation with two unknown factors. Insight into contemporary consumer behaviour is rather limited. Therefore, insight into future consumer behaviour is risky at best. Nevertheless, this is the book's objective. We attempt to give an answer to the question of what the future market of the consumer looks like, how the future consumer will react, and what this, in turn, will mean for future marketing activities.

Within this ambitious objective we will have to restrict our scope and will do this specifically with regard to five areas:

1. A focus on Western economies with their saturated markets and their expansive infrastructures. Markets in underdeveloped countries or regions are beyond our scope.
2. It is not our intention to present strategic conclusions and recommendations on individual products and services. Instead, we will limit ourselves to an inventory of general developments and their consequences. Readers who are interested in the impact of general developments on specific products and services should draw their own conclusions from the general trends.
3. We restrict ourselves with regard to the period for which we are making predictions. Although predictions for the very long term are the most interesting, these make no sense, since the uncertainty is so great that only unacceptable, superficial and non-committal statements can be made. A prediction for the very short term offers more certainty (in fact it involves a linear extrapolation from the recent past and present to the future), but is unlikely to provide 'added value' to the reader. So, when making a prediction, a balance must be found between curiosity and certainty. In this book, we focus on a period of approximately five years from the publication of this book. This time frame has not been chosen for specific reasons; it merely indicates a time perspective.
4. Another limitation is that we develop a single scenario. Using the arguments that are available now, we attempt to anticipate what lies ahead. We will check our prediction with the occurrence of actual market developments. These will allow us to assess the validity of the future scenario and to adjust it if necessary.
5. Our predictions apply to both business-to-consumer (b-to-c) markets as well as to business-to-business (b-to-b) markets. When we use the word 'customer', we mean both household customers (consumers) and business customers. Companies in b-to-b markets usually have fewer customers but more intense and enduring relationships with these cus-

tomers. Companies in b-to-b markets usually sell a greater variety of products and services to their customers than in b-to-c markets. The conclusions of our book are thus applicable to both types of markets. The words 'customer' and 'consumer' may be used interchangeably.

The question of the future situation of consumers is important for several reasons.

1. At the macro or aggregate level (the general level which represents a cumulation of individual choices), consumer choices determine the quality of life in society.
2. Consumers determine to a large extent the speed and size of economic progress. A decrease in consumer spending has a strong negative effect on economic growth.
3. Market structures and market processes are dependent on the way in which consumers determine their choices. The travel market provides an example. Here, the growing popularity of booking trips and vacations through the Internet leads to a weaker market position for travel agents. These changing consumer choices force them to reconsider their position, and to search for added value.
4. An analysis of future consumer behaviour is at least as relevant as an analysis of current consumer behaviour. Many market parties are dependent on the present consumer, but whoever wants to serve consumers in the future will have to anticipate future developments.

PREDICTION

Making predictions, how is this done? In the following section we first consider the problems associated with making predictions. Of course, it is not really possible to predict the future. At most, an attempt can be made in that direction. Different types of attempts are associated with different types of results and different types and levels of risks. Therefore, it is important to make a careful decision about the method to be used. The question of what the future will look like is key for several reasons:

1. It is a question for which it is impossible to obtain a definitive answer, at least at the point in time when we are interested in the answer. This moment will, by definition, always precede the actual future. The point at which the future becomes the present, the question becomes superfluous.

2. 'The future' is an undetermined subject. This makes it necessary to specify a time frame for questions related to the future. Policy makers often make a distinction between the short term, the medium term and the long term, but this distinction is as soft as butter. The short term typically relates to a period of several months; the medium term relates to a period of one to two years, and the long term is usually related to a period of more than two years. But there is no solid rule in this regard. This means that everyone who wishes to make an attempt at a prediction, needs to make an explicit choice about a point or period in the future (as indicated earlier, we focus upon the period of the next five years).
3. Although we consider that the question of what the future looks like is important, there is also some hesitation towards the answer. On the one hand there is a need for clarity about future events; on the other hand there is also a need for ambiguity. We do not always prefer to know with great certainty what the future will look like.
4. The future question may lead to a large number of different approaches to find a – provisional – answer.

We will further elaborate the last point here, because the quality of the method determines the quality of the result. The best-known approach is the intuitive one, also known as 'reading tea leaves' or 'inspecting the crystal ball'. From daily experience we know that intuition is an unstable basis for decisions and judgements, and therefore also for predictions. People have a tendency to attribute decisions that have produced positive results to the quality of their personal intuition. But they do not blame that same intuition when disappointing results are obtained. This makes intuitive estimates less suitable as a method for the prediction of future situations.

Also popular is the prediction of the future based on an extrapolation from the past. This involves the assumption that history occurs in a linear fashion and that the future will offer a logical sequence to the developments that we have already witnessed. Such an assumption does not take into account any developments that occur in a discontinuous fashion (by jumps), nor does it consider disruptions in the nice, linear development line. History has shown that whoever uses the linear assumption is often correct. The best predictor of tomorrow's weather is still today's weather. But the difference between 'always', 'often' and 'sometimes' can be crucial for policy makers and strategic decision makers. The same may be said about the difference between today and five years ahead so that the future may not simply be an adaptation of the present. The course of time has witnessed crucial moments of discontinuous change. Depending upon the prediction made, these changes may be very painful.

There are various methods for assessing possible future scenarios and developments. A well-known method is the Delphi method, in which various experts are requested to give their assessment of future development. After they state their opinions, the greatest common denominator of these opinions is once again submitted to the same experts with a request for amplification, a rejoinder or a correction. The procedure is repeated in a number of rounds until convergence takes place and a picture of the future emerges that is supported by the majority of the experts.

In scenario analysis, potential 'pictures' of the future are created of which the validities are continuously compared with each other and over time. Important signals identified in the environment are used to determine which scenario has the highest validity and predictive power. In this manner the scenarios are tested.

Trend analyses are performed by (market) research agencies and by trend watchers. By monitoring behaviour patterns, purchasing patterns, attitudes, opinions and interests, the general changes in preferences at certain levels of society may be determined. This involves preferences that relate to a longer term than the well-known short-term hypes, fads or the more seasonal fashions. The Delphi method, the scenario analysis, and trend watching may be characterized as qualitative methods. A more formal, quantitative approach is offered by econometric predictive techniques, in which historical data are used to make extrapolations to the future.

It is difficult, if not impossible, to provide a qualifying judgement about the various approaches. One method is not by definition superior to another. It is more important to select the method that is most suitable for the specific future question in consideration. The formalized, quantitative approach is preferred if:

1. it is possible to describe the object accurately.
2. it involves a more or less stable situation which means that the data available from the past may be applicable to the future.
3. the developments occur gradually and in a balanced fashion.
4. the complexity of the circumstances is not too great.

The previous discussion makes it clear that a scenario of a gradual, linear change is not likely to apply to market and marketing developments. It would be risky to use present insights and experiences in making an estimate of the future. In more chaotic cases that may involve discontinuous change, like we have here, a qualitative approach is called for. Within this approach, we prefer a scenario analysis over the Delphi method because it seems important to first develop a substantiated vision of the future.

The analysis of the future starts with knowledge of the present situation and with insights into how this situation has been reached. In the next chapter we describe a number of distinct developments within markets and in marketing. These developments will also be considered from the consumers' perspective. The question of how consumers experience the market, marketing, market supply and market demand will be addressed after various noteworthy developments have been discussed.

2. Developments in Markets and Marketing

SUMMARY

In this chapter, we review developments in markets and marketing. Markets are undergoing rapid changes due to internationalization, technological developments, the growth of ICT, increasing information overload, network formation, increasing prosperity and individualization, to mention just a few general trends. More specifically, market-related developments include: a growing customer orientation of companies and non-profit organizations, more attention towards long-term relationships with customers, a stronger emphasis on innovation, a stronger focus on contact with the customer, a higher interest in *fun shopping*, and the increased use of a psychological approach to marketing and market research. These developments lead to a number of downward 'spirals' in innovation, communication, distribution and prices. We explain why these 'spirals' imply unfavourable and threatening consequences for companies. They lead to several paradoxes that hamper the developments in contemporary marketing. Mass customization and mass individualization seem to provide an adequate response to the current threatening developments in marketing, but do they really?

INTRODUCTION

Some developments are related to the functioning of the market itself; other developments are related to the activities that are performed in the market. Therefore, we make a distinction between *market* developments and *marketing* developments. Market developments involve the structures and processes of the market; the way in which the supply side and the demand side are organized. Market developments are directly related to general societal and economic developments. Marketing developments are also related to the way in which suppliers present themselves towards consumers, and get into contact with them. Here, contact should be interpreted in both the literal and figurative sense. Direct contact exists in the physical, observable forms of distribution: shops, department stores and personal selling. Many services also involve direct contact between service providers and consumers. Contact in the figurative sense takes place in marketing communication through media, whether interactive or not. Contact in the figurative sense involves the intention with which suppliers present themselves to the consumer as a partner. In this context, contacts may vary from superficial and incidental contacts to stable, intensive and long-term relationships.

We will briefly describe the various developments, together with the possible consequences that these may have for consumers. Each description of a development may be interpreted as a position statement.

MARKET DEVELOPMENTS

In an attempt to give a more complete impression of the market dynamics, we discuss nine societal and market developments:

1. Internationalization of markets
2. Technological developments
3. Growth of information and communication technology (ICT)
4. Increasing information overload of consumers
5. Blurring boundaries between organizations and the formation of networks
6. Increasing prosperity and economic welfare of consumers
7. Individualization
8. Corporate social responsibility
9. Re-evaluation of time

Although these developments are at first presented as separate, independent trends, it should be noted that they are clearly connected, and support and stimulate each other. The nature of this connection will be discussed after the inventory of the separate developments.

1. Internationalization of Markets

One of the most sensational developments of the past decade is the increasing internationalization or globalization, coming as a direct consequence of international political-economic agreements. These agreements concern the lowering of customs boundaries between countries (within the European Union, and to some extent also globally). Other developments relate to the intensifying competition, the increasing openness in a cultural sense, the rapid growth of international travel and tourism, the marked improvement of general infrastructure, and the expansion of communication networks (see also Naert and Coppieters., 2000). This means that traditional barriers are being lowered or even removed, that international trade is expanding, that cultures are having more frequent and intense contact with each other, that products and services are being distributed over a greater territory, and that global brands are flourishing.

For consumers, internationalization means that they are confronted with a large number of new, foreign products, services and brands, with an enormous diversity among categories of products and services, and therefore with a variety of choice possibilities that, from a historical perspective, is unique. In principle, more choice options allow for better choices. After all, if supply is generous, there is a greater likelihood that the optimal alternative will be available, than if supply is narrow. But if supply is great, there is a risk that the market may become too complex to oversee. This high number of available alternatives makes it impossible, for the consumer, accurately to characterize the differences between these alternatives (Schwarz, 2004). Internationalization of markets is not only one of the consequences of increased competition. It also stimulates competition, as more suppliers enter the markets that often already have a high level of saturation.

2. Technological Developments

In the past few decades, new technological developments have taken off at a dramatically high pace. The introduction and use of the chip in various applications has significantly increased the functionality, safety, user-friendliness and usefulness of many existing products. Technological developments have led to 'intelligent products' entering the market, products whose existence could not have been imagined a few years ago. Examples include electronic payment systems, cellular phones, palmtops, electronic agendas/organizers, navigation systems, remote control of systems in the home and in the office, and 'intelligent' clothing.

Technology enables linkages between systems, which leads to even newer applications. The combination of various technologies makes it possible to assist car drivers to reach their destination through an individual navigation system, and may even assist them to park their car. The network of computers guarantees an unparalleled access to a multiplicity of information sources and huge amounts of information. Due to agreements at the international sector and branch levels, technologies that were originally functioning separately are now compatible and integrated. New functions have been developed that are better than the sum of the original functions: thus, synergy is created.

Technology enables *feedback* systems that can be used to monitor the actual functioning of products, thus allowing continuous corrections to take place, for example, remote control of equipment in the home (heating, cooling and safety systems). Meanwhile, quality has become a *conditio sine qua non*, instead of being the distinctive characteristic that it used to be.

To consumers, the quality focus and the technological leap forwards are a blessing, because the likelihood of 'bad buys' or a disappointing product is greatly reduced. Consumers can almost be certain that products will function as they should, and that services will deliver the promised effect. Quality may not have objective boundaries. In principle, products and services can be improved indefinitely. However, there are psychological boundaries to quality. At some level (the 'quality ceiling'), additional (objective) quality improvements will either remain completely unnoticed, or consumers will consider them to be trivial. The quality ceiling represents an intriguing paradox as, basically, quality is viewed as a main determinant of consumer buying. This may be more true for low levels than for high levels. At high levels, it may no longer be perceived and judged as such. By result, quality is becoming an increasingly fragile basis for consumer trade-offs. Technological quality by itself is used less as a criterion in purchasing decisions.

This progress in technology means that consumers are often unable to judge the technical quality of products and services. The *sophistication* of products and services is developing to such an extent that most consumers no longer have a complete overview of the number of choice options or functions, or they may know that there is a choice but they are not able to understand it. Often the functions of products can no longer be derived from their exterior design. Therefore, distinctive characteristics that may justify the choice of one of the alternatives are increasingly sought in areas other than technical quality. This helps to explain the increased interest in product design, product presentation (as distinct from the products themselves) and brand/company images.

3. Growth of ICT

A separate branch of technological development is related to information and communication technology (ICT). The Internet is the most obvious representative. ICT has a great impact on the total functioning of the market and even society, at least potentially. There are significant international differences in the application of ICT within markets. Commercial experiences still differ widely, but a structural increase of ICT applications (of Internet use) appears inevitable.

ICT developments will not only make more information available about products and services, but this information will also be available at moments and in situations that are the most useful for consumers. As well as providing information, the Internet also offers services that are unique to the medium. In a more simple form this involves the provision of information that consumers must pay for; in technologically more complex forms it even involves the provision of support in searching for information and making decisions: the *intelligent agent*. One of the implications of the introduction of the Internet is increased competition resulting from the facilitation of the comparison of purchasing alternatives. Suppliers who, until recently, were able to maintain high prices due to the lack of market transparency, are now detected more easily. Exposure leads to price adjustment through market transparency.

ICT (Internet) consequences for consumers are tremendous, although important segments of the demand side are not yet using the Internet as a tool for making purchases. One of the critical characteristics is the extended search capability, which allows the consumer to obtain relevant information regarding various purchasing alternatives within a relatively short time. This saves time, increases the role of information as a basis for decisions, is cheap, and is also comfortable, compared to the more traditional forms of information processing such as shopping, calling for information, and requesting written leaflets and other documentation.

On the other hand, it raises the question to what extent the increased availability of information is counteracted by the lack of clear organization and clarity. Thanks to the Internet, the number of choice options has greatly increased, as have the number of product characteristics that may be assessed. However, although the amount and quality of information has multiplied, decisions will not necessarily be better. There is more information to process, but the quality of the decision is not served by the disproportionate amount of information. In this context it is important to note that research carried out as early as the 1970s has shown that beyond a certain point, an increase in the amount of available information regarding a decision has a negative effect on the quality of that decision. See also Figure 2.1. In this figure, the amount of information beyond point A reduces the quality of the decision.

While the consumer may be in an improved position in terms of the availability and accessibility of information, the usefulness and functionality of the information may be reduced. Therefore, the question regarding whether the Internet has a positive influence on the quality of consumer choice remains unanswered. On the Internet, consumers have more power to select the information they need and want, and are not bombarded with irrelevant information as is the case with television and print advertising.

Nevertheless, the Internet may contribute to the consumer being smothered with information.

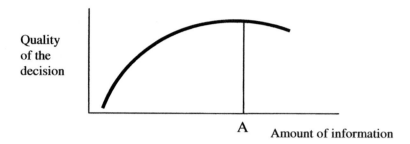

Figure 2.1 *The relationship between the amount of information and the quality of the decision*

4. Increasing Information Overload

'Customers do not want more choices. They want exactly what they want – when, where and how they want it' (Pine et al., 1995). A lot of variety and choice is not a goal in itself. It is only a means to match differentiated supply with a differentiated demand. The Internet provides an enormous increase in the amount of available information. Even before the Internet was introduced, when 'only' the 'traditional media' such as newspapers, radio and television existed, the concept of information overload was already being discussed: the problem that people (citizens, consumers) are confronted with more information than is functional for their decisions. Both the number of media and the number of choice possibilities (brands, types, options) for consumers continue to increase every day.

Depending on the goal, the type of product or service, and the circumstances, consumers may not even appreciate (part of) the offered possibilities. Examples are, possibly, commercial telephone calls, addressed and non-addressed (door-to-door) direct mail, free newspapers and billboards. The consequence of this is that the advertiser's initiative to communicate may be counteracted or even dominated by the consumer's initiative to refuse information. The Internet facilitates the consumers' initiative regarding information, thus allowing them to control the amount and the content of information they actually receive. The increasing number of media and the corresponding growth of the number of advertisements and other commercial messages mean that communication, as it is organized, is a phenomenon suffering a great deal of pressure. Whoever has a message to present, increasingly needs to consider whether this message even has a chance to reach the intended target audience, and if so, also has a chance to be processed cognitively or emotionally, and to be stored in memory for later use in a decision-making situation.

5. Blurring Boundaries between Organizations and the Formation of Networks

The high demands that are placed on producers require a high degree of specialization. Often it is no longer possible for organizations to maintain all specializations in-house and to keep financing these specializations which, by their very nature, require continuous upgrading in order to remain competitive. As a consequence, specialities are either *in-sourced* (integrated completely into the own organization) or *out-sourced* (placed outside the organization). Thus, two seemingly opposing developments co-exist in the market. On the one hand, we see the tendency toward specialization; on the other hand, some functions of companies are outsourced. Both tendencies may be subsumed under the overall trend towards further professionaliz-ation and merely indicate that a company may not benefit from having all particular functions under its own roof. What is more: specialization stimu-lates collaboration between experts. This makes them highly dependent on each other. Multi-functional companies are being replaced by networks. This, surprisingly, applies not only to organizations that provide mutual support to each other, but also to organizations that occupy different places and functions in the value chain. The chain consists of several links (parties) that all provide some added value. Although organizations often still oper-ate exclusively under their own brand, a brand often represents a conglomerate of different parties, businesses or business units that comple-ment each other. In this way, some organizations are able to bundle the input from several organizations and to present themselves (whether or not on behalf of the other organizations) as a *façade* (brand) to the market. In the car market, for example, car parts and components are supplied by dif-ferent suppliers from different countries, and assembled by a single party (brand) into a specific type of car. For example, Škoda cars are equipped with Volkswagen engines and technology. Chevrolet cars with General Motors' technology are produced in Korea.

For consumers, this development has limited consequences to the extent that they are often unaware of the precise functioning of the market. Nor are they aware of the way in which products and services are assembled. Obvi-ously, consumers benefit (either consciously or not) from its advantages: optimal supply and cost control. Further integration or network formation might lead to the situation in which consumers are involved with fewer rather than more parties (brands) in the market.

6. Increasing Prosperity and Economic Welfare

Despite the economic recession in Europe at the start of the twenty-first century, economic prosperity is high in most Western countries. Economic recessions do have an impact on welfare differences and employment levels. In most countries, there is economic growth and a rather favourable prospect of continued growth. For large segments of the population, free disposable income is considerable and allows for ample consumer decision freedom and spending possibilities.

Consumer confidence plays an important role in producing or directing economic fluctuations. Unfavourable political-economic news, such as terrorist attacks, makes consumers more hesitant in making large purchases and obtaining credit and mortgages. Pessimistic consumers tend to save more. Pessimism also causes investors to take less risk with their stock portfolio. Consumer and investor confidence is a major factor determining economic fluctuations.

7. Individualization

More than ever, consumers want to demonstrate their personal style and uniqueness through the use of products and services. Products and services are becoming accessible to an increasingly wide public. Thus, the possibility for a company to distinguish itself based on specific products, services or brands is decreasing. At the same time, consumers need to differentiate themselves from others. Individualization means that the market supply takes the personal wishes of customers into account. One way of doing this is by designing and offering tailor-made products. A bank offers customers the opportunity to design their own credit card by putting a personal picture on it. Products and services can be designed and assembled according to individual preferences. Often, services are more easily adapted to individual desires than products, but also products are increasingly being adapted to consumers (customization) rather than the other way around. This requires suppliers to focus even more than before on identifying (the background of) the problems, motivations, goals, wishes and desires of consumers. It also requires consumers to think more explicitly about their personal consumption goals, needs and wants.

Individualization needs to be met with increased flexibility of the supply side of the market. A supplier is expected to have the ability and willingness to make quick adjustments in the supply following the consumers' wishes.

Individualization requires some flexibility on the part of the consumers as well: consumers who reject standard products and require customized products, should be willing to pay the associated (higher) price.

8. Corporate Social Responsibility

A noticeable development in society is the increased emphasis on social responsibility. Companies are expected to be 'good citizens' and to take their responsibility seriously, because, otherwise, they may be confronted with damage claims and/or negative publicity. Recent examples are claims against tobacco producers and against producers of breast prostheses containing silicones. This development originated in the United States and appears to be migrating to Europe, although excessive damage claims such as in the US, do not (yet?) occur in Europe. The increased use of the judicial system is forcing companies to carefully consider the long-term consequences of their decisions. They need to take the responsibility towards customers and users of products seriously, and to attempt to prevent problems rather than correcting them afterwards.

This has a direct extension in the social responsibility of companies. Companies can no longer ignore environmental issues, the problems of Third World countries, child labour, fair trade, long-term health consequences, animal welfare, sustainability, or politically sensitive transactions. A strictly legal approach regarding these issues is, generally speaking, not relevant, because very little has been legally determined. Yet public opinion, important for the social embedding of an organization, cannot be ignored. This raises the question whether the increased attention to ethics is a cause or a result of the changing positioning of the supply side of the market.

From a customer perspective, this means a reduction of the risk that products are problematic from a moral, political or social perspective. The control and potential pressure by the market, the government or interest groups are so strong that serious violations are increasingly being prevented or eliminated. When a potential incident threatens to occur, social interest is so extensive that a company is wise to decide not to damage its reputation and to choose an alternative that is less problematic.

9. Re-evaluation of Time

The economic stability and the high level of economic prosperity in the Western economies should, in principle, enable a more stable balance between income and (free) time. Yet from an economic-social perspective, there is still a great deal of time pressure. In Europe, discussions are being held on extending the working week, cancelling early-pension schemes, and raising the age of retirement. There is a lot of attention being paid to effectiveness and efficiency, and targets are continuously being sharpened. Quantity and quality performance is under continuous pressure. Much is invested in time-saving facilities and instruments, both at work and at home. The result is not that the same work is completed within a shorter time, but that more work is accomplished within the same time. Extra time appears to be an illusion because it is immediately filled with extra activities. Company objectives often do not consider the actual possibilities for performance improvements. Task descriptions often offer little room for the slack that is required for creative work that, in turn, is essential for innovation. Work often requires more time than anticipated. As time is an inelastic concept, the pressure on free time continues to increase.

The other side of the same coin is that the available 'free' (discretionary) time is spent efficiently and carefully. An expression has been invented for this concept: quality time. This refers to time that has been specifically reserved to be devoted to activities that are highly valued at a personal level, for example, spending time with the children. Due to the amount of work and other obligations, many people feel the need to also plan and spend their free time carefully. Time is the new scarce commodity, which has two consequences for consumers. The first is that less time is reserved for activities that are not valued positively. For many people, this includes, for example, buying groceries and shopping for necessities. The second is that consumers devote a part of their (extra) income to saving time – for example by hiring people to take over unpleasant activities, such as gardening and household chores. Of course, they may also purchase time-saving products. Handheld, IT-supported organizers help the user to plan their time better – so that any time savings may be recorded, future time slots may be reserved, and loss of valuable time may be avoided.

In the past, services were only hired by non-wealthy consumers when it was inevitable due to a required expertise or due to a special situation. In principle, people, if capable, would do the tasks themselves. This way the scarce resource of money would be reserved for purchasing products (or perhaps for saving). People generally preferred to invest time and effort rather than spending money in order to save time and effort. More recently, there are some indications that these priorities are reversed, which can perhaps be explained by the fact that for many people, money has become less scarce than time.

This concludes a first inventory of existing market developments that are relevant to marketing. In the following section, the inventory will be continued, but this one will be more focused on developments in *marketing* itself. The demarcation line between market and marketing developments cannot always be drawn clearly, as the above examples already show. Yet a number of developments may be noted that are specifically related to the way in which suppliers position themselves in the market and present themselves to their customers.

Here we will again indicate the most salient developments and also provide a brief overview of their consequences for consumers.

MARKETING DEVELOPMENTS

Seven developments may be observed that influence the relationship, the interaction, and the communication between the supplier and the customer in the market:

1. Increasing customer focus by companies
2. More attention to long-term relationships with customers
3. More emphasis on innovation
4. A stronger focus on branding
5. Contact with the customer is becoming more important
6. More *fun shopping*
7. A more psychological approach to marketing and market research.

1. Increasing Customer Focus

An important development of the last decade is the increased attention paid to consumers' actual interests and desires. By customer focus we mean the intention and the active effort by companies and institutions to make the interests of customers the focal point in marketing policy. Instead of expecting that consumers will adjust to the offerings of the supplier, suppliers increasingly adapt themselves to customer needs, desires and preferences. We want to emphasize that this refers to an intention and an active focus; it does not necessarily refer to a successful attempt. After all, as indicated earlier, the crucial question is how consumer needs should be defined. Companies are often unable to do more than to estimate needs based on market data. Then, market supply is not determined on the basis of a predicted need. Rather, an estimate of a future need is made on the basis of past sales. If alternative A is purchased more frequently than alternative B, then this is interpreted as a larger 'need' for A ('revealed preference'). Many suppliers still do not understand that it is necessary to question to what extent alternative A actually matches the actual need (which obviously may be different from the mere preference for A over B).

This development means that companies are increasingly using the (added) value of the product or service as experienced by the consumer as a starting point, rather than the purely technical quality of that product or service. The fact that many services are added to products can be viewed as the consequence of this.

In the activities of the supplier an interesting shift may be noticed. While in the recent past the marketing emphasis was almost exclusively on the phase preceding the purchase and the transaction itself, now there is an increasing emphasis on supporting consumers' consumption experiences. Customer experience is a new focus of attention in marketing. The quality of the product is no longer the issue, but rather the quality of the experience that is the result of the consumption of that product or service (Pine and Gilmore, 1999).

2. More Attention to Long-term Customer Relationships

The emphasis on the interests and experience of consumers ensures an increasing focus on the development of long-term relationships with customers. Two transactions with the same customer are more valuable and cost-effective than two transactions with two different customers, even if the monetary value of the transaction is the same (Reichheld, 2001). In the past, the marketer was only interested in generating purchases, regardless of which consumers made them. Now, there is a clear interest in the person of the buyer who is able to make repeat purchases. It is generally known in marketing that acquiring new customers requires disproportionately more effort than maintaining present customers. For example, repeat purchases require less of the marketing budget than the first purchase. By consequence, the focus is no longer merely on customers per se, but on well-known, loyal customers. Long-term loyalty guarantees continuity of income and profit, possibilities for *cross selling* and lower marketing costs. On the other hand, it should be noted that the benefit of relationships may be reduced by more elaborate price- or service-related demands from loyal customers.

For consumers this is an important development as well, because they realize that the *commitment* of the supplier does not end with the transaction. The concept of *accountability* is becoming increasingly important at various levels of the value chain. Accountability refers to the justification of the added value and of the way in which that added value was obtained. It refers to the legitimization of decisions and activities. *Accountability* is strongly associated with responsibility.

An aspect of the long-term relationship is the customer lifetime value. This is the value of the customer for the supplier in terms of expected sales and turnover over a long period (Rust et al., 2000). The customer lifetime value or equity is an indication of the value of the customer for the company. The company may spend a proportion of this value to inform and serve these customers better and to increase their loyalty.

A long-term orientation provides suppliers with the opportunity to collect and use data on individual customers. It should be clear that such data (individual, over a long term) is more useful for optimizing supply than aggregated data that was obtained at one specific point in time.

3. More Emphasis on Innovation

Very frequently, products are being introduced in the market that present themselves as 'new' or 'improved'. Yet in the tradition of the innovation literature (Rogers, 1983), a new product is only a true innovation if it requires an adjustment in the lifestyle of the user. In all other cases, 'new' products only relate to an adjustment of the existing assortment. Innovation is the foundation of the continuity of most companies. An organization that does not innovate in a developing market will lag behind and will find it increasingly difficult to catch up. This creates an eternal treadmill in which organizations and consumers are required to adjust their positions and behaviours continuously.

Organizations cannot escape from the treadmill of continuous adjustment, and neither can consumers. Products and services that are new, or that are being presented as such, are so prominently present in markets that the notion of innovation seems subject to inflation. Consumers have become so accustomed to continuous real and claimed innovations that they may not even recognize or experience a real innovation. This leaves companies with no other choice than to innovate even more frequently or more significantly, and to announce even more intensely that the product concerns something truly new. And this, of course, aggravates the very problem.

Innovation is not just restricted to products and services. Marketing itself is subject to considerable change. New approaches, concepts and techniques are being developed as if marketing has an assembly line of its own. New concepts are being introduced in marketing practice on a continuous basis. Each one of these seems to hold great promises, but the fate of almost each of them is an untimely death. *Experience marketing*, *event marketing* and *viral marketing* are recent examples.

Marketing instruments also keep changing in an attempt to uphold effectiveness. The pressure to innovate is increasing. Store concepts, for example, have shorter life cycles than a few decades ago. Advertising campaigns are adjusted continuously in order not to fade away among other campaigns.

4. Brand Developments

Marketing activities are strongly focused on the development and maintenance of the brand (*branding*). The brand may be seen as the symbolic representation of carefully described products, services and organizations (*corporate brands*). It is the focus of marketing policy as it is responsible for the association of intrinsic characteristics and extrinsic perceptions. The brand and the brand image relate to the essence of the product or the service, lead to recognition and to the most important favourable and unfavourable mental associations. Consumers can use brands for simplifying purchasing decisions, as brands can combine and represent a large amount of information.

In a complex market environment consumers have a need for a clear identification of the supply. Brands play a central role, if not the most central role in this. The psychological function of brands is to generate and maintain trust, a concept that is gaining importance in contemporary marketing. Because of this development, it is very important that brands present themselves frequently in a favourable, explicit and consistent way.

Companies attempt to increase (and exploit) brand equity by assessing whether more products and services can be sold under the umbrella of the same brand name. This is known as 'brand extension'. The concept is important to the extent that strong brands may have the tendency to increasingly 'fill' themselves with new products and services, so that the brand eventually represents an assortment rather than a single product or service. While traditionally the brand name supports a product, now the relationship is reversed: a set of products and services supports the brand.

It is obvious that this will only happen to brands that are strong enough to carry the extra weight of the new products. Think of a cigarette brand such as Camel, which has a fashion and shoe line, and of a fashion brand that extends itself into cosmetics, like Chanel and Versace. In psychological terms, it is important to guard against the situation in which the brand concept is extended disproportionately, resulting in an unacceptable fading or dilution of the brand. An overstretched brand will lose its consistency and credibility, which leads to a less favourable brand image. When GM introduced a small Cadillac on the market, this had a negative effect on the large Cadillacs, because the exclusivity of the Cadillac brand decreased. The same risk may be noted for Jaguar and Mercedes.

In conclusion, brands are anchor points for consumer decisions. The loyalty that consumers demonstrate for certain brands may be partly understood by the need for consistency and convenience, and to simplify their decisions.

5. Contact with the Customer is Becoming more Important

In volatile markets, where consumers are sometimes 'accused' of a lack of brand and store loyalty, it is crucial to maintain contact with consumers. We may conceive this contact in two different ways. In the first place it is an opportunity for direct interaction – it allows the suppliers to present themselves to the consumer. In the second place, contact with consumers is necessary to build customer knowledge. Customer data may be stored in a database, an important, if not the most important tool for effective and efficient management of the market. If a company delegates the contacts with its customers, the database and the data maintenance to a third party (for example, an intermediary or a distribution system), it makes itself vulnerable towards the whims, peculiarities and interests of that party. An intermediary may deny access to a database or may sell the data to other parties. Also, the company that fails to have direct customer contact, lacks information on how consumers make decisions, evaluate products and services, and how consumers react to marketing communication campaigns. Customer knowledge is the equivalent of market power.

Therefore, market parties increasingly attempt to maintain access to customers. As it is becoming more difficult to reach customers with mass-marketing techniques, databases with information about consumers are becoming strategically (and not only tactically) important. Consumers are unlikely to notice this development. They feel no need to know how the market is organized. They probably do not even notice whether the database is handled by the original supplier or by a third party. But they do notice an increased knowledge of past purchasing behaviour, which is expressed by tailored offers, personalized information and special privileges.

6. More *Fun Shopping*

Fun shopping is an attractive pastime for many consumers. For them, shopping may serve the purpose of recreation, searching for divergence, of presenting new impressions, making social contacts, fighting boredom or, simply, spoiling themselves. This seems to contradict the increased 'franchising' or homogenisation of urban shopping centres. Well-known franchise formulas and brands are now present in all retail environments. Shopping centres are looking more and more similar. All over the world consumers encounter the stores of H&M, IKEA, McDonalds, Pizza Hut, Delifrance, Starbucks and Zara, with their well-known store formulas. And each of them presents their familiar products and store lay-out behind their familiar façade. Are shopping environments stimulating for fun shoppers?! Homogenization increases the predictability, and may decrease the attractiveness of shopping centres for consumers, some of whom see shopping as a form of leisure behaviour. In this regard, historical city centres offer a clear added value through their original character and architecture.

Due to the similarity of shopping centres, a part of the authentic, unique charm of European city centres has been lost. But by regularly adjusting retail formulas it may perhaps be possible to bring standardization and boredom to a halt, and to make shopping more attractive. This is even more important because shopping is increasingly associated with costs such as loss of time, parking problems, feelings of lack of safety, and other irritations (apart from the financial costs of purchases). The accessibility of shops is often limited by heavy traffic, parking space tends to be restricted and parking fees are often high. The combination of these factors leads to an increasingly unattractive market situation, while on the other hand the need for positive shopping experiences seems to grow.

Parenthetically, when shopping centres and malls are designed, the concept of fun shopping should not be confused with the mere presence of recreational facilities such as movie theatres and restaurants, which have no direct relationship to the shopping experience itself.

New channels may fill the gap: if shopping is unattractive, it may just as well be quick and cheap. The Internet is associated with high accessibility, attractive 'opening hours', low time costs and often low financial costs. The 'travel and parking costs' are merely those of the telephone. The Internet means a significant expansion of the distribution channels of financial and tourist services, and distance selling of books, CDs, airline tickets and software. For these services, consumers can now be served at a place, time and manner determined by themselves. For other services, the function of the Internet may be limited – consider the hairdresser and the window-cleaner – although even these service providers may improve the quality of the service provision through an Internet contact with their customers.

The Internet has a positive effect on the time costs and financial costs of collecting information and obtaining products and services, but it also makes the market more complex. Parties that originally could profile themselves in the market based on their specific sales territory, such as real-estate agents and insurance agents, now find themselves placed next to (or across from) many other competitors. Ten years ago this was unthinkable. Suppliers now attempt to create as many distribution options as possible for their own products and service, in addition to, or perhaps even instead of, the traditionally arranged distribution channels.

As direct access to the customer is an important condition for the creation of a relationship, there is great interest in the expansion of contact possibilities. For example, financial institutions attempt to maintain contact with the customer through every possible channel, even SMS.

7. A More Psychological Approach to Marketing and Market Research

These various developments are interesting phenomena in their own right, but their impact on consumer behaviour is especially important. Consumer behaviour in this context concerns the way consumers do (not) notice, experience, know, feel and think, and how they use that as a basis for (not) considering, choosing, deciding, purchasing, consuming and evaluating products and services.

Consumer behaviour changes under pressure of the environment. In this context it becomes necessary for marketing management and market research to understand how consumer behaviour develops. Originally there was more interest in a general characterization or segmentation of consumers based on socio-demographic and economic characteristics (buying power). Obviously there was also a lot of interest in the results of consumer behaviour – expressed in turnover or sales (what and how). But now, a clear need is developing for insights into the determinants of consumer behaviour. These determinants help understand which marketing activities are suitable. Such an understanding increases marketing effectiveness and decreases marketing costs. There is a striking growth in the use of psychological market research, both qualitative and quantitative. Insight into consumer behaviour helps suppliers to anticipate market developments. It helps them to increase the effectiveness of measures and to suggest new possibilities for innovations and investments.

MARKETING SPIRALS

Although the inventory of developments in the market and in marketing as outlined above is not complete, it is clear that the metamorphosis of the market is spectacular. The changes are dramatic and are taking place within a relatively short time period. The market is exploding. How can we summarize these developments, and how can they be extrapolated to the future of marketing? We summarize the changes by focusing on four circular effects, each related to one of the traditional marketing instruments.

1. The Innovation Spiral

The innovation spiral starts with the need for companies to offer new products and services in order to be noticed in the market and to distinguish themselves from their competitors. Such an innovative position allows companies to request a higher price (*premium pricing*). There is a continuous need to distinguish oneself from competitors, which leads to an excess number of attempts to be considered new, renewed or innovative. As this phenomenon is not limited to particular companies but relates, more or less, to almost all markets and companies, the drive to make progress is universal. According to the cliché: standing still in Western markets is like running backwards.

One of the results is that innovations are short-lived. They only have a short life cycle. An innovation loses its newness quickly and then continues its existence as a 'normal' product or even as a commodity. On top of this, consumers quickly develop habituation to new products and services; they even appear to be getting used to the high renewal rate. In some markets, such as the laptop market, consumers wait to purchase, because they anticipate an even newer generation of these products (or cheaper versions of the same product) in the short run. In addition, competitors turn out to be quick in copying a successful innovation and in presenting their own, slightly adapted version to the market.

The number of innovation attempts is so large, and the frequency with which they appear in the market is so high, that consumers have trouble identifying them as such. This modifies innovative products and services. The impact of the head start that a supplier hopes to achieve with an innovation, continues to decrease. The duration of the innovation, that is the time period in which the innovation is still rather unique, becomes shorter as well. This leads to an increasing innovation pressure. After all, the supplier does not want its company or its products to risk standardization. The latter effect closes the circle, starting a downward innovation spiral. This spiral is visualized in Figure 2.2.

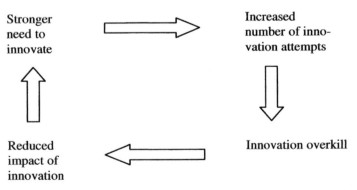

Note: There is a supplier and a consumer side to the spiral. The top half relates to suppliers; the bottom half to consumers.

Figure 2.2 The innovation spiral

The innovation spiral presents a problem for various reasons:

1. Innovations involve high investments. The phenomenon of the spiral increases the risk that the innovations are not fully appreciated and that the investments are not recovered.
2. Innovations that are not perceived or appreciated as such by consumers, do not distinguish themselves from the other products. They get sucked into the grey area of standard products (commodities).

The innovation spiral raises the question of how to escape. Marketing practitioners suggest a variety of solutions. The most frequent suggestion is to reverse the direction of movement in the cycle by offering increasingly simple rather than increasingly sophisticated products. However, the cycle is not one of mere technology. The obvious counter-argument is that if the company is successful doing so, others cannot wait to follow. And the cycle will spin as happily as ever.

2. The Communication Spiral

An innovation cannot exist on the basis of its objective technical qualities only. It is necessary to communicate its special position and features. Without communication, innovations are not viable. They have to compete with non-innovative products for the attention and favour of the consumer, even as products that do not present an actual, objective innovation, may still attempt to claim a certain position through their brand and communication policy ('Make it or claim it'). However, for communication, we encounter a circular, spiralling phenomenon as well (Poiesz, 1999). Because suppliers have an increased need to present their product to the market through communication, the number of commercial messages increases. For customers, a situation of *information overload* develops. Information overload involves the reception of more messages than the intended recipient is able to process. This forces customers to be very selective. In turn, this implies a reduction of the level of attention that consumers are able to devote to each message. Many suppliers notice that the effectiveness of their communication activities is under increasing pressure. As communication is vitally important for their product, they react with an even stronger urge to communicate. Thus, communication is intensified (more frequent exposure, more media usage, more elaborate and expensive formats and, of course, a higher budget). Consequently, for communication also, a downward spiral starts spinning. See Figure 2.3.

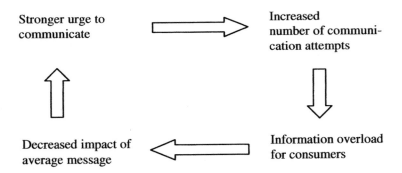

Figure 2.3   The communication spiral

The disadvantages of the communication spiral are obvious. As indicated, in an attempt to escape its effects, suppliers continuously try to use new media. Once a communication medium is obstructed by overload, other media are introduced, with the hope and the expectation that these will be able to reach consumers. However, history shows that each new medium eventually becomes the victim of the same information overload phenomenon. Several decades ago, only mass-communication tools were used. When these began to suffer from decreased effectiveness in the communication spiral, more direct media with personalized messages were introduced. But even that was insufficient to stop the downward communication spiral. Subsequently, telecommunications seemed to present the answer, until this medium became clogged as well. Neither an increase of the number of channels and the number of satellites, nor the introduction of the Internet is presenting the desired solutions. At first sight, the Internet appears to be a solution for the spiral, but now its limitations are becoming more apparent. Think, for example, of the low click ratios for Internet banner advertising.

3. The Distribution Spiral

Here, however, the arguments repeat themselves. For distribution also, the freedom to manoeuvre and to be effective is increasingly restricted. Because of the spirals discussed above, the need to have direct contact with consumers is increasing dramatically. This leads to an expansion of the number of contact possibilities, and to a more intensive use of existing distribution channels. Companies that originally used a single channel, are now using a *multi-channel* policy. Technology allows for new contact possibilities. Cell phones provide the most recent ones. The likely effect is that, more and more, consumers feel 'stalked' by commercial parties, which reduces the effectiveness of individual channels. Contact possibilities are being limited rather than expanded, and the downward distribution spiral is starting to spin.

A multi-channel strategy is often used to reach consumers that cannot be reached with single, traditional channels. Or it is used to contact consumers in different ways and at different times. Problems of coordination and consistency are likely to arise, as consumers are not likely to adapt to the distribution policies of companies. One financial company introduced a low cost Internet channel for its non-wealthy consumers and invested in a face-to-face channel for its wealthy clients. The effect was that the use of the channels was reversed. High-income and highly educated clients used the Internet, and the low-income, non-wealthy consumers came to the bank offices. 'Cheap' clients suddenly became expensive. Apart from this, commercial contacts in different channels should be mutually complementary and consistent. And all channels should be well-maintained and supported. But, the careful distribution of a product or service is a high cost operation that does not prevent a distribution spiral from starting to turn. Competitors, as always, are eager to follow channel successes of the competitors. See Figure 2.4 for the downward distribution spiral.

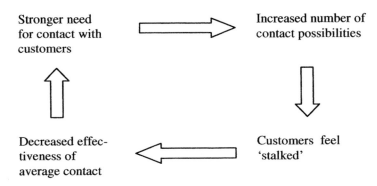

Figure 2.4 The distribution spiral

The inevitable result of the innovation spiral, the communication spiral and the distribution spiral is that it becomes increasingly difficult for individual products to differentiate themselves. The three instruments needed to achieve added value lose effectiveness. For companies that want to distinguish themselves in terms of quality or consumer experience, life becomes increasingly more difficult. Product innovations, communication and distribution no longer offer the added value that is required to distinguish the product from the competitors. Some suppliers choose a positioning at the

lower end of the market. They focus upon cost reduction, operational excel-
lence, and *economies of scale*. They seek to implement a clear market
function by striving for an increasingly lower price to be paid for a highly
standardized product (*commodity*).

4. The Price Spiral

The end result of the various spirals is price erosion and a price spiral,
which is closely related to the *commodity magnet* or *commodity trap* (Rangan and Shapiro, 1994). Due to the lack of added value, it is impossible to
ask a premium price. This restricts the profits that would be required for
investments to generate added value. Without financial reserves it is impossible to make extra investments in innovation, communication or
distribution. The product becomes increasingly standardized, which puts an
even stronger downward pressure on the price. The sequel to the story is
well-known: a downward price spiral is set in motion. A product that gets
caught in the spin cannot, or only with the greatest effort, escape from the
spiral. See Figure 2.5.

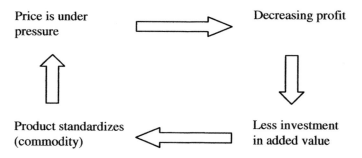

Figure 2.5 The price spiral

Four Spirals

Several comments should be made regarding these four spirals:

1. The spirals show a tendency to spin increasingly faster; they accelerate.
2. The spirals do not exist independently from each other, but drive each
   other forwards. They serve as each other's catalyst.
3. The weak link in the chain is the consumer, who is not able to follow
   the exponential growth of the marketing efforts, and therefore simply
   gives up: he or she stops acquiring sufficient information, making care-

ful comparisons, and making careful trade-offs and decisions. By consequence, products look increasingly similar, not only in an objective sense, but particularly in a subjective sense – as perceived and experienced by the consumer. In the absence of perceived quality differences, price differences cannot be justified, and consumers will tend to focus upon price and buy the cheapest product. Products that once were able to differentiate themselves from the rest, now slide down towards the 'grey' centre of the market, where they will either enter a low cost strategy or perish. Note that there is relatively little room in the market for low price products, especially in our Internet era. Companies will be forced to cooperate to split fixed costs and to attain economies of scale. This further restricts market supply variety. The market implodes and shows symptoms of constipation. Marketing no longer seems to make sense. The combination of the four spirals may be called 'the marketing spiral'. See Figure 2.6.

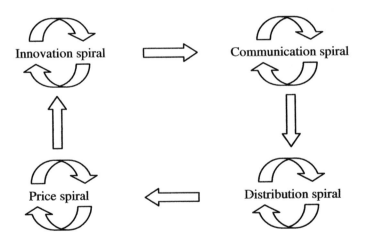

Figure 2.6 The marketing spiral

The marketing spiral means that the explosive growth of competition and marketing activities leads to a situation in which marketing is threatening to suffocate itself. It is biting its own tail and develops into a self-destructive phenomenon. The more attempts at differentiation that are made, the less real differentiation can actually occur in the market.

Metaphorically speaking, the market is like an enormous commercial gathering in a large reception hall which suffers from rich acoustics. In order to be heard and understood, everyone present is starting to shout louder and louder. Conversation is reduced to an enormous sound wave of indiscriminate noise that appears to fill the entire space. The end result is that no one can understand anyone any more.

Marketing presents a similar phenomenon. As such, it is a *prisoner's dilemma game*: in an attempt to achieve a disproportionate advantage for themselves, individual persons *together* create a situation that is disadvantageous for all of them.

The conclusion on marketing management presented above may appear somewhat too dramatic. It ignores the possibility that new marketing instruments still may be developed, that breakthroughs still may occur in the area of innovation, that collaboration still may lead to new market power, and that new markets still may be opened through internationalization. After all, among marketing failures marketing successes can be noted. But the concern is not a gross exaggeration, since there are strong signals indicating that consumers increasingly feel alienated from the market, market supply and marketing. It is generally claimed that a considerable percentage of new products fail (the figure of 80 per cent is often mentioned). Consumers either ignore or shrug their shoulders in the face of product renewals, and discard communication that was specifically tailored to them. Consumers are often incapable of explaining or even describing the nature of the added value of a product. Satisfaction with products often appears to be no more than the mere absence of complaints (satisfaction as the mere absence of dissatisfaction). Often, repeat purchases are more based upon the convenience of the routine decisions than upon a well-considered resolution to re-buy a specific product. Many consumer decisions are made carelessly because the required knowledge is lacking, because products have become too complicated, or because too many aspects ought to be considered. Or consumers may no longer worry about a 'bad bargain', as the average product quality is high anyway.

In conclusion: while the purpose of marketing is to synchronize market supply and demand, it is becoming less successful in doing so. Consumers buy products they do not need. Or they buy products with features they do not need. Or they do not buy products that would have satisfied them. Or they may even have features on products that they would like to use, but fail to understand. For example, software often contains features that the owners would appreciate if they only knew of their existence. The problem that marketing faces cannot be solved with incidental tactical measures. Even a massive change in tactics does not seem to suffice. There is an urgent need for a reconsideration of the marketing paradigm. Marketing needs a new strategy.

PARADOXES

A strategic reconsideration is only useful when it is based on a careful analysis of the total market situation and the developments that take place in that situation. So far in the inventory and analysis of these developments, no concrete strategic solution for marketing has presented itself.

On the other hand, we defined the problem more clearly by specifying the four marketing spirals. In addition to these spirals, there are several paradoxical developments that cannot be ignored when reconsidering the paradigm of marketing. These developments relate to the following contrasts:

1. Clustering versus differentiation
2. Heterogeneity versus homogeneity
3. Intermediaries versus disintermediation
4. Many choice options versus need for a single product
5. Needs become more important versus less insight into the nature of the needs
6. Pursuit of quality versus quality ceiling
7. Corporate culture versus external focus
8. Marketing as an activity versus marketing as an orientation

1. Clustering Versus Differentiation

Under the pressure of the individualization trend, suppliers have become increasingly focused on the differentiation of products and services. This requires a modular structure of organizations. *In-sourcing* and *out-sourcing* lead to a redistribution of tasks across companies. The reduction of strategically secondary tasks increases the dominance of their core competencies. Yet opposite movements also appear to occur. The past decade was characterized by a strong increase in the number of company mergers and structural collaborations. Companies enter into strategic alliances (cf. airlines) or even merge in order to create a more dominant power position in the market. Thus, differentiation and clustering occur simultaneously.

This paradox may be understood as an expression of macro and micro strategic movements on the supply side. Simultaneously, there are attempts to increase value and to reduce costs, albeit in different organizations. However, consumers do not want either high value or low prices; they ultimately want both. As the spirals have shown, value and price are both under pressure. By its very nature, traditional marketing created this problem and is, therefore, not capable of solving it. A new marketing is required to combine individualization, differentiation and low (or at least reasonable) costs.

2. Heterogeneity Versus Homogeneity

Strong national and international competition, and the continuous pursuit of differentiation and added value increases the heterogeneity in the market. The overall quality level has reached a point that may be described as *quality overkill*: products and services offer a quality that many customers are no longer able to notice, let alone appreciate. Quality overkill means that actual, objective heterogeneity is transformed into subjective homogeneity. This result is the most noticeable lower in the value chain, that is closer to the end user or consumer.

A more or less homogeneous supply means that consumers have a lower need to compare products carefully before purchase. The quality of the supply is high, and the differences between products and services are small. Thus, the costs of making careful trade-offs may be higher than the benefits of a superior purchase. Consumers will devote less time, money and effort to their purchases, unless the purchasing process itself is worthwhile. Here we may refer to the term *'fun shopping'*, which stands for the pleasure in the act of shopping itself. Although the supply itself is becoming more homogeneous, the context in which it is presented still offers some opportunities for differentiation. It turns out that consumers are often unable to select the product with the best objective quality, but derive the subjective value of that product from the brand and the (store) environment in which it is presented.

Both the supply side and the demand side need product differentiation, so there is no real contradiction here. The paradox is that heterogeneity created (perceived) homogeneity, a problem that cannot be solved by conventional marketing.

3. Intermediaries Versus Disintermediation

The complexity and unpredictability of the market make it difficult for suppliers to find the right consumers, and vice versa. This creates room for intermediaries and brokers. These have the task of matching the appropriate parties according to supply and demand. In some markets the intermediary has long been a well-known phenomenon. For example, in the insurance market we may refer to the insurance agent. The general practitioner may be regarded as an intermediary between the patient and the medical specialist. Wherever market developments occur rapidly, or where the complexity is great and the transparency is limited, the need for new 'market guides' arises. The 'infomediary' is an example of an intermediary that arranges the information supply to match it with the needs of the other party to facilitate the information processing and choice of a customer.

On the one hand, the need for support and therefore for intermediaries is increasing. But, on the other hand, the function of intermediaries is decreasing. The pressure on price forces some companies to ignore them altogether and to contact consumers directly. The disappearance of traditional intermediaries relates not just to people, but it may also be related to various levels within the value column. For example, *factory outlets* skip the intermediary function that is traditionally fulfilled by retailers. The absence of a channel is always cheaper than its presence. Also information technology reduces some of the functions of intermediaries. The result is that intermediation and disintermediation co-exist. To the extent that this is a dilemma, it is certainly not solved by marketing as we know it now.

4. Many Choice Options Versus Need for a Single Product

Differentiation leads to a large number of choice alternatives. Freedom of choice is considered an important issue in Western countries. However, while consumers consider a certain degree of freedom of choice positively, there is no need for alternatives that make the total supply difficult to survey. The costs of the choice process may exceed the potential added value of an optimal choice alternative. Zeleny (1996) already argued that the consumer does not need a wide-ranging supply of choices, but a product that has been tailored towards him or her. Pine (1993) formulated this even more directly: 'Customers do not want choices, they want exactly what they want'. In his book, *The Paradox of Choice – Why More is Less*, Schwartz (2004) directly refers to the inverted U-shaped relationship between freedom of choice and consumer appreciation of this freedom.

This paradox poses the fundamental question concerning how marketing should perform. Western economies are based on the principle of the free market. This principle, in turn, is based on free choice. But what does it mean for the system when free choice, above a certain level, is not what consumers want? Present-day marketing apparently does not fully support the free market principle. It may even counteract it.

5. Needs Become More Important Versus there is Less Insight into the Nature of the Needs

Needs of consumers are becoming more important, but it is also becoming more difficult to determine what they actually are. The 'lower' needs of the needs hierarchy (physical needs) have been satisfied for most people in Western nations, and the 'higher' needs, such as recognition and personal growth, have therefore become more prominent. In the literature, needs have been mapped in different ways. It appears that none of these methods is appropriate for direct application to Western markets, in the sense that they are capable of predicting successful product innovations and adaptations in the total set of products and services.

Perhaps a better insight may be derived from a combination of the various approaches. For a (provisional) combination of the needs hierarchies of Maslow (1954) and Alderfer (1972), see Figure 2.7. Maslow distinguishes five levels of needs. The two lower levels relate to basic existence needs such as hunger, thirst, sex, safety and protection. At the third level, relations to others, affiliation and love become important. The two higher levels relate to personal growth: recognition and respect, and self-actualization. Alderfer makes a classification into three levels: existence, relatedness and growth (ERG). The five needs of Maslow fit into the classification of the three levels of Alderfer.

Two principles are assumed in the models of Maslow (1954) and Alderfer (1972). The first principle, fixation, states that as long as a need is not satisfied, people are fixed on that particular need. The second principle states that when a need is satisfied, people move to the next higher need. The highest level of self-actualization and personal growth means that people at that level can fully realize their potential and talents. It is assumed that the happiness and wellbeing of people at this level is higher than at lower levels.

As a result of the theoretical vagueness surrounding the concept of need, needs are not a good predictor of particular purchasing and consumption decisions. It appears that, sometimes, they are to be interpreted as a result rather than as a cause of consumer choice. Thus, needs precede and follow consumption experiences. Due to this circular relationship, it is more difficult to use them as 'predictors' than to refer to them as 'descriptors' (revealed preferences). In addition, consumers find it more difficult to articulate their own high-level needs than their low-level needs. To put it differently: the more important needs are in marketing, the less support they provide in the formulation of marketing policy.

Again, the paradox is that the product supply should be based on needs, but that in reality the situation is reversed. Once a product is purchased, we 'explain' it by saying that it apparently matches a need. We erroneously conclude, then, that needs may be used as explanatory concepts for consumer purchases. In present-day Western markets, 'need' is a misleading concept.

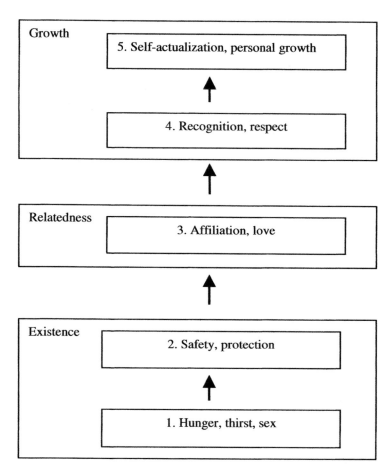

*Figure 2.7 Combination of the needs hierarchies of Maslow and
         Alderfer*

Our conclusion is that in new marketing thinking, the concept of need
deserves rehabilitation. This can be done by way of a renewed attempt at
theoretical elaboration. However, this only makes sense if the result may be
applied in practice. There is no need for needs as a post-hoc explanation. A
more vital approach may be to focus on consumer problems, dissatisfaction
and insufficiencies. Here we do not mean problems related to particular
products or services, but more general problems associated with being a

consumer. Here we can think of inefficiencies, uncomfortable situations and otherwise sub-optimal situations. We will return to this issue later.

6. Pursuit of Quality Versus Quality Ceiling

Quality is experienced as an important factor, but it is increasingly difficult for consumers to assess product quality. The paradox is that while added value is becoming more important, it is also becoming impossible to achieve this with the help of traditional quality thinking. The developments in quality thinking may be characterized according to the progression in the following set of statements:

> *Do the things right.*
> *Do the right things.*
> *Do the right things right.*
> *Doing the right things right is no longer good enough.*
> *Doing the right things right is no longer relevant (but don't you dare do less!).*

The last line is a logical extension of the previous ones and signifies the need for a change in marketing thinking. A strong focus upon products, services, brands, communication, distribution and prices may prevent truly innovative marketing thinking. The marketing innovations that do get presented often seem no more than mere variations of existing themes.

7. Corporate Culture Versus External Focus

For a long time, marketing has been contained in departments and in functions. More recently, the importance of marketing is reflected in the recommendation to view marketing as part of the total organization. In this sense, it is not only a set of activities, but also part of the company culture. Over the past ten years, there has been a notable increase in attention to the issue of organizational culture. 'All noses point in the same direction' is the motto. There should be a collectively supported *commitment* to the organization and a *commitment* amongst the employees themselves. Corporate culture is the shared vision regarding the objectives, the direction of organizational development, the values, the rules and the operating methods of the organization. Culture is a phenomenon that is relatively invisible and intangible, yet it is interwoven with all organizational activities. Although corporate culture is actually an internal issue, it can certainly be noted in the environment through the corporate image and reputation.

The paradox is that while corporate culture is receiving more attention and even represents a core theme at the level of top management, there is a contrasting development in which employees are increasingly being expected to act in a customer-oriented fashion, to be externally oriented, to identify with customers, and to be creative, innovative, flexible, critical, independent and mobile. The paradox means that employees should be committed in two directions: internally and externally, even if this involves conflicting goals. Actually, they need two noses. A related conflict is the one between shareholder orientation and customer focus. Shareholders want short-term profits. A customer focus may require long-term investments. Companies and marketing are dependent upon shareholders, customers and employees. In the present view on marketing, these interests diverge. Diverging interests are ineffective and inefficient. As diverging interests seem to be an inevitable by-product of traditional marketing thinking, a spontaneous solution is not to be expected. For this, a new approach to marketing seems to be required.

8. Marketing as an Activity Versus Marketing as an Orientation

The essence of marketing is that a product or service should be optimally supported to reach the consumer. In this regard the interests of the supplier and the consumer are linked. Originally, in a *one-to-one* interaction between supplier and customer, it was not necessary to develop a separate marketing activity. As outlined in Chapter 1, the supplier was located close to the customer (both literally and figuratively). The communication regarding the product or the service was optimal, the delivery or distribution itself did not present a problem, and the price was clearly agreed upon beforehand. With the introduction of mass production, market saturation and competition developed. The distance to the customer increased (again, both in the literal and figurative sense). It became necessary to establish marketing as an independent activity, which became more important as the market grew in complexity. Various segments required individual attention and a differentiated marketing policy. This did not solve the problem of the increasing supplier–consumer distance, however. A beautiful, but also painful example is the often troublesome relationship between R&D departments and marketing departments. Both are in existence to serve the customer. But their combined understanding of the consumer is so limited that miscommunication between these departments is more the rule than the exception.

An organization's existence depends on the creation of added value. Because marketing is focused on managing added value towards the customer, marketing is increasingly becoming a strategic activity rather than a supportive activity. Yet this strategic activity often is still housed in a separate marketing department (or 'department of marketing and communication' or even 'department of communication'). By the *strategic lift* of marketing, the traditional (and artificial) boundaries between the marketing department and the other departments of the organization are disappearing, and marketing activities are once again merging with other company activities.

Organizational marketing, in the physical sense, becomes less visible. Obviously, it does not disappear, but it develops from an activity of a specific organizational unit into an orientation within the entire organization. The paradox lies in the realization that marketing is becoming more important, but also less visible. Marketing becomes a less distinct discipline, with all the apparent risks involved.

A PROVISIONAL CONCLUSION

If we consider the various paradoxes, it may be argued that there are many parallel developments that are tumbling on top of each other in a chaotic, spiralling motion. It appears that each position in each paradox may be supported by concrete market examples. The complex relationships between the developments as well as the speed with which they take place, makes it almost impossible to anticipate the future. Yet the task of this book is to try anyway.

We will first indicate the most central trends within the many developments described above. After all, whoever finds the complexity confusing will do well to choose a higher level of aggregation in order to create his/her own simplicity. The risk of getting lost in the details may be avoided by focusing on a more general level of analysis. We may do so in several different ways.

At the most general level, the issue is the identification of one single trend. At this level, the trend identified should contain or summarize all other trends. Taking into account the various developments in the market and in marketing, we arrive at the conclusion that there is actually one single development that supersedes the other trends. This is the trend of an increasing focus on the individual: individualization.

This trend subsumes customer orientation, the desire to monitor customers as individual persons over a longer term, the continuous differentiation and optimizing of products and services on behalf of increasingly smaller segments, as well as the pursuit of contacts with consumers in their specific situation at various critical moments in their time.

May individualization serve as the single source of inspiration for the development of a type of marketing that may avoid the marketing spiral? We will address this question by explaining the meaning of mass customization and mass individualization. For this, we will refer to the insights of Van Asseldonk (1998) in the following section.

The need for individualization arises from the level of economic prosperity that allows people not only to satisfy needs but also to achieve this in a way that connects with their personal lifestyles. For example, need satisfaction may match the person's need for variety and his/her need to continuously undergo new, enriching experiences. Van Asseldonk (1998) compares two fundamental marketing strategies that find their origin in individualization: *mass customization* and *mass individualization*. The distinction between the two lies in the manner in which the product is being individualized. *Mass customization* refers to the optimal synchronization of individual products towards individual consumers, and it is based on the principle of *economy of scale* (advantages of scale). By using increasingly complex forms of segmentation it is possible to achieve economies of scale. Therefore, mass customization is not possible without databases of customer information.

Mass individualization, on the other hand, abandons the principle of segmentation. This approach focuses on a modular structure within organizations that is set up in such a way that it allows the individual consumer to assemble an individualized product late in the production and distribution chain, and even at low costs. In this vision, efficiency is not obtained through economies of scale, but through the ingenious way in which the production chain is organized.

Mass individualization relates to the combination of more drastic differentiation and efficiency. The goal is individually tailored products and services at a low or reasonable price. The *economy of scale* is no longer used as a basis for cost control. Instead, companies may generate revenue based upon the differences between consumers (instead of being based on the similarities). There is a transition from homogeneity (large segments) to heterogeneity (individuals).

It is clear that insight into why and how consumers make their choices is becoming an increasingly important condition for synchronizing supply and demand. Over time, this insight has become more sophisticated. Traditionally, only crude, aggregate level information was available: it concerned the market in general. Subsequently the insights referred to increasingly smaller market segments. Until databases were introduced as a technological tool, much detail was not possible due to limits of an organizational, financial and even human nature. According to Van Asseldonk (1998), there is a difference between mass customization and mass individualization in the way in which knowledge is obtained and in the intention with which databases are used. In mass customization, knowledge remains focused on similarities between consumers: on tracing the segmentation possibilities or on bundling at the end of the production chain. The bundling occurs at the demand side of the market: consumers are considered to be able to assemble their own individual package, product or service in a self-service buffet type of system. With mass individualization, the data file is focused on suggesting combination possibilities higher up in the production and distribution chain. In this case the bundling occurs on the supply side of the market, while differences between consumers are taken into account as much as possible. Here, consumers receive an individualized package and do not have to assemble it by themselves.

Due to the individualization trend, databases with customer data will become the beating heart of the market and marketing. The rapid technological development that allows for further differentiation requires a change in marketing thinking. In fact, it concerns a reversal of the principle of mass production for mass markets towards modularly organized production for individual consumers.

At this point it is interesting to determine to what extent this prognosis fits with the development of marketing in the course of history. In its rudimentary form, marketing once started with individual suppliers that tailored their supply to the wishes of individual customers: *one-to-one marketing*. Over time, the supplier develops an efficient manufacturing process so that many customers may be served by a single supplier (*one-to-many marketing*). At the aggregate level of the market, this caused competition. In a competitive market environment, suppliers are forced to focus their attention on differences between price–value relationships. Thus, in a next stage of development, the market divides itself into roughly two types of companies: suppliers who focus on creating added value for a relatively high price (by focusing on either innovation or customer intimacy) and companies which take position with a *commodity* or a standardized product for the lowest price possible. Further economic growth leads to an increase in demand for individualized need satisfaction, so that segmentation is stretched to its financial and technological limits.

This is the point at which the tension between differentiation and efficiency is at its highest level. Although further differentiation might involve an increased individualization of the supply, it would also include a higher price. According to Van Asseldonk (1998), this is the point at which the supply should reorganize itself, abandon thinking in smaller and smaller segments, and reorganize the production and distribution so that the direct competition between differentiation and efficiency is eliminated. This gives consumers the impression that the supply has been tailored specifically to them as individuals, and suppliers take the consumer's personal wishes into account as much as possible.

In its latest phase of development, marketing actually returns to its original situation: *one-to-one marketing*. After all, the consumer has no need for a large number of suppliers who are each responsible for their own product or service. Consumers benefit from a transparent organization and a high level of clarity. They need products and services, not suppliers. The number of suppliers that address the consumer directly is reduced, restoring the concept of one-to-one marketing. This development may be summarized by specifying the various stages of marketing development in their chronological order. See the outline of Figure 2.8.

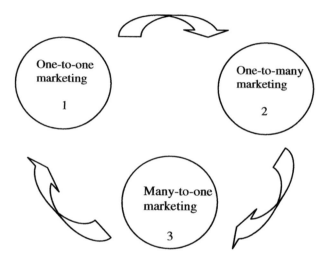

Figure 2.8 Development of types of marketing

From the circular development of marketing we are back to square one. There is one significant exception: the use of ICT to build complex manufacturing systems that may deliver highly personalized goods and services.

The concept of *many-to-many marketing* exists as well. This is, for example, the case for the auction sites such as e-Bay that are available on the Internet. Many suppliers present themselves with offers to many customers. Many-to-many marketing is an interesting consequence of the use of the Internet but, for reasons to be explained later, will not become mainstream.

Do the concepts of mass customization and mass individualization offer the tools to escape the marketing spiral? At the most general level, this question can be answered affirmatively. The problem of market saturation is avoided by serving individual consumers in a situation that is relevant for them, at a time that is convenient for them, and with the help of a product that has been completely tailored towards them. Yet this does not answer the question of which general principles should provide the basis of mass customization or mass individualization. It should be clear that it is possible to assemble products and services differently through a fundamental adjustment of organizational structures and processes. Yet, what should the assembly itself be based upon? Which guidelines could apply in this case? Perhaps individualization is too general a concept to suggest the more specific conditions necessary for new marketing successes. Stated differently: how can marketing provide support for the optimization of individualized need satisfaction?

Individualization as a singular, general trend in itself does not clarify how this should occur. A singular trend is apparently too general. Therefore we propose to descend towards a somewhat less generic level. So what are, at the next level, the most general trends? These are to be viewed as part of individualization, and should relate to the paradoxes referred to earlier. Here we pose three central developments, each related to individualization, that determine the face of marketing. With these three developments we will attempt to construct near future marketing scenarios. Here we will merely indicate them, and in the following chapter they will be explained more extensively:

1. The first development is the continuously increasing sophistication of products and services. Over the course of history, products and services have changed not only qualitatively, but also in terms of their nature. Which developments may be identified, and what kind of extrapolation can be made in this regard? We already noted the individualization of products. Another, upcoming trend is the combination of products, services, and products and services in a single offer to consumers: product packages.
2. The second development refers to a change from purely short-term transaction oriented contacts with consumers towards long-term contacts or relationships with customers.
3. The third development is based on technological developments (ICT). This trend serves as a catalyst for the other two developments. It ensures that they can take place in such a way that the individual consumer is served in an optimal fashion. We will return to this shortly.

It is important to note that each of these three developments may be viewed as part of the individualization trend. In the end, the transformation of products and services arises from the wish to improve supply continuously (in spite of the spirals). Long-term relationships reflect the wish not to limit the responsibility for customers to a single moment or to a limited period. Individualization is supported by knowing the customer better and by adopting a more long-term responsibility.

Finally, the technological development is focused on matching the multitude of various customers and the multitude of products, services and brands in a manner that is tailored to the individual customer.

The three trends may be summarized by stating for each the two main consecutive developmental stages:

Product Sophistication

1. Focus on the core ('no frills') product/service.
    The product/service has one function, to which no additional features, attributes or benefits are attached.
2. Attention to the 'augmented product/service'.
    The augmented product consistes of the core product plus a set of 'layers of menaings', each referring to a particular value added to the product or service. The word 'brand' is often used as a synonym for 'augmented product', but augmentation may be created by additional services as well.

Relationship

1. Short-term transaction focus
    No attention to the relationship between the transactions. Whether one customer buys 100 items of a product or 100 customers buy one item each is considered an irrelevant issue by the marketer.
2. Interest in repeat purchases and loyalty.
    Transactions are perceived in a historical perspective and with reference to future transactions. The focus is more on the customer and customer loyalty than on the sale.

ICT

1. ICT serves to make supply processes more efficient and thus cost effective. Also consumers may benefit, although their interest is secondary to that of the supplier. For example, the use of barcodes.
2. Support of product sophistication and relationship formation.
    In this sense, the ICT dimension is secondary to the first two dimensions.

A matrix may be drawn to combines the first two dimensions (Figure 2.9). The reason for doing so is that in the real market, the developments are not taking place in isolation, but co-exist. Of course, their stages do not necessarily overlap, so that a matrix presentation is in order .

Product sophistication

		Focus on core product	Focus on augmented product
	Transaction focus	1	2
Relationship formation	Focus on repeat purchases	3	4

Figure 2.9 Marketing development matrix

The description provided before, and the summary presented above, suggest that market developments take place in two directions simultaneously, ignoring ICT development for the moment. This means that the progression from Cell 1 to Cell 2 and the progression from Cell 1 to Cell 3 are ultimately combined in Cell 4. It is in this cell that fierce competition exists. As many suppliers focus on both extending the product/service and the relationship with the customer, there is heavy congestion in Cell 4. The density is growing here. Cell 4 is home of the marketing spirals.

It will be necessary for marketers to think strategically beyond this matrix, as the matrix itself no longer provides any solution. It is clear that the mere addition of tactical marketing instruments in the areas of products, services, communication, distribution and pricing, are subject to the spirals. Marketing tactics also suffer the problem of high visibility to competitors. Successful tactics are likely to be copied, especially in areas where these tactics are needed for differentiation. Tactical improvements and innovations will not do the trick. The solution is to be found in strategic innovation. In other words: if we view the matrix as the marketing box, marketers will have to think out of it.

Before doing so it is important to discuss in more detail how consumer behaviour develops relative to the trends. More in particular, we need to consider how consumer behaviour may change if consumers are held captive in the pressure cooker of Cell 4. This will be dealt with in the next chapter.

3. Consumers in the Pressure Cooker

SUMMARY

Customer understanding is critically important for marketing. In marketing practice, the notions of the consumer and the consumer decision process are often idealized. In marketing, it is often implicitly assumed that consumers have the motivation, the capacity and the opportunity to make the decisions that are in their best interest. However, reality shows that the ideal, rational consumer is difficult to find. Obviously, consumers do make purchase decisions, but these are often made on the basis of other criteria than marketers (implicitly) assume. Marketers are more than willing to admit that rational consumer behaviour is exceptional, but often fail to take the deviations from rationality into account. This is an alarming observation in a period characterized by marketing spirals.

INTRODUCTION

Insights into consumer behaviour are crucially important for marketing. This was true in the past, it is important today, and it will become even more important in the future. One way to escape from the marketing spiral is to outrace it, but this requires huge investments. The other way is to reduce its detrimental effects by understanding its dynamics, that is, by understanding the driver behind them: the consumer. Consumer understanding is required in order to anticipate and possibly steer future developments. With consumer behaviour knowledge, we understand why and how consumers choose products and services, and how relationships of suppliers with consumers develop over time. It is also important in order to establish the medium or media by which consumers may best communicate with suppliers.

The recent marketing literature presents various inspiring themes that might be relevant in this respect. While the attention used to be focused on product and market characteristics as determinants of marketing successes, it changed by taking consumer reactions to marketing activities into account as well. *Market focus* is gradually changing into *customer focus*.

It is surprising to note that, even though the concept of customer focus is frequently used by marketers, its precise meaning and intention remain unclear. Organizations that show customer focus in their banner, often do not even take the trouble to define the concept, let alone use it as a basis for marketing policy. 'Customer focus' is usually no more than old wine in a new bottle. Paradoxically, companies do have to become more customer oriented in order to survive in a highly competitive market (E.M. van Raaij, 2001). Ideally, customer orientation should be based on knowledge of customer behaviour and its determinants in order to understand customer decisions, to design effective marketing techniques, and to predict future consumer behaviour. Also in the development of products and services, the preferences and behaviour of consumers should be taken into account. To what extent does the product or service fit with the lifestyle of consumers? And for which particular needs, desires and functions will the new product or package be important? We propose that the ultimate form of customer orientation is behaviour orientation, that is the attuning of marketing measures to the nature and determinants of consumer behaviour.

At a minimum, customer orientation means that a company takes into account individual differences between consumers in, for example, existing possessions, preferences, motives and usage habits. A company that focuses on the 'average customer' is, by definition, not customer focused. It is fortunate to observe that the size of segments to which companies apply the notion of 'average consumer' is getting smaller and smaller, thus gradually alleviating the problem of focusing on a simple average. Some companies even identify micro-segments.

Behaviour orientation implies that no normative judgements are made with regard to the rationality of consumer decisions. A behaviour orientation allows for the possibility that consumers perceive an objectively superior product as inferior, and vice versa. The consumers' opinion is the one and only truth. For marketing, this observation is a blessing and a tragedy at the same time. True customer focus takes into account that consumers may not have an adequate perception of the market, the market process, or the market supply. It also takes into account that these perceptions may not result in adequate evaluations, and may even produce irrational decisions.

To determine how consumers will react to future marketing developments, it is useful to first describe how consumers behave in the current market and marketing situation. Figure 3.1 presents an idealized consumer behaviour process. This process indicates that various decisions are made that are linked together hierarchically. The process presented in the figure suggests that consumers orient themselves to the available alternatives prior to purchase, and that they arrive at the purchase after a choice/decision, that usage or consumption is followed by evaluation (and perhaps maintenance or repairs), after which the product is discarded, replaced or exchanged. That is, if the product has not already been consumed and used up.

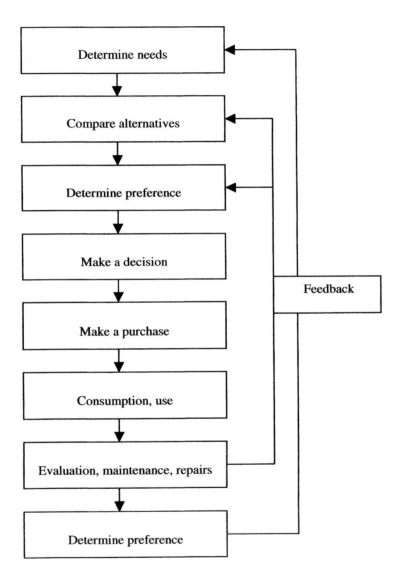

Figure 3.1 The (idealized) decision-making process of consumers

As indicated, this is the idealized process. Real life consumer behaviour may deviate considerably from this. Although consumers are perceived to be decision makers, they may be observed to often make superficial, fairly impulsive decisions that do not necessarily match their own priorities. In doing so, they do use information, but sometimes this involves information that does not do justice to the actual quality of the relevant product. What is more, as early as 1979, Olshavsky and Granbois indicated that there are quite a few reasons to doubt the inclination of consumers to process information and to make well-considered decisions. They indicated that consumers often budget carelessly and that they often make important decisions without being well informed. They follow a decision-making process such as indicated in Figure 4.1 either incompletely, superficially or in a distorted manner. For example, in the case of impulse purchases, the decision to buy is made before the formation of an evaluation.

When introducing the marketing spirals, we presented possible reasons for such deviations of normative, rational decision-making. These reasons can be summarized in three main determinants:

1. Consumers may lack the motivation to engage in elaborate decision-making. This is not the place to provide a full inventory of possible reasons for a lack of motivation, but several more general examples can be mentioned: the quality of most products and services is so high, that it may not be worth the trouble and the time to make careful comparisons. In many cases, consumers are familiar with products and services, so that a repetition of an extensive decision-making process is not called for. Information gathering and decision-making may be a tedious and unattractive activity.

2. Consumers may not have the ability or mental capacity to engage in elaborate decision-making. Ability/capacity refers to consumer knowledge, understanding, processing and mental tasks. For the consumer, it is difficult to know and evaluate all options available in the market, to really understand the various features and attributes of products and services, and to combine these into decisions that reflect personal priorities. Even if consumers would be motivated to do so, their mental ability may be too limited. This is not a matter of intelligence but of the number of items a person can evaluate at one point in time. A complicating factor here is the difficult language that is used in the presentation of many products. Advertisements, websites, manuals and even salespersons use terminology that is often not understood by consumers. Apart from mental capacity, we may identify financial capacity. To what extent do consumers have sufficient financial resources to buy the product?

3.   Finally, consumers may not have sufficient opportunity to make rational decisions. Making decisions takes time. If a person had to compare three brands of a product on the basis of four characteristics each, the task would be very time consuming. Consumers do not have the time to make elaborate decisions for the majority of their purchases. Under time pressure, consumers look for negative evidence of the alternatives in order to select an option that does not have a negative aspect. This is called the 'negative evidence' heuristic (Wright, 1974). In addition, the circumstances under which the decisions are to be made tend not to be ideal, and this is an understatement. In stores, the noise of other consumers, sales personnel and background music, time pressure, and the multitude of stimuli that impinge upon the consumers' various senses hamper active and effortful decision-making, but stimulate simple decision rules (heuristics).

Motivation, ability/ capacity and opportunity can be viewed as necessary conditions for behaviour (such as consumer decision-making) to occur (see Poiesz, 1999). It may be doubted whether a sufficient level of these conditions is available in contemporary consumer decision-making situations. In Cell 1 of the marketing development matrix (Figure 2.9), the product is simple and the transaction is simple. If rational consumer decision-making takes place at all, it is most likely to occur here. For more elaborate products and services, as in Cell 2, the decision is more complex. The same applies to decisions that take place with a time perspective (like repeat purchase decisions). In principle, the most complex decisions should be found in Cell 4, but it is here that it is hardest to meet the three necessary conditions. In this cell, the density of marketing activities is such that they ruin each other's effectiveness. Also in this cell, consumers lack the motivation, capacity and opportunity to know, follow and evaluate everything that is going on. The decision-making that takes place is no more than a caricature of the decision-making as displayed in Figure 3.1.

At this point it is confusing to note that consumers do make purchases, suggesting that they make decisions after all. So if they do not have the motivation, capacity and opportunity to engage in more or less deliberate and elaborate decision-making, how do they make their choices? And what does this mean for marketing?

The confusion can be solved by pointing at the various escapes that consumers have creatively invented for those conditions in which sufficient levels of motivation, capacity or opportunity are lacking. Below, we will present an inventory of these escapes. The inventory does not claim to be complete, but it shows how consumers may continue to act as consumers even though (the quality of) their decision-making is seriously hampered.

COMPLEMENTARY PURCHASES

Perhaps only a few phases of the diagram that was presented in Figure 3.1 actually take place, and possibly even highly superficially. There are also other reasons why consumers are often not able to make careful decisions. Typically, products and services are not bought separately but in an interrelated combination. Consumers acquire assortments of goods. In this regard, *critical goods* determine the choice and purchase of other, complementary goods (Arndt, 1976; Gredal, 1966). The purchase of a car dictates car-related products and services such as petrol, insurances and car accessories. The purchase of carpeting determines the style of the furniture, curtains, and other products in the home. The same applies to fashion: several basic garments in the wardrobe determine the acquisition of complementary items and accessories. The purchase of certain software determines available possibilities and desirable expansions. Dependent on past purchases, consumers are caught in a certain pattern of possessions and purchases (Solomon, 1992). Little research has been performed on patterns of complementation in possessions and purchases. There has been some research into 'consumption ladders', however, that is sequences of purchase of durable goods (Van der Zwan, 1965) and financial services (Paas, 1998).

Complementors are products that match a previously purchased product and that make the previously purchased product more attractive and more useful (Brandenburger and Nalebuff, 1996). Recipes provided with food products, as provided by the supermarket, can be viewed as complementors. Consumer purchases are often complementary and connected with each other. *Interlocking purchases* is the term used in this context, often in relation to cross-selling, that is selling complementary products and services to owners of a certain product. Complementary products and services can make the possession and use of the earlier product more attractive and more useful. Complementary purchases have lower search costs, less waste and testing, and fewer trials and mistakes than non-complementary (separate or 'loose') purchases. Non-complementary purchases are often done 'incrementally', without either a clear objective or an overall picture of what someone wants to achieve with the purchase.

Therefore, previous purchases and possessions not only expand consumption experiences, but also restrict the possibilities for new purchases. Possessions orient consumers towards a (more) limited set of complementary possibilities. Thus, consumers differ in the degree of freedom for their purchase and consumption behaviour. The result of sub-optimal past purchases may keep consumers 'captive'. Past purchases are then seen as *sunk costs*, costs that the consumer does not immediately want to or is even able to write off (Thaler, 1980; Arkes and Blumer, 1985). People want to 'recover' (write off) the acquired purchases in a reasonable number of years. Therefore they continue to orient themselves with new purchases towards the (sub-optimal?) purchases made in the past. New possessions are bought like 'overlapping roof tiles', meaning that consumers deprive themselves of the option to make a clear transition to a different pattern of possessions, even if they would like to. A metaphor may clarify this.

A consumer has spared neither effort nor expense to make a special soup. Yet he does not like the soup. Instead of throwing it away (because of guilt about the sunk costs), he adds new, expensive ingredients in an attempt to make it tasteful after all. The attempt fails and the new composition is even more horrible that the first. Again, new attempts are made to restore the damage. The story repeats itself until the consumer gives in and puts the soup in the freezer to be taken care of later. After a year, it is discarded after all without having been given another try.

Many consumers (and incidentally, also many entrepreneurs) keep going for too long on a 'sub-optimal' road without taking the drastic step of stopping and taking a different direction. Because of sunk costs, it is often too difficult for people to concede that a situation is sub-optimal and that changes are needed. In this way, people remain 'locked in' in unsatisfactory situations. There are many examples of this in business and government projects: the British French Concorde supersonic aeroplane, and the Kalkar nuclear energy plant in Germany.

CONSUMPTION HEURISTICS AND BIASES

Consumers may escape from elaborate decision-making by using 'mental short-cuts' to arrive at a choice (heuristics and biases – see Kahneman and Tversky, 1974). These techniques help them to circumvent the actual decision-making process and still come up with an outcome. For example, consumers may make a choice based on the assumed popularity of a product without knowing or understanding its true qualities. Thus, the consumer who has often seen a product or brand in a television commercial may erroneously conclude that it is popular and is of good quality. Obviously, the subjective, indirect inference of quality may or may not match the actual quality.

Habits may acquire the function of heuristics. When consumers are asked why they purchase a particular brand, they may shrug their shoulders and say that they have always bought this brand. Or consumers may buy a brand because the package looks carefully designed, or because it has more shelf space in the store than other brands. Then, 'loyal' behaviour is not based on a conviction that the brand is to be preferred.

Procedural Knowledge

People use particular, routine procedures for arriving at certain purchases. For example, some consumers may exhibit store loyalty and always go to the same store for purchasing electronic equipment. Or they may be brand loyal: in this case it is not the conviction of the superior quality price ratio that is the basis of the choice, but the loyalty to the brand. Other consumers may follow a standard routine when going through a Consumer Report comparative test. They may first look for the acceptable price bracket and then for the brand name. After the choice is made, they look for corroboration of their choice in the description of the brand characteristics.

These escape behaviours may reflect another, deeper problem (Van Raaij, 2000). People/consumers may have insufficient insight into their own goals, preferences and *biases*. The lack of self-understanding leads to heuristics and biases. Well-known biases are loss aversion, the tendency to select 'safe' and secure alternatives and to avoid possible losses. Another bias is time discounting, taking too short a time perspective into account for a decision.

Loss aversion of investors results in a preference for a certain profit over the chance of an even higher profit at a later point in time. This is called the disposition effect (Shefrin and Statman, 1985). With loss, the reverse is the case: in this case a small chance that no loss will be suffered is preferred over a certain, but smaller loss. We see this in the casino, where gamblers who are losing will take large risks in order to compensate for their loss.

Other human shortcomings that may become apparent in consumer decisions, and which may 'help' them to escape from elaborate decision-making are overconfidence, illusion of control, and its psychological opposite: decentring.

- Overconfidence: Provided with a lot of information and good documentation, many people strongly believe in the quality of their own decisions. But more information does not always lead to better decisions (Jacoby et al., 1977, 1984). Too much confidence develops, as well as too much certainty that good decisions are being made, especially because the available information has not always been completely integrated into the decision-making (Russo and Schoemaker, 1992).
- Illusion of control: The availability of a lot of information also gives one the feeling of controlling the situation. The environmental factors that are not being controlled are often underestimated. Think here of car driving and accidents (Langer, 1982); drivers overestimate their

driving competence and tend to underestimate the probability of an accident.

- Decentring: This is a consequence of frustration in the interaction with equipment and information technology. This is a relevant issue in the case of Internet purchasing. People no longer feel as if they are the boss and the centre of their universe, but instead they lose control and are enslaved to their equipment and situations. They no longer feel master over the situation and the technology, but experience the technology as hostile and 'oppositional'. As a result, consumers may not use relevant databases and decision aids, because they cannot handle the available equipment and usage instructions.

Therefore, we can state that consumers' decision and purchase freedom is not only limited by financial and social conditions, but to a large extent also by their own past behaviour, and by their psychological characteristics. The overall conclusion is that conditions in Cell 4 prevent consumers from making elaborate decisions on the basis of personal priorities and trade-offs, and force them to use decision escapes and heuristics. This seriously affects the quality of their decisions. In fact, there may be three generic types of problems:

1. Consumers purchase products that they should not have bought if they had made a decision according to their personal preferences and priorities. Costs in terms of money, effort and time are made without a corresponding benefit. This leads to added costs, but no added value.
2. Consumers do not purchase products that they would have liked to buy if they had known about their consumption effects. They do not know what is available in the market or misjudge purchase options. Generally, this is not viewed as a serious consumer behaviour problem, but in fact it is, and may seriously affect the interests of consumers and producers alike.
3. Consumers use products that they have bought in a different way from their expectations at purchase. For example, audio equipment is purchased on the basis of the number of its functions (a heuristic for product quality). After purchase, the number of functions proves to be prohibitive for effective usage.

The conclusion of sub-optimal consumer decision-making requires an adjustment of Figure 3.1 into Figure 3.2.

In Figure 3.2, the phases of need determination, information collection, preference formation and evaluation are not included. They have made way for more or less forced acquisitions, automatisms in behaviour, and impulse buying. The feedback has no other function than to maintain this system of biases and heuristics.

In this case there is no careful decision-making process that results in need satisfaction in conformity with the personal priorities, either for the short term or for the long term.

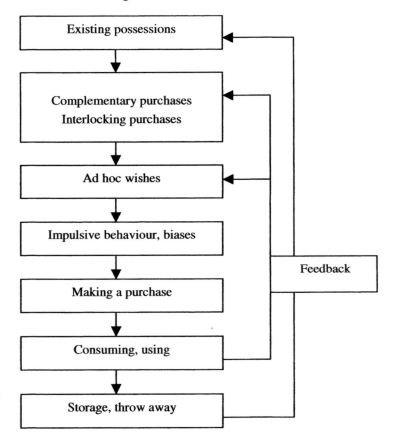

Figure 3.2   The (modified) decision-making process of consumers

IMPLICATIONS FOR MARKETING

It is clear that these changes in consumer behaviour will, in turn, affect the very marketing developments from which they originate. Thereby, the circle is closed. Marketing affects behaviour and behaviour affects marketing. The more marketing intensifies, the more consumers escape its complexity and dynamics; the more marketing tries to reach consumers anyway, the more extreme consumers' evasive behaviour, and so on. We have seen this in the marketing spirals, and it is evident from the behaviour that consumers show. At the same time, we may observe some distinct blindness on the part of the marketers. They either ignore the problem because they do not see it, or they strategically look the other way because they do not know the solution. As many marketers frankly admit that they are experiencing greater and greater difficulty developing effective marketing measures, we opt for the latter explanation. The remainder of this book is aimed at finding a strategic answer to the turmoil that surrounds us all, recognizing that mere tactical improvements may not present the solution. The strategic answer should allow companies to escape from the marketing spirals and provide a solution not only for themselves but for customers as well.

4. Marketing Developments: A Synthesis

SUMMARY

In this chapter, an attempt is made to find a strategic solution to the marketing spirals. This is done by making an extrapolation of three major marketing trends: the increasing level of *product sophistication* (from core products to meta-packages), the stronger emphasis on longer relationships with customers (from ad hoc transactions to lifelong relationships), and the growing impact of information and communication technology (ICT). The first two factors are combined into the 'value matrix' – an extension of the 'marketing development matrix' (Figure 2.9), while ICT enables these developments as a support instrument. Based on these combinations, a number of added value strategies may be developed. Companies will enter into long term, even lifelong relationships with their customers and will offer a meta-package of goods and services. This meta-package is presented as a meta brand: the 'Virtual Guardian Angel' (VGA). The VGA reduces market complexity – and its associated hassle, stress and time – for customers. The VGA will assist consumers in realizing important goals and values in life.

INTRODUCTION

Chapter 2 concluded with the suggestion that three central trends may be considered as the 'essential elements' of individualization:

- Increasing product sophistication and product bundling.
- Extension of the duration of the relationship of suppliers and consumers.
- Growing impact of information and communication technology (ICT).

With these trends, we developed the marketing development matrix (see Figure 2.9) and elaborated, in Chapter 2, on the implications of the marketing situation in the matrix cell that best describes the current situation. We showed how consumers escape from the situation and engage in suboptimal buying behaviour. Thus, it was indicated that the implications of the marketing spirals have detrimental effects for both marketers and consumers. On this basis we called for a strategic solution as, apparently, tactical solutions merely add to the spirals.

We used the three trends to summarize all relevant marketing developments. Based on these three trends, we will now present an extrapolation towards the future. As stated in Chapter 1, we will not focus on very long-term scenarios. It is impossible to imagine with even the slightest certainty what the world will look like in ten or fifteen years from now (apart from the notion that it is going to be quite different from now). Also, for most market sectors, industries and companies, this period is far too long in terms of strategic policy. We will, therefore, restrict ourselves to a prediction for the medium term.

In Chapter 2, we presented an initial examination of three trends independently. For a well-argued extrapolation to future situations or scenarios it is essential to describe the trends more completely and to consider them in their mutual relationships. After all, the spirals from which they were derived were not considered to be mutually independent either. It is our intent to use the combination of the three trends as an inspiration for near-future scenarios. For this, we will present a more extensive description of the various phases of these trends.

INCREASING PRODUCT SOPHISTICATION

At the most general level, the development of products and services over time may be characterized by four phases. The first phase has already taken place and is still going on. On top of this, the second phase is in full progress. The first signs of Phase 3 may have already been noticed, and Phase 4 is starting to appear on the horizon.

Phase 1: Core Product

The first products and services that were produced were exclusively related to the specific, almost tangible function they were expected to fulfil. A chair was a chair and a table was a table. No more, and no less. The barber cut hair, with a highly visible result. Products and services did what they should do. We call these products and services *core products*. They were evaluated based on the extent to which they were fulfilling the fixed, primary function specified prior to the purchase. If a product improvement or decoration was present, it was more related to the need of the producer to demonstrate his or her own craftsmanship than to the consumers' need. Additions were not necessary for differentiation purposes, as differences between competing products were apparent. Complementary services and guarantees did not yet exist. Whoever wanted a special design had to make a special order. There were no websites, premiums, coupons, frequent flyer programmes, savings stamps, special packaging, sweepstakes or scratch cards. Added psychological value was not necessary, because consumers were capable of judging the quality of the product themselves.

Phase 2: Augmented Product

As the market supply continued to increase relative to demand, competition called for the need to include some added value in products and services. Products were packaged more nicely, in the literal or figurative sense. The supplier paid more attention to decoration, improvement and renewal. The original functional core product was differentiated by *branding* and by an additional 'layer of meaning' (McCracken, 1986). This layer connects a story to the brand and communicates the implicit or explicit message that this product is better than or at least different from competing products. In the literature, this is called an *augmented product*. In other words, it is an expanded or dressed-up product. In principle, a new layer could be arranged around an existing layer. When competitive pressure increased, a growing number of 'layers' around the core product could be observed. In the course of time two problems became evident, however:

1. Competitors copy successful products and add similar layers of meaning to them. Then product/brand differentiation quickly disappears. The mere addition of concrete product characteristics (packaging, design and additional functions) is no longer sufficient.
2. Product differentiation possibilities are reduced to the extent that the number of layers increases. This leads to a situation in which new layers have the tendency to be less and less concrete. These more abstract layers are related to additional service aspects such as expanded service, money-back guarantees, longer guarantee periods, and even abstract values such as harmony and peace (Coca-Cola). The adoption of these layers by competitors forces the supplier once again to search for more differentiation with the help of supplementary associations and meanings. The product acquires new layers of meaning continuously, which eventually leads to the somewhat odd relationship between intrinsic characteristics – that are related to the primary functions of the product – and the added characteristics. A situation may develop in which the former may no longer be related to the latter. For example, a car as a collection of technical and design characteristics may claim an association with freedom. It cannot be deduced from the

number of cylinders, the ABS system, the catalytic converter or the exhaust system why this car in particular should give its owner the feeling of freedom. Finally, over time, the balance in the relationship between concrete and abstract characteristics may completely tip over to the latter. If this happens, the relevant product no longer exists on the basis of how it performs, but on what it means to the owner. Brands, as carriers of meanings and associations, determine the position of a product in the market, even when the products that they represent are no longer distinguishable from competitive products in an objective sense.

Due to the never-ending competition, a situation arises in which the layers of meaning keep accumulating, leading to top-heavy brands. New layers of meaning no longer have any, become less credible, are too expensive, or can simply no longer be found. Certain brands still make an effort to connect with core values of consumers such as friendship, harmony, safety and adventure, but the number of core values is limited (Rokeach, 1960), leaving little room for differentiating brand claims.

And so, despite (or perhaps even because of) abstract differentiations, the market has become very crowded. It may no longer be be possible to use the traditional techniques to imagine new differentiating layers. Overall differentiation decreases, and homogeneity of supply increases. We have already indicated in Chapter 2 that a lack of differentiation or a lack of added value leads to a negative price spiral. Whoever is not able to claim exclusiveness, is reduced to a standard product, a commodity.

In short, the augmented product has some unintended side effects. Because brands are disproportionately focusing on the newest (and therefore the most abstract) meanings, the exterior layers become alienated from the intrinsic product or brand characteristics. Consumers no longer perceive the relationship between the value that is addressed by a brand (for example 'freedom', 'adventure' or 'harmony') and the actual functional brand qualities of a soft drink ('to quench thirst'). The only way to establish the relationship is by frequent and continuous repetition of the association in communication. It becomes more difficult – and therefore more expensive – for the supplier to create the desired association. For the consumer it becomes more difficult to distinguish brands at this abstract level.

Perhaps the most frustrating side effect is that the added value that originally was generated by the new layer gradually dissolves into mediocrity. Consumers get used to the extra service, the guarantees, the free toothbrushes, the discount coupons, and the gift wrap. The first car dealer who provided coffee in the showroom had a unique selling proposition. Yet car dealers these days that do not provide coffee for their customers are perceived as very discourteous. Over time, the so-called *satisfiers* (product characteristics that lead to satisfaction if well provided but not to dissatisfaction if not provided) shrink to so-called *dissatisfiers* (product characteristics that if not fulfilled lead to dissatisfaction, but not – or no longer – to satisfaction) (Herzberg et al., 1959).

The side effects may create the phenomenon of *floating brands*, brands whose associations are not directly related to physical characteristics. Just like over-inflated balloons, these are very highly susceptible to outside influences (competitive winds) and are easily 'blown away'. Similarly, a floating brand is vulnerable to all sorts of external influences. Because such a brand is not filled with directly supporting functional characteristics that allow for credible associations, a 'pin prick' or a minor incident is sufficient to make it collapse. A financial institution that positions itself as The Bank (with the emphasis on 'the', like *the* ABN-AMRO bank in The Netherlands), and which is not associated by consumers with distinct characteristics or clear benefits or values that legitimize the claim of superiority, is very vulnerable to any imperfections in the relationships with customers, due to the contrast effect with expectations.

To summarize, an *augmented product* in a very mature market is not enviable. Regardless of how much has been invested in its positioning, differentiation possibilities will reach a ceiling, after which the product can only slide down into homogeneity and be sucked into a negative price spiral.

Phase 3: Category Packages

The crucial question is what a product or service is still able to do in order to be seen as truly different and to be appreciated by consumers. Because the product or service itself no longer offers any room for differentiating added value, we have to consider this from a completely different angle. The product or brand itself can no longer be extended in a psychologically meaningful way. Yet competition is relentless and a solution is urgently needed. Therefore, we are forced to look for added value in what appears to be the only possibility that is still open: a unique combination with other existing products and services, that is product bundling (Stremersch and Tellis, 2002). The combination of functions of various products may create synergy: entirely new and even innovative functions. The first products and services that are suitable for this process are products and services that consumers perceive as complementary to the core product. With the purchase of a new car, a full tank of petrol is delivered free (the reverse combination being less obvious). In making a holiday reservation, the consumer receives a free vacation booklet from the travel agency. With a can of soup the consumer receives a potholder, and the purchase of a tube of toothpaste yields a free toothbrush. These examples involve products that the consumer considers to be complementary: the added product is the logical extension of the core product. Complementarity is an advantage because the consumer needs little information on the nature of the relationship between the two products.

Yet complementarity also leads to a disadvantage: the more a product is viewed as complementary, the more likely it is to be perceived as a mere additional layer. This, again, reduces its potential to differentiate. This leads to the conclusion that added value should be found in the combination of products and services that the consumer does *not* experience as an obvious supplement. Non-complementary products and services would therefore be preferable. But how can the degree of complementarity or, conversely, the degree of the uniqueness of the combination be determined?

Before discussing this, we need to present several assumptions. We assume that consumers use mental categories of products and services. A single category includes different products and services that more or less relate to the same function or benefit. Consumers experience differences between them as small or even negligible. The larger the perceived difference between two categories, the more differences consumers will perceive between the products/services and the less they will experience a combination as being logical and familiar.

We assume that categories are arranged in a hierarchical order: larger categories contain smaller categories. And the larger categories are part of even larger categories themselves. Thus, the between-product differences are determined by the distance between the products within this hierarchy.

Let us refer to financial products and services as an example. At the lowest level of this hierarchy are the various individual products and services: glass insurance, home insurance, car insurance, travel insurance, disability insurance, life insurance, checking account, savings account, investment account, foreign currency account, pension and mortgage. We assume that consumers combine the individual financial products into different mental categories or accounts, such as insurances, savings, payments, loans, investments, mortgages and pensions/retirements. These, in turn, may be combined into still higher order categories, such as one category of financial products/services that relates to the short term and one category of products/services that relate to the long term. Finally there is one single main category or account: the category of finances that contains all financial products and services.

But even a main category may be combined again with other main categories such as clothing, food, transportation and furnishing. The overall hierarchy is composed of various categories between which consumers experience large or small differences. For example, consumers will experience fewer differences between food products or between clothing products than between food products on the one hand and clothing products on the other hand. Soon we will see why this is important.

The size of the differences between categories is a continuum: it ranges from small to large. The larger the difference, the more unusual is their combination. We designate a very small difference between the categories – a light bulb with a fitting – as 'complementary'. Such a small difference is, in fact, a variation of the *augmented product*. When the difference (the perceived distance) becomes so large that the consumer no longer perceives a product to be the logical extension of another product, we may refer to the types of offer as presented in Phase 3: the phase of the category-specific packages.

In the search for differentiating added value, an independently operating product has a decreasing amount of 'room to manoeuvre'. There will be an increasing use of bundles of products and services that belong to the same category. To the extent that these combinations occur so frequently that they are taken for granted, the perceived differences within the bundles will continue to decrease and the perceived differences between them will continue to increase. A guarantee of a free repair of a minor car problem offers added value, until the consumer gets used to it and takes it for granted. The more self-evident a characteristic, the less likely it is that it may serve as the differentiating added value.

In order to surprise, impress and truly please customers, new product bundles will be formed. For example, a car manufacturer may do this by extending the notion of mobility. Customers may receive added value in the form of privileges at particular car rental companies in the event that their own car is not available. The added value then is no longer located in the characteristics of the original products, but in the synergy of the chosen product/service combination. In this Phase 3, the combination is still within the category experience of consumers (mobility). For example, in this phase, products and services will be combined that the consumer perceives as belonging to the category 'living', or to the category work, leisure time, transport, health or education.

We use the term 'category package' for this concept. The combined products/services belong to the same category and their combination creates synergetic added value. Several other examples may be given. Within the category of insurances, an insurance company ensures that the components in the insurance package are optimally integrated. This avoids risky gaps in the coverage. Also, the consumer does not have to pay double premium for overlapping insurances. In the category of medical services, care and prevention may be seen as separate activities, but it is also possible to link them together for individual clients/patients. In the category of home care, maintenance and cleaning may be combined. Similarly, the category of safety shows the combination of a theft alarm and the automatic notification of the police in the event of burglary. In the market, the number of these and similar examples is increasing slowly but steadily. For example, the following are being combined into a single supply: mortgages and life insurances; investments and pensions; savings, investments and insurance products; television sets and DVD recorders; espresso and coffee machines; and telephones, fax and copy machines. Even the Internet, radio, television and telephone are becoming an integrated bundle of services. This is an example of technical complementarity. The potential number of synergies seems to be unlimited.

Category packages are not yet used widely in the market. Or, from a marketing technology perspective, the concept has not yet been well developed and accepted. An example that provides an exception is that of the *All Finance* or *Allfinanz* concept. This contains a number of financial products and services that have been synchronized for both the short term and the long term, which allows for a link with fiscal and pension advice.

Considering the large number of products and services and the endless possibilities for combining them, the number of initiatives to arrive at attractive combinations is actually still quite limited. And we do not mean mere 'layer of meaning' initiatives such as the bookseller who is also selling CDs, the chemist's that also includes glasses in its assortment, or the butcher who also sells charcoal for the barbecue.

We are not referring either to the presentation of insurances by supermarket chains or the presentation of supermarket products by petrol companies. In fact these examples only involve industry or category blurring in which the emphasis is primarily placed on the advantage for the supplier. By expanding their assortment, suppliers may succeed in increasing their sales. Although there are advantages for the consumer, these are limited to saving time and financial costs due to the availability of more products within the same location. But the advantages are not yet sought, nor presented, in terms of the added value of the synergy. Yet this is the focus of our attention. In the case of the *All Finance* concept, the added value consists of synchronization amongst the financial products and services to such an extent that:

1. There is no overlap between the separate components. The consumer does not pay too much.
2. Gaps and omissions in the entire package are avoided, so that undesired surprises and risks are avoided.
3. Not only short-term, but also long-term interests of consumers are served.

Consumers are able to transfer the time, attention and care for their finances to the supplier and no longer have to pay much attention to it. The 'hassle' has been delegated to the other party. The added value is located in the savings of time and effort or energy (and perhaps even money), and the reduction of uncertainty about the quality of the purchase.

Note that brand and line extensions do not necessarily result in category packages. Brand extensions involve the offering of other products under the same brand name. There are three types of brand extensions: line, benefit and value extensions (Van Raaij and Schoonderbeek, 1993). For example, the brand Camel offers cigarettes, fashion and shoes. This is a value extension, because the brand Camel is a strong brand exploiting the value of 'adventure'. A line extension involves the addition of product variations in colour, taste or size under the same brand name, for instance Cherry Coke as a line extension of Coca-Cola. Benefit extensions involve products with the same benefits, such as Weight Watchers food products. Although line and value extensions are focused on using the market position and lead to several types of products from a single supplier, this does not mean that they constitute a category package. Cigarettes and shoes do not form a natural product package. Benefit extensions come closer to a category package. People with a weight problem may become members of the Weight Watchers organization, may participate in local groups, and may use Weight Watchers products.

What does synergy-oriented marketing mean for the future? We expect that hybrid products/services will take off and that the difference between the products/services (measured in 'distance' between their respective categories) will increase. The development is towards larger, broadly composed bundles of products and services for which the consumer still experiences the differences amongst them as sizeable and relevant. The trend is in the direction of 'meta-packages'.

Phase 4: 'Meta-packages'

The concept of 'meta-package' refers to the synergistic combination, within one single concept, of various products and services that do not originate from the same category. The notion of meta-package designates a particular conceptual level, that is the level above that of individual products and services. It should not be confused with a mega-package. This involves the mere sum of a large number of products. Thus, a meta-package may not be a mega-package.

In a meta-package, the true value of the market supply is located in the total package, and not in the sum of the individual products and services. By focusing on functional combinations between products and services from various categories, suppliers are able to create substantive added value compared with the existing supply.

A classic example is provided by the inclusive trip as arranged by a tour operator and offered through a travel agent. Although airline companies, bus companies, hotel owners, car rental companies and local suppliers of excursions each have their own, specific and independent products and services, the tour operator uses these components to assemble a unique service for which the combination is better than the mere sum of its parts. The consumer saves not only time and probably even money, but also has the guarantee that the different elements are merged into a logical overall package. Although consumers, in principle, can select and purchase the individual components separately, they would probably not succeed in creating the synergistic effect that the tour operator is able to deliver.

A recent example of a meta-package is the linkage of a mobile telephone (GSM or cell phone) to the Internet and to bank-related services. Compare also technical combinations made possible through the Internet: radio, television and telephone. Another example is the collaboration between a pharmaceutical firm and a publisher, in which the publisher answers consumer questions on health, and publishes information on diseases and general treatment. In this concept, the attention is not only directed at care in case of illness, but also on the prevention of illnesses through information and support.

Additional examples may be presented. We can imagine the application of the idea of meta-packages to employment counselling services and temporary employment agencies. As another example, 'home products' are being developed that use living in the broadest sense of the word. 'Home' in this case is a combination of owning, leasing or renting a home, the 'guarantee' of a safe environment, the attractiveness of the outdoor environment, the maintenance of that environment, the availability of medical provisions, garden maintenance, surveillance during absence, and the possibility of supplementary services such as home cleaning and maintenance.

Meta-packages make one-stop shopping or single supplier–consumer contacts possible. Products and services offered as a combination can be considered simultaneously in a consumer's decision and can be arranged by one supplier, that is to say, if the consumer experiences the combination as a unit. If the consumer is convinced that, despite the combination, separate decisions need to be made regarding the individual components, the package concept does not apply.

To be entirely clear with regard to the distinction between mere product combinations and synergistic meta-packages, let us compare, for example, a funfair – as a temporary collection of various attractions – with a permanent theme or amusement park such as Disneyland. At the fair, visitors make a decision about each individual attraction and need to pay for each individual ride. By contrast, at the entrance of the amusement park, visitors pay one overall entrance fee. For this fee, visitors can use the available amenities based on their own preferences and as much as possible. The attractions have been composed in such a way that there is a large variety of choice options with little overlap amongst them, and sometimes an attractive order in which the attractions can be visited.

Because the theme park has a fixed structure (as opposed to the fair), the guidance of the visitor is strongly optimized. Information is available on the attractions and the routes, visitors may inform themselves beforehand about the individual attractions, the park is maintained professionally, and the design is optimally arranged. The structure in the organization and the professionalism of the process make a strong customer focus possible. At the fair, however, the market is still in its earliest development stage: suppliers are strongly product-oriented and transaction-oriented. They are not interested in consumers but in their money. No distinction is made between one visit by five different customers, and five visits by the same customer. The supplier could not care less. In contrast with the fair, the theme park can present itself as an integrated entity to (potential) customers, and can engage in a brand and relationship policy. Visitors perceive themselves not only as paying customers, but feel themselves, to some extent, as guests and members of a club. The personal connection to the theme park is supported through merchandising activities. Now, the market often is much like a fair. However, only when meta-packages are formed will it start to look more like a theme park.

The example raises a question regarding the linkage of products and needs. Undoubtedly, there is a certain degree of linkage; otherwise the products would not be purchased. Yet specific products may not be linked to specific needs – as if there is a 100 per cent fit. In other words, it is most likely that an optimal fulfilment for a specific need does not exist, and a specific product probably does not cover a specific need completely.

If a specific product is purchased because it is a better fit for a customer need than another product, there is no guarantee of a complete overlap. At best, the overlap will be relatively favourable (see Figure 4.1a). Incidentally, suppliers of products show a tendency to assume that a complete overlap exists if the product is being purchased (see Figure 4.1b).

At the most general level – the level of total supply – the pattern of overlap between needs on the one hand and products on the other hand is very complex. In fact, the exact nature of the overlap at this level is unknown. This allows room for the following possibilities:

1. There is an optimal match between products/services and needs.
2. There are various products that satisfy the same need.
3. Several products satisfy various needs.
4. Some needs are not being addressed by the existing supply of products.
5. Existing products satisfy needs only partially.

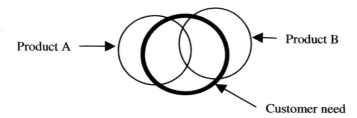

Note: The overlap of the need and product A is larger than the overlap of the need and product B.

Figure 4.1a Actual overlap between the need and products A and B

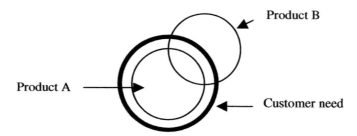

Figure 4.1b The overlap of the need and A as assumed by the supplier of product A, if A has been purchased and not B

In sum, it is likely that there are gaps (unmet needs) and overlaps (over-satisfied needs) in the fit between needs and products/services (between demand and supply). Shortages and surpluses co-exist. One would think that market principles would be able to correct the lack of balance. However, the corrective effect of market functioning is either absent, partial, slow or simply late. In the meantime, the customer continues to purchase separate products and services that may or may not fit needs and that may or may not overlap in function.

On the one hand, the current market supply is a blessing due to the enormous number of choice options. The market is like a gigantic buffet, and consumers move along to fill their plates. On the other hand, the abundance is also a matter of concern, since the supply of options continues to change. Literally thousands of dishes are presented in a random, arbitrary order, making choice difficult, and increasing time and opportunity costs. The chocolate sauce is positioned next to the mackerel, the cauliflower next to the dumplings, yoghurt next to the sweetbread and the Chablis next to the peanut butter. Behind each dish, producers compete for the guests' attention and preferences. They shout and gesture to persuade consumers that their particular dish is the very best available. Consumers fill their plates at the first section of the buffet table with attractive items, but have the uncomfortable feeling that they may later encounter dishes that they, in hindsight, might have preferred over the ones selected now. Suppliers early in the line have an advantage over 'later' suppliers, because if consumers' dishes are filled, they will stop collecting more items.

After finishing the meal, they are informed that they could not possibly have chosen a less healthy combination of food and drinks. They receive the advice to pay more attention to restrict the amount of cholesterol, sugar, salt, calories, colourants and alcohol. But when the consumers are standing in front of the buffet table the next time, the supply has been changed ('NEW!'). No nutritional information is presented. Instead, suppliers have decided to identify the source of the plates more clearly. They introduce brand names. Now, each dish is provided with a little flag indicating its origin. The number of brands is such that this helps a little, but not a lot. Anyhow, the suppliers have decided to *upgrade* their marketing activities in order to attract the consumers' attention. Now they use increasingly larger flags, flashlights, megaphones, sirens and banners. Next to the dishes there are scratch cards, bonuses, customer affinity cards, discount coupons and other relationship gadgets. One supplier mentions that he sponsors a cycle team, while another claims to support the World Wildlife Fund. Yet consumers still do not know whether they have filled their plate in a way that best suits their personal tastes and interests, and whether they have chosen good combinations.

The organizers of the buffet decide to change policy again and to arrange the dishes and drinks in the order in which they are to be consumed: from appetizers to main courses to desserts. This does help. Also, dishes that are most suitable to be combined from a culinary perspective are placed side by side. For each combination, a particular wine is recommended. At the same time, the organization decides to inform consumers beforehand about these combinations, so that they do not need to walk past the entire buffet first and then return to make a selection. Now, consumers are satisfied, the suppliers do not need to convince consumers and can spend their energy on product quality rather than communication. The amount of food that is left over afterwards due to overabundance is significantly reduced.

How does a meta-package take shape? A meta-package is the result of the efforts of various parties. The suppliers themselves may, based on their expertise, imagine creative concepts that are better suited to their target audiences. Consumers may also articulate their own appreciation about the combinations received or about the proposals presented to them. It is important that suppliers no longer restrict their products and services to their original functions. Just like wine, whose quality is to be judged in relation to the situation (appetizer, table wine, dessert wine, and so on), the functionality of other products and services should be determined with the particular goal and context in mind. By focusing on consumption goals, it is possible to approach the actual needs more closely. A consumer does not want to have the Internet, a telephone and a copier. Rather, the consumer wants to communicate effectively and efficiently. Consumers want pension advice that is wrapped in fiscal considerations and that takes their current assets into account. They do not want three separate pieces of advice to be integrated by themselves: one about pensions from a financial advisor, one about fiscal consequences from a tax consultant, and one about asset management from another consultant. Simply, because, in this case, three times one is less than one times three. Patients will never spontaneously identify the partial needs associated with every link in the chain of medical services. They simply want to be cured and to be reintegrated in the societal process. They are more interested in the full process leading to cure and reintegration than in the various aspects and phases of this process called medical services. Similarly, consumers are not so much interested in a pure accumulation of products and services, but rather in the advantage of the synergy that may develop between them.

The synergy should lead to logical, organic combinations that are a better match for individual consumer needs than the original units. The value of a dish in a buffet is not determined by its own characteristics only, but also by the specific combination with other dishes. A meta-package can help the consumer to connect with a need not only at a certain point in time, but also over time. A combination may be very suitable as an appetizer. But if this combination is served so generously that there is no more financial or physical room for a main course or dessert, the notion of the meta-package was too narrow.

It is easy to translate this metaphor to other domains. Take the example of combined financial products: here the consumer's need should be defined more broadly than 'short-term financial advantage'. It may concern the value of the package in the long term. Or it may concern the contribution of that package to the satisfaction of various needs over time. The real contribution of the package may also lie in the fact that consumers are tired of the financial 'hassle' and no longer want to deal with the question of whether they have arranged their affairs as well as possible. Thus, financial needs may not have a one-to-one connection with financial products. Rather, needs should be defined at a more general level in order to be psychologically meaningful. Financial needs, then, may not relate to mortgage options, loan variations and investment alternatives, but to psychological comfort, time saving and uncertainty reduction. Mr Johnson does not care whether he has the optimal financial product. He would not be able to judge it anyway. Instead, he wants the perfect excuse for not having to deal with it.

In conclusion, we state that the development of products and services over time indicates a trend in which these products and services become increasingly more *sophisticated*. We use the word 'sophisticated' to emphasize that we do not merely address the formation of more complex products and services. Complexity in itself would be too simple.

So the core product has developed into an *augmented product*, which consists of a bundle of different meanings. The augmented product is followed by category packages. Category packages are bundles of products and services belonging to the same overall function – as perceived by consumers. Examples of categories are food, finance or literature. Under the pressure of continuous competition these will eventually find their sequel in meta-packages, consisting of products and services that originate from different categories. Meta-categories or packages are related to domains such as household entertainment, mobility, leisure time, work and health. The borderline between packages and meta-packages is not very strict. The boundary is defined by the consumers' perception that the combination involves products (and/or services) that have not been presented before as belonging to the same category.

Examples for each phase may be found in the market, with obviously the fewest examples being available of meta-packages. Various signals point to the development of the specified direction. Health care institutions team up with housing organizations. Companies may outsource all maintenance services to one party to take care of buildings and facilities, as well as cleaning, decoration, repairs, gardening, and even watering the plants. Software intermediaries may form and expand elaborate packages of compatible hardware and software products. In the holiday markets, all-inclusive packages are becoming more popular. Travellers can enjoy themselves and have nothing to worry (to think?) about from departure to return. We expect that market supply will increasingly offer such packages and that new total concepts will become available. Due to their effect on the behaviour of consumers, it will be appropriate to characterize them as 'discontinuous innovations' (a term introduced by Rogers, 1983). More and more, these packages are being based on the characteristics of the *connection* between the components and decreasingly on the characteristics of the components themselves.

Therefore, the search for added value will be completed in four phases. Strategically speaking, hardly anything can be gained from Phase 1 (core product) any more. Phase 2 (augmented product) is characterized by high pressure on the effectiveness and efficiency of marketing measures (no wonder that the concept of *accountability* appears in this phase – 'Justify what you are doing, because we no longer believe in an automatic result'). Paradoxically (or maybe not), the more difficult it is to legitimize marketing activities and expenditures, the higher the need for justification. Phase 3 (category package) does offer some strategic room to manoeuvre, although at this point it appears to be more a case of experimental rather than systematic attempts to redefine market supply. If a company is prepared to discuss its own historical market and marketing definitions, it may be able to create new strategic possibilities in Phase 4 (domain packages). In that case, a broad view is required for strategy formation, not restricted by the own current market, nor by mental rigidity of strategic decision makers.

Unfortunately, the continuum that has just been outlined is not free from inflation. It involves a dynamic development, which means that what might be interpreted as an innovative combination at time 1, may be taken for granted by the consumer at time 2. Innovations dissolve into normal products: *satisfiers* inevitably evaporate into *dissatisfiers*. The race against commoditization continues. We expect it to be run along two dimensions: product sophistication and long-term relationships. Of these, we have now described the first. For the sake of clarity we should note that this dimension, in itself, cannot provide the strategic solution we are looking for as the dreaded spirals may develop with regard to product/service packages as well.

LONG-TERM RELATIONSHIPS

The second basic dimension relates to the nature, the intensity and the duration of the contacts between supplier and customer. Over the past decade, the attention to the concept of relationships has increased significantly in marketing (Vargo and Lusch, 2004). Why is a relationship important and how should it be interpreted? Which advantages exist for suppliers and customers?

Advantages for Suppliers

It is not surprising that suppliers are inclined to develop long-term relationships with their customers. They do not need to incur costs in order to reach their target audience: after all, it is familiar and accessible. A loyal customer is a consumer who seems to be convinced of the added value of the relevant supplier. This is important, because we have noted that the traditional marketing instruments are losing their functionality and effectiveness. The disproportionate costs that have to be made to persuade new customers of the added value do not need to be made for existing customers. Their loyalty only needs to be reinforced and supported (Reichheld, 1996; Buchanan and Gilles, 1990).

Another advantage of long-term relationships is that more information can be collected about the customer over time. It becomes clear which fluctuations customers demonstrate and what causes these fluctuations. The required dosage of marketing instruments can be better defined. In a steady relationship there is more stability and there are more certain purchases. This is called a strong 'consumer franchise'. It has a cost reducing effect, for example because it is not necessary to maintain inventories for absorbing unanticipated fluctuations in demand.

The possibilities for *cross-selling* are an important advantage of long-term relationships. Cross-selling is selling additional products from the same supplier to a loyal customer. Because the consumer is known, it is possible to determine at what point an expansion of the products/services package is appropriate. It is possible to approach the consumer at the right time and the right location for this purpose.

Finally, a long-term relationship underscores the chosen positioning. If a supplier has a high percentage of loyal customers, it suggests that the market position is legitimate and has been earned. This increases the status, the power and the reputation of the supplier in the market, with favourable side effects.

To complete the picture, it should be noted that long-term relationships do not always lead to more favourable outcomes for the supplier. By intensifying the relationship, the buyer increases his/her knowledge of the supplier's processes and, consequently, may identify possibilities to cut costs or increase services. Very loyal customers may not only contribute to the continuity of the organization, they may be very demanding, thus increasing costs and decreasing client-related profits (Keiningham et al., 2005).

Advantage for Consumers

For consumers, a steady relationship also has advantages over wildly vary-ing contacts in the market. In the first place, the relationship provides a fixed point in the otherwise chaotic and dynamic market. Therefore, loyalty may not only be the consequence of a positive choice, but it may perhaps also be partly explained as a negative choice, avoiding uncertainty, incon-venience and repeated decision making. For consumers, the long-term relationship offers the advantages of the status as a regular customer. Often this involves financial advantages and privileges. The customer also en-counters fewer search costs and may even be able to profit from the possibility of *cross-buying* – the customer counterpart of *cross-selling* (cross-buying is the purchasing of additional products of a supplier from whom purchases have already been made). In fact, cross-selling should be based upon cross-buying, not vice versa.

As in a social environment, relationships in a market environment may differ in intensity, quality and duration. A number of related characteristics have been suggested in the literature. For example, it is important that the relationship is not based on the dominance of one party over the other: in that case the one party is dominating the other party based on power. This occurs, for example, by indicating the minimum number of products that must be purchased, such as with a book club. In that case there is a 'forced' relationship, and the parties do not engage in the desired behaviour. It is not unlikely that, given any freedom of action, the dominated party will termi-nate the relationship. However, a power balance is not sufficient either. Both parties also need to feel that the other party treats them in a fair way. A relationship will not last long if one party feels that it has a less favour-able balance between results and investments than the other party. Neither party should have the idea that the other party is profiting disproportionately from the relationship. The inputs and outputs of the relationship should be in balance for both parties involved. Finally, it is important that a number of psychological characteristics support the relationship. For example, there should be mutual trust. This refers not only to the trust that the other party will deliver the contractually agreed performance or payment, but also to the trust that the other party will devote itself to looking after the interests of the partner – even when this has not been agreed beforehand.

Other characteristics that are also important in social relationships are: openness (no hidden agendas), empathy and the willingness to give the other party 'credit' if, for whatever reason, that party is temporarily unable to fully meet the agreement ('credit' has a non-financial meaning here). The important issue in analysing the quality of relationships is the ongoing reciprocity. This means that the relationship must be evaluated continuously from the perspective of both parties. A relationship is not a one-sided phenomenon. Characteristics such as trust are not characteristics of the relationship, but of the parties who form the relationship. So whoever wants to assess the extent of trust in the relationship should assess this twice if there are two parties involved. In a true relationship, there is always a vice versa. This applies not only to trust, but to all relevant relationship characteristics. A relationship can only exist by virtue of the relevant parties, and therefore both of them must be acknowledged in the assessment of relationship quality.

A good relationship is characterized by the willingness and intention of both parties to continue and perhaps to intensify the relationship. There is mutual involvement and commitment. Both parties know that they want to continue with the other party and both parties also know this about each other.

In the market, mutual commitment is based on the advantages that a steady relationship with a customer creates for the supplier and on the advantages that the customer experiences in the relationship. This mutual commitment may lead to a situation in which it would even be expensive for both parties to end the relationship. After a relationship of many years, a supplier may be fully aware of the characteristics, needs and desires of a particular customer. The supplier may have fully tailored his own production and processes towards this customer. It would be unwise for this supplier to ignore the investments made and the favourable situation for future sales. Conversely, it would not be wise for the consumer to discontinue the relationship and start all over again with another party that is not yet aware of his characteristics, needs and wishes. It would take a long time before the old situation were reinstated. Therefore, in a good relationship the parties may be seen as each other's hostages, with the understanding that the hostage situation was created by their own free will.

A word of caution is due for the case where the supplier refers to a 'lock-in' of customers. A lock-in is based upon deliberately created switching costs. The term 'lock-in' suggests that one party forces another party to purchase against his/her own interests, as if the client is prevented from escaping from the relationship. As in marriages, a lock-in does not work well in commercial relationships either – at least not for a longer period of time. If the provider of electronic cameras locks in buyers by forcing them to purchase expensive accessories, these buyers will think twice before purchasing another product from the same supplier or brand. In fact, a lock-in reflects a short-sighted strategy.

Development of a Relationship

Relationships may vary not only in nature, but also over time. Dwyer et al. (1987) specified a relationship development process that consists of four phases. In (1) the awareness phase, the parties become aware of each other's existence. This is followed by (2) the exploration phase in which the parties exchange information. The result is the exploration of mutual expectations expressed in the establishment of rules, guidelines and roles. Then (3) the expansion phase follows: both parties know how to understand each other and the conditions for collaboration are favourable. While the parties become increasingly familiar with each other, the relationship deepens and broadens in each additional phase In the expansion phase, the orientation is on maximizing the advantage for both parties (a *win–win* situation), and there is no contrast in interests because an unfavourable situation for one party is unfavourable for the other as well. Therefore, a problem experienced by one of the parties is interpreted as a collective problem. Both parties continue to invest in the relationship ((4) the commitment phase). It should be possible to deliver a performance without immediately requiring a similar counter-performance. The exchange of information is intensive, since both parties need to and want to remain familiar with the wishes of the other party. Feedback is essential. Negative feedback (dissatisfaction, complaints) may help to identify and correct the imperfections in the relationship, and their expression should even be stimulated. Therefore, if a customer does not express any complaints, it is important to determine what this means. After all, it may be either a positive or a negative signal. It would be a positive signal if it means that the product or relationship is functioning very well. It is a negative signal if the client is not satisfied, but expects that complaining will not have any result. In that case, the absence of a complaint is a signal that the relationship is not functioning well. In a good relationship, both parties feel responsible for the joint result, which implies that important decisions have to be taken together. The latter may occur, for example, through in-depth consumer research.

In principle, there are alternative partners available on the market for either party. However, the relationship will be continued for as long as its advantages, increased with the switching costs associated with a transition to another party, are larger than the expected advantages of a relationship with another party. The phase of separation or dissolution occurs if the consumer and/or the supplier experience the advantages of the current relationship as being few, if the switching costs are low, and if another party offers more advantages/fewer costs.

So, when the quality of the relationship has to be evaluated, it is important to determine in which development phase the relationship is located, and which characteristics are relevant. It should be noted that while certain quality characteristics are necessary for a good relationship, the mere existence of these characteristics does not guarantee a good relationship (Poiesz, 1999). The duration of a relationship is such a characteristic. In principle, the better the relationship is, the longer it will last. Conversely, however, the length of the period during which the relationship has existed is, in itself, not a guarantee of relationship quality. The number of transactions over time is not a sufficient indication of relationship quality either. This supports the argument that the quality and intensity of a relationship should be considered in addition to its duration.

Development Phases of Relationships

If we can use these last two characteristics (duration and quality/intensity) as a starting point, the duration of the relationship presents a good basis for tracking the development of the relationship over time. Therefore we propose to distinguish four phases within this development. These stages or phases are located on a continuum, and cannot be strictly separated:

Phase 1: Ad hoc contact: no relationship
At this phase there is a very temporary contact, out of sheer necessity, between a supplier and a customer. Both parties are exclusively interested in the product or the service at that moment, and not in the potential significance of the other party for future transactions. Sometimes a relationship is suggested by the way the supplier approaches the customer, but once the transaction has been made, the suggestion appears inconsequential. Then, customer focus does not arise from a long-term involvement of the supplier, but from a short-term focus on the transaction. In that case relationship techniques are no more than superficial sales techniques. Car dealers tend to be guilty of this offence. The customer is placed on a pedestal as long as no deal has been closed, but as soon as the sale has taken place, the customer is expected to join the ranks of an anonymous and insignificant clientele.

Phase 2: Short-term relationship
During a transaction, the supplier is focused on creating the next transaction. The consumer sees advantages in not having to search for an alternative again. The consumer wants to limit search costs, but is not necessarily focused on a long-term contact. The contact between the two parties is still strongly driven by each party's own advantages that both imagine they will achieve through the relationship. Many examples may be found in the market. When purchasing a product, a discount is given towards the next purchase. A service provider offers a subscription for regular services (car

wash, maintenance and repair). A supermarket chain gives the consumer a customer card that entitles the customer to special, periodical discounts. Various fashion and shoe shops have a similar approach for customers who make several purchases over a long time frame. Different suppliers participate in customer loyalty programmes in order to bond customers. Airline companies reward their loyal customers with frequent flyer programmes. Although these programmes are a part of customer relationship management (CRM), it is usually more a case of 'bribing' customers by providing advantages (implicitly indicating that the added value of the original product or service is insufficient to bond the customer). In fact, the transaction takes place under changed price conditions. Therefore, measures like these cannot be viewed as belonging to a relationship strategy. They only stimulate repeat purchases. Because suppliers are unlikely to differentiate between repeat purchases and loyalty, they too easily assume that true loyalty is involved. They tend to be very surprised when the consumer switches to the first supplier who has a slightly better 'loyalty programme'.

Phase 3: Long(er)-term relationship
In this phase, both parties see the relationship as more than a pure sequence of transactions. The relationship is no longer viewed as an instrument for achieving the next transaction, but as a result of a dedication that is focused on long-term effects. Relationships as a marketing technique make way for relationships as an expression of partnership. Instead of a one-sided bond that, in essence, is commercially motivated (such as in Phase 2), there now is a mutual *commitment*. The objective is a positive result for both parties, which also means a positive result for the other party.

The customer is not lured with the promise of financial advantages, but with activities that demonstrate the involvement and customer focus of the supplier. The attention of the supplier is not just focused on the phase preceding the transaction, but also on the consumption phase as it is here where added value is supposed to materialize. The consumer evaluates the experienced (surplus) value and provides feedback. The supplier uses this feedback seriously and it motivates him or her to action. The contact is individually oriented. The focus is on *this* customer and not on an arbitrary one. The supportive role of ICT is important in storing information on the customer and in using this information in contacts with the customer.

Phase 4: A lifetime relationship
The intention of a relationship that is focused on lifetime duration is to maintain the relationship to such an extent that a consumer will remain a customer indefinitely. Increasingly, financial institutions calculate the importance or value of an individual consumer on a lifetime basis. The

lifetime value of a customer may be determined by the purchases he or she makes over a lifetime and the profit that this generates for the company. Imagine a customer who, from age 25, purchases a new Volvo every five years. This involves ten to twelve cars with a total value up to €400 000. It motivates the organization to do something for the customer in order to retain him or her as a loyal customer. This viewpoint includes, among others, that a supplier should be able and willing to invest in the customer at different points of the relationship. For example, financial institutions are often prepared to accept the negative return of younger population groups. In fact, they only cost money. The *return on investment* is gained when that same customer uses the services of the same institution in later years. Therefore, a bank that sees a young customer leaving after ten years has a double disadvantage. In Phase 4, individualization has been implemented more than in previous phases. Again, ICT supports it with databases and analysis.

It should be clear that even though relationship policies become increasingly important, they are just as subject to spiral effects as the trend towards product/service packages. So the ultimate strategic way out of the spirals cannot be expected from loyalty programmes either.

INCREASED IMPACT OF ICT

The third dimension that, in our opinion, is a critical determinant of the developments in the near future is information and communication technology. Information and communication technology (ICT) will turn out to be a decisive factor for further individualizing marketing. Several development stages may be noted within ICT as well, although in reality these stages represent a continuous development in which no strictly separated stages can be distinguished.

Phase 1: ICT as Support

The first application of ICT to support marketing had the purpose of streamlining existing processes. The introduction of the bar code, for example, created a significant increase in efficiency, both within the organization (maintaining inventories, order picking) and in the contact with the customer. Waiting times at checkout counters were drastically reduced, and most errors were eliminated with the arrival of bar code scanning. ICT is used in this phase as a tool to facilitate, improve and accelerate internal processes of the organization, and not yet to stimulate the relationship and communication with clients.

Phase 2: Linking Functions and Databases

Subsequently, we observe that companies are collecting information regarding consumers and their purchasing behaviour in a more systematic fashion. The bar code is not only applicable to products, but also to people. By combining data from both sources, insight is created into the specific purchases made by consumers. *Customer tracking* is the tracking of customers at an aggregated level. In markets that are focused on one-to-one relationships between supplier and customer, such as in the automotive branch, suppliers create databases to track customers over time. Suppliers receive more information about their customers, and the information that customers receive about the supply has been more specifically tailored towards them.

If a company has access to data about individual customers, it becomes possible to treat a customer as a real person when there is a new contact. This is a large step forwards for parties who have direct contact with the customer, because during this contact they can directly consult the relevant data in their database. If someone makes a telephone call to the supplier, he or she may notice that the person on the other end of the line is familiar with the history of purchases, requests for information and any complaints. This application of the technology not only makes the process and the contact more efficient, it also ensures a clear personal touch during the contact. Thanks to ICT, customers may be promoted to human beings.

Phase 3: Almost Unlimited Information

In a later phase of development, when the Internet was developed, ICT started to play an important role in the preparation for a purchase. With the Internet, customers have access to a very sizeable source of general and commercial information regarding products and services. This source may be consulted at a time and place to be determined by the customer. The costs that were traditionally associated with the collection of information – telephone costs, postage stamps, parking costs, transportation costs, and especially also time – are strongly reduced. Information is available more easily and more completely. In this phase, the initiative for communication is gradually moving from the supplier to the customer. With further technological developments, ICT will be able to combine these functions. Data regarding products and services are being combined with data regarding individual customers, their purchasing patterns, and needs for information.

In this phase, the *intelligent agent* (IA), or knowledge robot, is developed, which is the software that can autonomously accomplish a task for a person or other entity. Intelligent agents are for instance able to execute tasks for the consumer based on information provided by the consumer. The intelligent agent, linked to a database or the Internet, is able to determine the most favourable purchase for a particular consumer based on his/her preferences and preconditions. The Internet bookstore Amazon.com enables consumers, upon request, to receive purchasing suggestions about books and CDs based on feedback that other, similar readers have provided regarding their experiences.

Intelligent agents or 'bots' (the name derived from robots) may be classified in terms of their domain, operation and function. Because new bots will come on the market regularly, the overview of intelligent agents in Box 4.1 is necessarily incomplete. See botspot.com for the most recent information. Many of the functions are also executed by general search engines such as Google.

In Phase 3, consumers consult the information provided by intelligent agents whenever they want, and it assists them to make better and more efficient decisions. In the transition from Phase 3 to Phase 4, the functions of ICT become more individualized. The 'consultation' function changes into a 'conversation' function in which the bot 'remembers' individual information from earlier transactions and consultations, and uses this information in answering queries and questions in the conversation with the client (Van Raaij, 1998).

Phase 4: ICT with Active Input

Because more insight has developed regarding customers, their backgrounds and their decisions, the supplier is able to start playing a more active role through ICT itself, whether requested or not. A relatively small technological step forward makes it possible to provide consumers at the right moment and the right place with purchasing suggestions that match their specific need patterns. The consumer him/herself is able to determine to what extent ICT fulfils this function, so that privacy is not an issue to be concerned about.

The intelligent agent becomes a 'personal assistant' to the client. The intelligent agent 'knows' each particular individual consumer as well as possible, it knows his/her priorities, and knows which products and services have led to the greatest satisfaction in the past for a particular consumer. The intelligent agent may also make comparisons with other clients with similar value or preference profiles, and forward their experiences with products and services to others in the form of purchase suggestions and recommendations. In this phase, interactivity is a continuous two-sided information exchange.

BOX 4.1 OVERVIEW OF TYPES OF INTELLIGENT AGENTS (SELECTION)

- *Knowledge bots* provide a wide range of services, e.g., general information. An example is: Ask Jeeves!
- *Academic bots* are agents designed for use by academics in educational institutions. They research information available in the online academic community, for instance Google Scholar.
- *Commerce bots* perform searches for commerce-related topics on the Internet. These agents are probably the most widely used bots at present. There is an increasing trend to make use of commerce bots by businesses for buying and online trading.
- *Communication or chatter bots* for communication with other parties and other communication bots. Examples are: Alice, Eliza and A Life Messenger.
- *Search bots* provide a refined, state-of-the-art method of searching the web. Their advanced functionality rests on the fact that they can operate independently of the user and continue searches even when the user is off-line. This means that consumers can multi-task while the bot is searching for them. There are search bots for general and specialized interest, software, people, news, weather, publications, literature, etc. Examples are: www.albany.net/allione, Katipo, Minder, PAWS.
- *Stock bots* monitor financial information and email to the user the latest release of stock prices, trends, press releases and current news on particular stocks and shares. These bots are available at www.personaltools.com/psm.
- *Asset monitoring bots* monitor a given portfolio of stocks and shares, and give financial advice and recommendations: Kasbah.
- *Work bots*: Office Atavar, BusinessVue.
- *News bots* are especially relevant for journalists engaged in information retrieval from the Internet. News bots allow the user to create custom searches for news clippings and articles on specific issues. Bots exist that will search the subdirectories of newsgroups. This allows the user to monitor all newsgroups for keywords and selected data sets. Collated information will be emailed back to the user or to a predetermined webpage. Examples are: Alert! and Morning Paper.
- *Shopping bots* search for products, deals, and compare prices on the Internet. Examples are: Bookfinder, Bottom Dollar, CNET Shopper and MySimon.

> • *Fun & game bots* are designed to enhance the user's fun through games, virtual environments, and virtual reality characters. These bots are available at botspot.com/search/s-fun.htm.

Some attributes are typical and characterize the intelligent agent or bot (nml.ru.ac.za/carr/~paula/Iamain.html). An agent or bot should be:

- *Autonomous*: The agent must be pro-active, exhibit the ability to work and implement actions independently of the user and spontaneously, often on a periodical basis.
- *Adaptive*: The agent must possess the ability to change and improve according to its environment and accumulated knowledge and expertise.
- *Communicative*: The agent must be able to collaborate and communicate with the user and other agents. This is a fundamental attribute, because it is the essential difference between intelligent agents' software and traditional software.
- *Goal-oriented*: The agent must continually strive towards the completion of tasks and the attainment of goals.
- *Customized*: The agent must be able to adjust and adapt to the different needs of different users.
- *Integrated*: The agent must be able to support an understandable, consistent interface with the client. The agent should also find solutions that integrate actions in several domains. This means that the intelligent agent searches for the best and integrated solutions for its customers over a broad range of domains for the short term and the long term.

Intelligent agents can deliver their services in a number of domains:

- *Financial management* in general (spending, saving and credit) and specifically portfolios of shares and options, as well as tax returns and insurances.
- *Rental and contract management* of rented and leased goods and services, renewal or cancellation of subscriptions and contracts.
- *Mobility function* while travelling with regard to travel time, navigation (GPS), optimal routes and addresses.
- *Intelligent cars* that monitor the driver and the engine, and determine energy use, optimal routes and positions.

- *Intelligent houses* that monitor the inhabitants, serve as an alarm system for senior citizens, as a support system for the inhabitants, and for the purpose of energy saving.
- *Intelligent clothing* that protects the wearer and warns of positions (GPS), options and dangers.
- *Agenda and organizer function*: to call a meeting, make appointments, note and arrange obligations, negotiate about place and time of meetings with other agenda/organizer bots.
- *Workflow management*: the planning and organization of work, household chores, leisure time and other activities.
- *Medical bots*: Provide medical information in emergencies, as well as medical monitoring of people (cholesterol, blood pressure and so on).
- *Buying and selling* of goods and services (virtual garage sales; consumer-to-consumer marketing; participation in auctions).
- *Co-buying*: bundling the purchasing to bargain for a lower price from suppliers (buying co-operatives).
- *Digital comparative testing* of goods and services, and giving recommendations to consumers.

Intelligent agents are able to fulfil the following functions:

- Search the web for information within a domain to answer questions, find choice alternatives and specify these further.
- Filter and select relevant news from sources such as the Internet and other media, including spam filtering.
- Warn the consumer of important news, events and deadlines: alert services.
- Notify and notice new relevant developments within and between domains.
- Match the attributes of information suppliers with the demands of customers: information brokers.
- Translate information, also from 'foreign' languages such as Russian, Chinese and Japanese.
- Negotiate and bargain with people, institutions and other intelligent agents (intelligent agents need to have a specific discretion and power of attorney in order to independently complete a contract and to make purchases).
- Customize goods and services.
- Draw attention to, signal and provide requested and non-requested recommendations and opinions.

- Provide communication support: sort, filter, remove, forward and, if possible, answer email, to be expanded to chatting, telephone, SMS and MMS.
- Serve as a digital library: looking up (retrieval), systemizing, categorizing, tabulating and summarizing of Internet information.
- Select virtual entertainment, theatre and film, if desired including interaction with the consumer. The consumer may sing along in the show (karaoke) and play in the film.

Customers may not be interested in these separate functions but only in the 'end results' that are associated with them. Intermediated processes and results are not interesting for most customers.

In short, ICT is starting to play a more central role in the purchasing and consumption processes of consumers. Over time, ICT will deliver a greater contribution to the interaction between suppliers and consumers, with clear advantages for both parties. Many Internet initiatives have perished as a consequence of the Internet bubble which burst at the beginning of this century (2001–2003), but now the initiatives are being taken again in a more sophisticated manner. ICT and the Internet are nevertheless playing an increasingly important role in supplier–customer interactions. We assume that the technological development cannot be stopped and that therefore it is not a question *whether* ICT will play an important role in the interaction between suppliers and consumers, but *when* and *how*.

ADDED-VALUE STRATEGIES

Now that we have described the three central developments (product sophistication, long-term relationships and ICT), it is important to determine to what extent they provide synergy and added value. It is important to note that each of these developments offers this possibility only to a certain extent. After all, they are the greatest common denominators of the general market and marketing developments that we have noted in Chapter 2. So, while we have taken the opportunity to extend the three central trends a bit further in time, it is important to note that none of them provides a lasting innovative perspective by itself, and none of them provides a solution to the marketing spiral.

This raises the question of which strategies organizations could follow in their pursuit of added value. In doing so, we will indeed use the three trends as a starting point, but we emphasize their combination rather than their separate functions. Which possible combinations exist? We have three main strategic directions. If we assume for simplicity's sake that for each direction there are two options (it is adopted or not), then in principle we have eight main strategies. See Table 4.1 for a schematic overview.

Strategy 1 is a pure transaction strategy, although it can be questioned whether this is a strategy at all. None of the three main developments are used.

In *Strategy 2*, salvation is sought exclusively through ICT, but there is no idea which specific strategic role or function ICT should be fulfilled. It is assumed that merely the supply of the technology will lead to the optimal match of supply and demand and to an increased flexibility of the market process. Such optimism about technology can frequently be observed. For instance, many companies believe that the mere acquisition of CRM (Customer Relationship Management) software means that customer relationships will be managed and that customer focus will be established.

Strategy 3 focuses exclusively on generating long-term relationships with clients. A lot of attention is paid to managing customer contacts, but it is not clear to which differentiating added value this will lead in the long run. The possibilities offered by ICT are insufficiently utilized in this strategy. Relationship management is interpreted as handling a large index card inventory that forms the basis for a collection of so-called customer-friendly measures. In order to stretch the relationship as much as possible, the supplier is even prepared to go as far as rewarding the customers (or bribing them) for continuing the relationship. This may occur with a customer affinity card that entitles the customer to special advantages and discounts. It is important to note that these rewards are also given away to customers that are already loyal. This makes such measures very expensive, especially if customers already exhibit a high loyalty.

In *Strategy 4*, the relationship with the customer becomes professional and is managed with ICT support, so that a true Customer Relationship Management (CRM) system is used. This provides added value, but here the question also arises whether CRM will be able to provide the required differentiating added value in the long run. After all, competitors may employ the same technology to create long-term relationships with their customers. In that case, CRM simply becomes a new competitive domain, subject to a downward spiral. The speed of developments and copying will in *no time* lead to a diminishing return on relation-oriented investments.

Strategy 5 is in contrast to Strategy 4. A search is made for new combinations of products and services, although the scope of this search is limited because the packages are presented as though they are separate products. The integration of a car radio and a DVD player, or of a television and a DVD recorder, involves combinations of products that originally led separate lives. Yet consumers only perceive their combination to be an innovation for a short period of time. The same applies to a combination of different services in the supply of a tour operator. The fact that, for instance, the transfers from and to the airport are included, indicates an increase of the product package. Yet within a short time, consumers will experience it as a deficiency if airport transfers are not included in the package. Then, these transfers no longer provide added value.

Strategy 6 uses ICT as a tool for creating combinations of products and services. However, this still occurs from a short-term perspective. For example, for certain customer segments, a supermarket chain might assemble special packages of products for which it is assumed that they will be appreciated by the segment. Strategy 6 is, however, not a very likely strategy because ICT is only used for product combinations and not for matching these combinations with consumers.

Table 4.1 Possible strategies as combinations of the three main developments

	Product sophistication	Long-term relationship	ICT
Strategy 1	No	No	No
Strategy 2	No	No	Yes
Strategy 3	No	Yes	No
Strategy 4	No	Yes	Yes
Strategy 5	Yes	No	No
Strategy 6	Yes	No	Yes
Strategy 7	Yes	Yes	No
Strategy 8	Yes	Yes	Yes

Strategy 7 combines product sophistication with a long-term orientation, without making use of ICT. An example is the travel agency that, through its very attentive staff, informs customers in time about attractive travel offers that are especially geared toward their personal desires. Here the intention is positive, but the implementation suffers from a lack of professional ICT support.

In *Strategy 8*, the added value is found in a combination of product sophistication, long-term relationships and technology. This strategy is based on the idea that it is less useful to create complex combinations of products and services in an ad hoc fashion. It is only possible to invest in relationships if it can be assumed that specific customers will not restrict themselves to one single transaction. The strategy is also based on the idea that there is little use in pursuing long-term relationships if the continuation

of the relationship involves continuous (that is, expensive) attempts at per-
suading the customer. Instead, customers should be motivated themselves to
continue the relationship.

In Strategy 8, ICT is not considered to be a goal in itself, but is a necessary (not sufficient) instrument for supporting the combination of the other
two intentions. The main goal is to pursue such a synergetic effect that it
creates a new form and range of added value. Therefore, we will apply the
concept of *synergetic marketing* to Strategy 8.

Synergy is the key word here. Synergy comes from the Greek συνέργέώ
(synergeoo, to collaborate). Synergy develops when two parties are both
better off through collaboration, or if a combination leads to the creation of
added value that exceeds the mere sum of the components of the combination. Synergy develops in a consumption pattern if the separate parts fit
so well together that a qualitatively superior combination emerges. Consider
the consumer who creates good combinations with relatively few clothing
items. Synergy develops between two parties if the result of their collaboration is more positive than the sum of their individual activities. So, synergy
may be identified at the product level and at the marketing level.

Four aspects or types of product synergy may be distinguished:

1. The total may create a certain synergy, $1 + 1 > 2$, that is the sum of two
   products or services is more than the simple summation of the products
   or services separately. There is added value in the combination of two
   or more products and services.
2. Synergy may exist between the components of a consumption package:
   the components form a qualitatively superior *combination*. Quality and
   good design are often created with the right proportions.
3. Synergy also occurs when a great deal is achieved with few resources:
   efficient combinations. An example is an insurance package without
   overlapping insurances and covers. So, for example, a travel insurance
   that does not cover expenses that are already covered by health insurance.
4. Synergy may also exist between the consumption package and the
   behaviour or the lifestyle of the consumer: *suitable combinations*. Consumers knowing clearly what kind of functions appliances should fulfil
   for them, only choose or at least prefer the functions that they need.

It is obvious that synergy may also be related to each combination of these
four types or aspects.

As indicated above, synergy may also exist at the level of marketing.
Here we speak of synergy when the three main marketing trends coincide,
as described in Strategy 8. In the next sections we will show how synergy

will allow for an unprecedented marketing strategy that, in turn, provides an opportunity to escape from the marketing spiral indefinitely.

Synergetic marketing is presented in Figure 4.2 as the combination of three (more or less) overlapping circles. This representation shows that the strict classification into eight cells does not cover all possible varieties.

The area of overlap of the three circles indicates the degree of synergy and the extent to which added value has been created. Note that we no longer search for added value at the level of aggregates, such as markets or market segments, but at the level of individual consumers.

In the ideal case, product sophistication is only realized at the level of the individual client. After all, the ideal package of client A is likely to be quite different from the ideal package of client B. Individual consumers may differ even more from each other in relation to the packages than in relation to individual products and services. Also relationship formation can only be considered at the individual level.

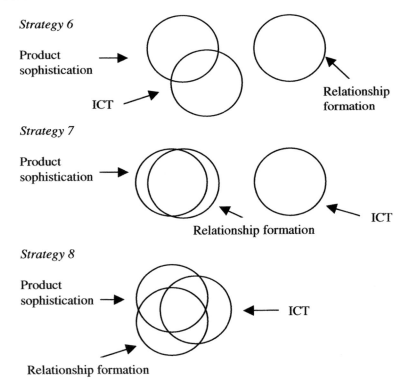

Figure 4.2 Combination possibilities based on the three main trends. Represented are strategies 6, 7 and 8

In summary, we consider synergetic marketing as the ultimate form of a sustainable customer focus:

1. The individual customer is used as the starting point.
2. The emphasis is on added value and on truly satisfied customers, not on customers who are prepared to accept what is provided.
3. The supplier's perspective is subordinate to the customer perspective in the determination of the functionality of the supply. This will, eventually, also benefit the supplier, because it raises customer satisfaction, reduces trial and error costs, and fosters continuity of demand.
4. Products and services are not evaluated on the basis of their own merits, but on the basis of their contribution to an integrated package of products and services (product bundling).
5. The focus is not on the value of a package at any one specific moment, but on the value of a package over time.
6. Feedback from customers is one of the pillars of the concept. It is strange that in a time that overflows with communication, market supply is still created almost entirely without direct customer interaction. Market communication is largely one-sided and (due to the overload described earlier) is becoming increasingly ineffective. The solution appears to be equally simple as effective: replace part of the one-sided communication with real interaction or two-sided conversation, to the benefit of both suppliers and consumers.

Because product sophistication and relationship formation are the most important in terms of content (the ICT developments are supportive), we put these determinants in a *value matrix*. We use this matrix as an instrument in our search for new, strategic added-value options.

VALUE MATRIX

For both product bundling and relationship developments we distinguished four phases. Combined, they form the value matrix consisting of 16 cells. See Figure 4.3.

With the matrix of Figure 4.3, it is possible to determine what the developments mean. For clarity's sake, in the matrix the developments take place from left to right and from bottom to top. The 16 cells of the matrix indicate strategic positions where companies may be located, which they may choose, or from which they may migrate to other cells. As indicated before, an organization may fully dedicate itself to extending the life span of the relationship while ignoring the possibility of further product expansions.

The reverse may also occur: a company that, perhaps in collaboration with other companies, works on assembling an integrated package of products and services, but does not choose relationship formation as a strategic focus. The matrix may be used to determine a company's current position, its desired position, and the route that it should follow to migrate from the current to the desired position. These three points pose fundamental strategic questions for a company. The answers to this question may be combined with more market-specific, company-strategic considerations.

	Core product	Augmented product	Category package	Meta package
Life time	13	14	15	16
Long term	9	10	11	12
Short term	5	6	7	8
No relation-ship	1	2	3	4

Figure 4.3   The value matrix

The Value Diagonal

Because the various phases of the dimensions indicate the developments over time, the matrix connects the past, the present and the future (expectations). The 'southwest–northeast' diagonal has a special meaning, since it combines the two developments. We state here that the diagonal that consists of the Cells 1, 6, 11 and 16, represents the optimal developmental perspective for an organization. In these cells the two trends provide optimal mutual support. Individualized package formation supports relationship formation, and relationship formation supports individualized package formation. And so on. ICT facilitates and boosts the circular interaction of the two developments. The added value for consumers increases along the diagonal from the least to the most added value. For this reason, the diagonal represents the key idea of synergetic marketing and will be the guiding principle in the discussion of the matrix. Cell 16 represents the ideal market situation with the maximum added value for consumers. And it provides an optimal market position for a company. Here, neither party exploits the other party to its own exclusive benefit. Their interests coincide completely. Current marketing practices show that many companies do already develop in the two directions indicated by the matrix: they do migrate from left to right and/or from bottom to top. Migrations in the other direction are unlikely. Even the reduction of an assortment of products and services to the core business of a company may be viewed as an attempt to add value. Also the simplification of a highly sophisticated product (Philips: 'Sense and simplicity') can be regarded as a migration from left to right in the matrix. In other words: Cell 16 represents the final goal of marketing. It is the critical reference point to which all company missions and marketing strategies may be compared. We do, therefore, expect that marketing will eventually develop itself until the situation of Cell 16 has been achieved. Competition, basically, is the battle to reach this finish first. According to the matrix, not all routes to this point are equally efficient.

ICT developments provide a necessary condition in the progression towards Cell 16. Without ICT support, the production of packages for individual clients in mass markets is inconceivable. With ICT, it is. The matrix may in fact be viewed as an unfolded cube, with ICT as the third dimension.

Obviously, this development toward Cell 16 will not take place overnight. We assume that the three developments will increasingly embrace each other. Over time, they will become more tightly intertwined, until the specific contribution of each of the main themes no longer may be distinguished within the combination.

We will now describe the cells of the diagonal. A description of all cells of the matrix seems superfluous as their content can be derived from the combination of the descriptions of the relevant entries. Due to the particular importance of the diagonal cells, we will discuss these separately. See also Figure 4.4. Due to the special significance of Cell 16, we will describe this cell in most detail.

Cell 1: Separate Transactions

This cell represents a simple, traditional situation that can be found in every market. Both supplier and consumer are focused on ad hoc transactions. The relevant product or relevant service is clearly defined. A product or service is seen as a bundle of characteristics or attributes. A consumer purchases a pencil at the shopping mall, buys ice cream at the ice cream vendor, hires a plumber for a leaking tap, or lets his or her children take a ride on the merry-go-round at the fair. The transactions are characterized by simplicity and a one-time occurrence. Neither one of the parties has the intention to anticipate any potential future transactions. A purchase in Cell 1 does not exclude new transactions, but the parties involved do not pay attention to their possibility.

In Cell 1, both parties are exclusively focused on their own benefits and costs. When the (market) situation allows it, suppliers will ask higher prices. If the customer is able to achieve a discount accidentally, he or she will not worry whether the price is a mistake disadvantageous to the supplier's interests. The interests of the supplier and the customer are antagonistic – opposed to each other. Fairness is not relevant. The profit of one party is the other's loss, and vice versa. They are involved in a zero-sum game. The customer does not feel the need to lose him/herself in the operational ups and downs of the supplier, nor is the supplier interested in the background and motivations of the customer. Which party makes the transaction is irrelevant. The supplier is strongly oriented towards the short term. He or she only pursues customer satisfaction in order to prevent the hassle of complaints. The supplier is not really interested in customer satisfaction, as long as the customer feels positive enough about the product to purchase it. The supplier is not interested in the customer's appreciation of the product once it is purchased. The supplier who receives suggestions for product improvement from the customer will shrug his or her shoulders. Feedback only costs time. The focus is on minimizing complaints, not maximizing satisfaction.

Cell 6: Satisfaction as a Base for Repeat Purchases

In Cell 6 both parties are aware that after this transaction another transaction is possible, from which both may benefit. The transaction involves an *augmented product*. In Cell 6 the emphasis is on satisfaction and repeat purchases. These are convenient for both supplier and customer. The supplier does not know why repeat purchases occur. Convenience, comfort and the simplicity of the decision are the most important reasons for customers. With repeat purchases, they avoid having to continuously make a new decision about something that is not all that interesting to them. The supplier only knows a few general characteristics of customers, such as roughly where they live (postal code), purchasing frequency, average purchase amount, and possibly some socio-demographic or other background characteristics.

Conversely, the customer knows virtually nothing about the supplier and is not able to judge the quality of the supply. The employees that are in direct contact with the customers are trained to be nice to them. After all, selling is a technique. *Mystery shoppers* (researchers that pretend to be a client) make telephone calls or visit the store in order to assess whether they are well serviced.

	Core product	Augmented product	Category package	Meta-package
Life time				16
Long term			11	
Short term		6		
No relation-ship	1			

Figure 4.4   The value diagonal

Customer focus/friendliness is based on a commercial intent. Companies consider it to be important to come across as customer focused, but only because this may contribute to their own result. How the customer really feels is irrelevant to the supplier. The supplier is happy as long as the customer keeps purchasing. Customer-oriented actions are actually tricks that present an artificial image of the supplier. There is no relationship formation and therefore also no true loyalty. At least there is no feeling of loyalty to a brand or a supplier. As soon as another supplier presents a better offer, consumers will switch.

In Cell 6, the supplier sees satisfaction as a stepping-stone towards the next purchase. The idea that satisfaction might be the goal of marketing is defeated by the dominant thought of short-term company results. But complaints are taken seriously and, within reasonable boundaries, addressed. (However, complaint handling is located low in the organization, at a convenient distance from higher management.) The supplier is interested in the characteristics and the needs of customers since this means that marketing activities can be more focused, and new layers of meaning can be created around the *augmented product*.

Cell 11: Reciprocal Commitment

In Cell 11 purely repeat purchases are no longer sufficient. The parties are now committed to each other. Customers are convinced that they prefer this supplier, and the supplier wants to keep this particular customer as a client. The supplier knows who the customer is and has succeeded in binding the customer to him/herself through an ever-innovative combination of products or services – within the same category (such as living, transportation, care, education, and so on). An intelligent agent is deployed to support the process. The customer does not feel the need to orient him or herself towards alternative suppliers, since there is full trust in this supplier. The supplier places emphasis on *cross-selling*, while the customer is focused on *cross-buying*. Neither party wants to disadvantage itself, but guards against overburdening the other party. Over time, the supplier builds up knowledge about the customer, which is used to optimize the package and, where possible, to expand the package. The supplier is dedicated to customer satisfaction. The customer is actively stimulated to provide positive or negative feedback. Complaints are now considered to be useful management information for the improvement of products and services. Customers' backgrounds, preferences and experiences are analysed in depth. The supplier is prepared to invest in the relationship, for example by providing exclusive privileges to the loyal customer, sometimes even for free. In turn, customers are prepared to make positive word of mouth recommendations to others, to the benefit of the supplier.

The supplier is interested in the characteristics of the customer, and the customer is interested in supporting the supplier, who does his or her utmost to please the other party. Mutual distrust, as in Cell 1, is no longer an issue. The parties trust each other, and depend on each other.

Cell 16: Home Base of the '*Virtual Guardian Angel* (VGA)'

Cell 16 is the most special cell. In our opinion, this cell represents the situation to which marketing is ultimately progressing. Here, products and services no longer exist as bundles of characteristics. Rather, products and services themselves are characteristics of integrated packages. Customers no longer need to know the specific characteristics of these products and services, as single attributes no longer matter. In a specific combination, a particular characteristic may provide a positive contribution for one customer but a negative contribution for another. For example, the price of a specific product may be high relative to the prices of other similar products in the market. However, this expensive product may actually be precisely the complement to the package that best matches a particular customer's preferences.

Suppliers and customers do what they can to exchange as much relevant information as possible. The parties involved are focused on achieving a positive result in the long run, not just for themselves but also for the other party. Both parties experience a long-term responsibility for each other. This leads to a collaboration that is in sharp contrast with the antagonism that markets have shown for many decades, and that still occurs in Cell 1. This antagonism was based on the assumption that the supplier is in principle striving to achieve an unfair advantage at the cost of the customer (*caveat emptor*; let the buyer beware).

In Cell 16, customer satisfaction is equally essential as in Cell 11, but it is related to the synergetic added value and no longer to individual products and services that are components of the package. The object of the relationship is no longer a product, a product category, or a spending category, but a complex whole of totally different products and services that create an attractive and trustworthy unity. For example, living, finances and care have been matched to each other. The customer is enabled to delegate the arrangements, the hassle and the decisions to the supplier. The result is that the components are optimally matched to each other, and moreover are matched to the needs and wishes of the consumer. Therefore, a simultaneous, triple synchronization takes place of:

1. Products and services among each other;
2. The total result matched with individual customer needs;
3. The short term with the long term.

Let us consider the example of the open buffet again. The development towards meta-packages meant that dishes would be matched to each other. Yet this only relates to the matching as determined by suppliers. Although customers are being informed about the new combinations, the choice still needs to be made by the consumers themselves. This implies the risk that consumers make choices that they may regret at a later stage.

Here Cell 16 would present the solution. Due to the continuous exchange of information between suppliers and customers, knowledge and insights develop that can be used to serve customers better. The evaluation by the customer of the chosen package at day 1 may be used to provide a more tailored advice at day 2. After a period of several weeks, the supplier knows exactly which dishes and drinks the customer evaluates in a positive or negative way, which combinations are preferred, which amounts are requested, which variation in eating patterns are considered to be important, how open the customer is for culinary experiments, what overall price the customer is willing to pay, which food supplements are desired, which ingredients should be avoided, which dishes lead to indigestion, and so on. Based on the evaluation expressed by customers with a comparable preferred nutritional pattern, an estimate may be derived regarding which combination of dishes has a good chance of creating enthusiasm. If the customer wants this, there may be a hook-up with his or her medical database in order to avoid an unhealthy diet. An approach that emphasizes the ongoing interaction with customers is thus completely different from an approach that is focused on merely expanding the package.

As consumers trust the selections made for them in Cell 16, they do not check alternative selections that could have been made. In this way, opportunity costs (and thus regret) will be reduced. This is an important benefit in an economy with so many alternatives (Schwartz, 2004).

For both parties, the continuation of the relationship is the central focus. After all, over time a situation has developed in which the supplier and customer feel directly connected. The supplier obviously does not want to lose his or her customer, but the customer also prefers to continue with this supplier, because 'buffet decisions' have been taken over from him. This not only saves time and *opportunity costs*, but it also provides a noticeable added value. The package may be expanded over time. Because the supplier knows the culinary and dietary interests of the customer, a special wine tour may be assembled. The reaction to the tour indicates the customer's preferences for particular types of hotel accommodations. New connections are then relatively easy to arrange. The package has the tendency to grow spontaneously. The meta-package may eventually become a mega-package after all.

It is obvious that the system cannot be implemented with an index card box or Rolodex. The information about customers, their experiences and their feedback about characteristics of products and services should be stored in a relational database that allows numerous possibilities for data analysis. Technically speaking, there are few barriers, but the expertise regarding data mining and database marketing is developing rapidly. Analytic techniques that are specifically designed to handle extremely large databases have been developed already.

Thus, the supplier will not just propose or take complex decisions on behalf of the customer. The role of ICT is crucial. It will be impossible to perform the complex considerations that are involved with the (meta) packages without technical support. The evaluations and ambitions of an individual customer need to be matched to the specific characteristics of products and services in their mutual connection. Individual guidelines are used for individual customers to ensure the quality of the supply.

Various guidelines are possible for the evaluation of the desirability of a package offer or a package adjustment:

1. The comparison of the package characteristics with the priorities as indicated beforehand by the customer;
2. The evaluation, afterwards, of consumption experiences;
3. The comparison with the evaluation by similar others;
4. The comparison with the evaluation by experts;
5. A combination of these guidelines, based on a weighting to be determined for each individual customer.

Therefore, customers need to provide information on their consumption experiences, their consumptive and other ambitions, and their possibilities for achieving them. In Cell 16, the intelligent agent has reached such a level that the agent is able to provide a clear opinion or make a decision for an individual customer. The role and significance of the intelligent agent extends further in Cell 16 than in Cell 11. In Cell 16, the intelligent agent functions as a *stand-in* for the consumer, of course with the agreement of the customer. The customer is protected from unwise expenditures, from not meeting deadlines, from failing to make necessary investments, from the unneeded acquisition of products, and from the unnecessary hiring of services. In this phase, suppliers may also make recommendations regarding the use of leisure time.

In Cell 16, consumers have at their disposal a special ICT facility that represents the different suppliers and that contains the database. We want to give this facility its own name so that it may express how sizeable its impact may be on the life and the functioning of the customer. We call this instrument the *Virtual Guardian Angel,* or VGA. The VGA functions as an intermediary between the customer and the suppliers that collectively compose a package. The VGA is the face or 'brand' towards the customer. The suppliers, in different compositions, are 'hidden' behind the VGA and are not noticed by customers. The positioning of these suppliers is no longer important, since the functionality of their products depends on the match with other products in the integrated meta-package.

Price becomes a less prominent characteristic. After all, customers cannot judge the price of the overall package anyway. By comparison, consumers are not capable of judging the price of the air bags, the gearbox, the suspension, and the brakes of their car. For these products, consumers have accepted that these belong to the package called 'car'. If provided with the possibility to do so, they would probably decline comparing different technical parts on the basis of price–quality ratios. The purchase of the parts has been delegated to the car manufacturer. In the same vein, but at a more abstract level, consumers will get used to delegating decisions regarding meta-packages to VGAs and will accept whatever price is asked. Added value is translated into the willingness to accept this price.

Because the VGA makes a selection from the total supply, it takes over brand positions of the original suppliers, and it is more likely that it will develop its own positioning. The VGA is actually a technical facility that is provided with a brand name and a brand position. The current suppliers or brand carriers move towards the background. Investment in their brands becomes a business-to-VGA marketing policy. The need for mass marketing techniques declines. There is no steady pool of suppliers for a specific VGA. Different criteria may apply for different groups of customers, for which an optimal set of suppliers will be established each time.

Note that suppliers may keep a brand policy towards consumers in order to create and maintain a preferred position with consumers, in this way bypassing the VGA. The objective of this brand policy is a pull strategy intended to maintain some consumer preference and to increase the likelihood that the brand will be included by the VGA in a product package. But the impact on consumer preference needs to be extraordinarily strong in order to overcome the impact of VGA delegated decision-making. Most suppliers will neither have the type of product or service, nor the necessary resources. Highly specialized niche players may be in the best position to remain noted by consumers.

For the sake of clarity let's compare the current market structure as represented in Figure 4.5 with the VGA-based market structure in Figure 4.6.

We do not intend to suggest with Figure 4.6 that the VGA automatically arranges the distribution of the package by itself. This might be possible, but it is not the meaning of the picture. The VGA continuously receives information from the customer on the evaluation of the package presently provided. In turn, the VGA has contact with suppliers in the market and intelligent agents on the Internet. The VGA therefore is an intermediary into two directions. Through the VGA, consumers may also state their preferences with regard to delivery formats, channels and times (Figure 4.6).

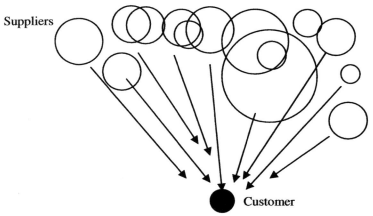

Figure 4.5 The current market structure

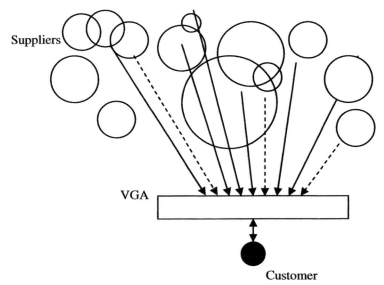

Figure 4.6 The position of the Virtual Guardian Angel

Until now, the VGA has been discussed as if there were only one. However, this would be too simple a representation of reality. More than one VGA may be created, since products and services may link together at numerous places in the market. Because this is not being coordinated from the top or beforehand, but occurs in the market on an ad hoc basis, it is likely that several VGAs will be established for different consumer segments and for different domains. The phenomenon of crystallization provides a useful metaphor: under ideal conditions, crystals form in saturated liquids, but it cannot be specified beforehand exactly how and where they develop.

It is very important to note that a VGA is unlikely to just happen overnight and to burst into existence. Rather, a VGA may be expected to have a gradual, but exponential growth curve. It may start relatively slowly on a very small scale (small package, relatively short relationship), where it is aimed at the development of initial customer trust. This takes time. In this period, competition is likely to be fierce when it is apparent that other parties have a similar ambition. Once trust is established, it forms the basis for the circular, accelerating relationship between package formation and relationship extension. Note that the expansion period can be relatively short (as compared to traditional business development), as the VGA does not need to manufacture or construct the total package by itself. For expanding its supply of products or services, it 'only' needs to target and invite selected suppliers, coordinate their activities, compile the packages, and organize customer information and feedback. Thus, in the realization of a VGA status, organization and coordination are more important than manufacturing. A VGA itself may contribute only a fraction of the total package.

Over time, the VGA may play different roles. First, the VGA may indicate to the customer what options are attractive to him or her. Then, the VGA may be allowed by the customer to present a short list of options. Next, a preferred option is suggested by the VGA, only to be confirmed by the customer before actual delivery. Finally, the customer may delegate the purchase to the VGA without his or her prior knowledge.

While the VGA status is likely to develop exponentially, competition is likely to decrease exponentially. Once a customer is firmly associated with a VGA, there is a strong mutual bond between supplier and customer. Comparisons between VGAs are highly unlikely as the supplied packages will be incomparable. The VGA status implies lack of competition. In synergetic marketing, the winner takes all.

Privacy

Customer information is vital to the VGA. Due to the fact that customer information was and is not always handled prudently by all (commercial) market parties, the privacy issue is important. The consumer should trust that the information is not used in another way than intended. The principle of the VGA only applies to the extent that the customer gives explicit permission to use personal information for the purposes outlined here. Privacy and freedom will not be compromised. There will be a learning process on the part of the customer who, at first, may be hesitant to deliver personal information and evaluations to an unknown party. If the VGA is able to provide guarantees in this regard and the customer notices that the provided package truly leads to positive experiences and satisfaction, this suspicion will decrease and trust will increase. Over time, the willingness to provide information will grow, assuming that the VGA will indeed deliver on its own promises. The current lack of interest or even refusal of many consumers to participate in market research should not suggest that customers are unwilling to provide information per se. At present, the unwillingness to provide information may be explained by the fact that providing information does not lead to personal benefits. Consumers are unlikely to experience a personal effect of their participation in market research and of the feedback provided in satisfaction research. In the case of the VGA, the provided information directly feeds into adaptations and improvements of the individualized package.

Personal freedom is guaranteed as no one but the customer determines to what extent the VGA will serve as a provider. With regard to this point, customers may be expected to differ considerably. Some consumers insist on selecting their own vacation destination, others would like to receive a shortlist and yet others prefer to have it selected, planned, organized and executed. In principle, all variations are possible.

Finally, we need to emphasize that privacy is only a concern in a relationship characterized by antagonistic interests. In the 'old' market situation, there is often a conflict of interests between suppliers and customers. In the case of a VGA, both parties benefit equally from the relationship. Therefore, the relationship is the joint responsibility of both parties and will be experienced as such. Customers do not want to leave their VGA or VGAs. And VGAs will not jeopardize the trust invested in them.

The synergies that are created by the VGA may be visualized as follows in Figure 4.7.

For completeness and clarity we give two more examples before concluding this chapter.

Travel

Tour operators are successful in connecting the various components of a package tour in an optimal way. These components relate to airport transportation, the flight, accommodation, meals, excursions, car rental, information, and so on. The package keeps expanding. In creating the value

mix, tour operators in the past have only focused on a 'horizontal' development in the value matrix: the expansion of the package. What they still
have not done adequately (but which technically was difficult to achieve in
the past), is to build up a relationship with their customers by matching the
packages to individual needs and wishes, supported by ICT.

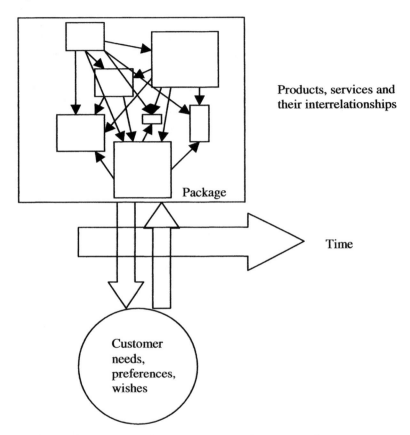

*Figure 4.7   The synergies created by the VGA: between package
components, between the meta-package and the customer's
needs and and wishes, and over time*

Consumers are probably willing to provide ample information about
themselves and their preferred vacation trips. This information might be
linked to combinations of travel packages. Obviously this can only be
achieved in a learning process (fed by the experiences acquired), and this
learning process would turn out to be very functional – for both supplier and

customer. By indicating priorities and providing feedback on their vacation trip, consumers allow information to be stored in a database that can be used for the recommendation or selection of future trips.

The following scenario may then be presented. A few years from now, the consumer receives a signal from his VGA: a specific holiday trip has been pre-booked for you: a trip of a particular duration in a certain period to a specific location in a four-star hotel or resort accommodation, and meals are already included. Two of the five possible excursions have already been booked. The consumer has never before been to that location. He has never even heard of the location, the accommodation or the package. It was formed on the basis of the following information about this specific client:

1. In which period he or she wants to go on vacation;
2. For how long;
3. Which destination and which type of vacation (culture, sports, adventure, nature, and so on) have led to a very high degree of satisfaction in the past;
4. How much variation or surprising elements he or she wants to have included in his or her vacation trip.
5. Also, the selection of the tour is made by making reference to the satisfaction expressed by other consumers with similar profiles of personal characteristics (such as income and budget), family characteristics, travel preferences and travel experiences.

Although the trip has been booked (including cancellation insurance and travel insurance, the transport to the airport and the local transfers), the client can cancel without cost, ask for an alternative or even decline altogether. The reason why is included in the database, to be considered in future bookings.

In this construction, consumers do not need to remember that they should request travel guides and that they should visit the travel agency in a timely fashion. They do not need to worry about the availability of aeroplane seats or the suitability of the accommodation. The tour operator not only has the advantage of the optimal support of the consumer, but also the advantage of the financial planning and communication.

Actually, in Western Europe in the past decade, travel agencies had an excellent position to develop a VGA status in the travel business and become a powerful party. There was frequent contact with customers, and the same customers often returned to the same agency. This provided an excellent strategic opportunity to build customer knowledge and to generate market power but, apparently, the opportunity has not been exploited. At present, travel agencies experience fierce competition from the Internet (direct bookings) and are often forced to take defensive actions.

Clothing

This is a somewhat stereotypical example of a couple. The wife likes to look and shop for fashion clothing. To her, fashion shopping is *fun shopping*. The husband has a whole-hearted dislike of shopping for clothes, and especially dislikes the strenuous search for the right shop, the right rack, the right pieces of clothing, the fitting and repeat fitting. The shops are being arranged more attractively for the *fun shopper*. The husband decides to join a VGA that specializes in clothing. This VGA makes an inventory of his wishes and purchasing pattern in the domain of clothing, checks the preferences of the wife for her husband's clothing, determines the proportion between work and leisure clothing, as well as the available budget. Depending on the indicated preferences, the consumer receives a supplement to his wardrobe several times per year. The consumer tries it on and may refuse and return certain items of clothing. The evaluation of the shipment is stored in the database together with earlier evaluations. The profit for the customer, measured in time and reduced frustration, is tremendous. Over the seasons and over the years, the VGA learns the preferences of the customer to perfection, and it can even expand the service provision towards other products. In connection with the leisure clothing, sports clothing and sporting equipment might also be arranged. Once related preferences and experiences have entered the database, a new avenue may be followed: for example toward sporting events and sports-related vacation trips. (The latter shows how the two examples may eventually merge under the umbrella of one VGA.)

The number of examples that are suitable for combinations is endless. But after several examples, it is clear that there are two critical strategic elements for the development of VGAs: the initiative for the development of a meta-package and the availability of a database. The supplier that is able to put these elements together will achieve a clear strategic advantage. The power associated with access to a database can be very substantial. Therefore, a customer database may be considered the most powerful strategic and tactical marketing instrument of the future.

SYNERGY

In order to determine their marketing strategy, companies could in principle choose a position in any cell of the value matrix (Figures 4.3 and 4.4). But this does not change the fact that there are more obvious and less probable cells. It also does not exclude the possibility that certain cells can be more recommended than others. Similarly, there are more and less desirable roads towards the goal of customer focus, depending upon the type of organizational strategy. Yet, we consider the diagonal of the value matrix as the avenue of the most efficient and attractive combinations.

To the extent that a strategy is further removed from the diagonal, it will be more difficult to classify it as striving towards a durable/sustainable customer orientation. In summary, in the value matrix there are actually five different strategic patterns that characterize organizations:

1. The static approach, in which the organization occupies a position in a certain cell of the value matrix and maintains this position. No further development takes place.
2. The package strategy, in which the emphasis is on the expansion of the supply and product bundling. This may be represented as a 'horizontal' movement in the value matrix.
3. The relationship strategy, which focuses on further expansion of the duration of the relationship. This is the 'vertical' movement in the value matrix.
4. The hybrid approach with an unpredictable pattern of horizontal and vertical movements in the value matrix. This approach is strategically inefficient and results in the risk of a position off the value diagonal.
5. The approach of synergetic marketing, with which the organization purposefully attempts to follow the value diagonal into the direction of Cell 16. One of the characteristics of the diagonal is that the three main strategy components are kept in balance and are synchronized in their developments.

We assume that the most effective and efficient strategy is focused on realizing or maintaining a balance between the product package strategy and the relationship strategy. In that case both strategies support each other. This means that an approach that is focused on long-term relationships will benefit most from a product strategy that results in synergetic packages. Conversely, an approach that is focused on the development of synergetic packages will benefit most from a policy that is oriented towards long-term relationships. According to the value diagonal, it makes no sense, strategically speaking, to invest in CRM (Customer Relationship Management) without having it accompanied by developments along the two dimensions. Along the diagonal of the value matrix, the synergetic effect of the collaboration between the supplier and customer becomes increasingly clear until the optimum is reached in Cell 16 of the matrix.

The disadvantage of long-term relationships – that customers may be increasingly demanding – is overruled by the capacity of VGAs to continuously outperform customers' desires. Once the package offered becomes static, the customer will become more critical, and rightfully so. But if the package is continuously improved or expanded, the customer has no reason to complain or to question the added value. In fact, the notion of the VGA suggests that in the new marketing, added value is no longer enough. What is required – and offered – is the continuous expansion of added value.

It was suggested that the prices of individual products and services in the package are no longer an issue. This, of course, cannot mean that the financial part of the relationship should be neglected. We feel that a solution may be found in the notion of a subscription. The consumer subscribes to a particular VGA or to a particular quality level provided by a VGA. In return for a certain amount of money paid periodically, the consumer receives the guarantee of a package. The amount of money transferred may not only imply a certain quantity and quality level, but also a particular emphasis on innovation. For example, by paying 15 per cent more, the consumer is entitled always to have the most recent versions of specified electronic equipment. Although this is not elaborated further here, it is not difficult to see how this might be facilitated by financial constructions such as leasing.

Ultimately, to prevent the consumer from being too vulnerable financially, the subscription to a VGA may be combined with a co-ownership of the VGA. If a consumer possesses shares of the VGA, the risk of paying too much to the VGA to make too much profit, is reduced by the fact that the consumer is also at the receiving end when the profit is shared. Alternatively, a financial surplus may be used to accelerate innovation. Consumers may subscribe to those VGAs that are known for their innovative nature, but then will have to accept a higher subscription fee or a lower profit share.

5. Developments in Customer Behaviour

SUMMARY

To a certain extent, customer behaviour develops as a response to the supply of goods and services. In the reverse direction, the supply of these goods and services adapts to changes in customer preferences. Information is the critical link between supply and demand. But, as we have seen in Chapter 3, a problem arises with regard to this essential instrument. When considering the potential purchase of goods and services, customers often cannot use the information provided. The first reason is that the amount of information is too large to oversee, and customers are often even incapable of processing the amount of information that can be overseen. The second reason is that information that may be processed is often not understood by its complexity or esoteric nature. This reduces the customers' ability to make optimal decisions and, consequently, to match supply and demand.

We will consider how customer behaviour is affected by the various developments, but we will also describe the conditions that allow customers to circumvent the problems inherent in present day (Cell 6) market functioning.

STAGES OF DEVELOPMENT

Cell 1

Customer behaviour in this cell can best be described as simple in nature. In Cell 1, ad hoc decisions take place with regard to commodities to which no layers of additional meaning (no branding, guarantees or extra services) are attached. Purchase decisions are likely to be routine and, in the case of consumers, often relate to the maintenance of sufficient household supply. More elaborate decisions (regarding more complex, more important and more expensive purchases) do not take place here. There is no clear pattern among the purchases. The purchases in this cell are to a large extent unplanned and are prompted by store environments. Functionality of the individual products and services – do they deliver the required benefits? – is considered most important.

Cell 6

The purchases in this cell are characterized by a slightly larger emphasis on the position of the product or service within the total set, and by some more attention to the effects of the product or service over the long term. Purchases are made somewhat more carefully because brands within the same product category differ in terms of associations and references to social effects. There is a closer relationship with the lifestyle of consumers. Products and services are combined in a somewhat better way, but this is primarily based on superficial characteristics such as complementarity, colour and style.

Cell 11

The fit between products and services (products, products/services and services) is considered to be more important here. Consumers believe that they know their own preferences, but this self-knowledge often is quite incomplete. When a lot of information is available, consumers think they are very well able to make decisions on their own. Yet that same information often turns out to be confusing, and assistance is required. This is available in the form of an intelligent agent (IA) to which an increasing number of tasks and decisions is entrusted. At first this is experienced as a bit odd and possibly even somewhat uncomfortable, but soon consumers arrive at the conclusion that the advice is helpful.

Since consumers have also become used to delegating tasks to equipment, such as the self-regulating thermostat, the consumer quickly gets used to the support provided by the IA. Decisions of the consumer are increasingly supported by the IA. Suggestions by the IA may be followed blindly, as trust in the IA increases with experience.

Cell 16

In this cell, decisions are related to more general consumptive objectives. Consumers are often not able to indicate which general objective they are attempting to achieve with the available resources. Therefore, it is impossible to make consumer choices in a well-founded manner. With the VGA, certain specific objectives and a specific lifestyle may become more explicit. Decisions are increasingly delegated to the VGA. The feedback that the consumer gives to the VGA becomes increasingly functional. The VGA ensures that, where relevant, related purchases take place in a more simultaneous and planned fashion rather than in a subsequent and ad hoc fashion. To the extent that consumers in this cell still make any decisions, the emphasis will be on decisions at the higher level of abstraction of plans, goals and lifestyle, rather than at the lower level of distinct products and services or even product and service characteristics.

TRANSACTIONS

A consequence of the decreasing attention to the actual transfer and payment is that the transaction itself becomes more diffuse. The product or the service will more often become a part of an interconnected set of products and services and of a more expanded and long-term relationship with a service provider that consists of a series of interrelated transactions.

Where more long-term connections exist in the current market between suppliers and consumers, we observe that the transaction itself has become less prominent. At some point in time, both parties have agreed on quality, delivery and payment, and this is taken care of as smoothly as possible. Consider for example the membership of a sports club or a subscription. The payment occurs in a fairly 'invisible' way through bank statements, credit cards, or automatic debit. Let's refer to the diagonal of Figure 4.4. In Cell 1, the delivery and payment preferably occurs at the same location and at the same time. Here the consumer is watching closely that they will not be cheated, and the supplier is paying close attention to whether the payment is received in time. In Cell 6, the parties have known each other for such a long time that they basically trust each other. After delivery, the payment could perhaps wait for a while if necessary. For example, payment obligations might be added to the credit card debt of the customer. Consumers may have a special credit account with their department store. In Cell 6 they are often not able to judge price–quality relationships due to the numerous layers of meaning that have been added around the core product or service. In Cell 11, the supply is even more difficult to assess, and consumers no longer know exactly what they are paying for. Products and services have been merged into one offer. This is not to make the world more complicated for consumers, but to achieve synergetic effects. Consumers judge prices intuitively; they are not able to judge the package as a whole. The same applies to Cell 16 as well, but here in an even more extreme way because products and services from different categories have been combined. Paying per transaction appears to be less relevant than making a periodic contribution. Consumers do not know exactly what they are paying for, but they trust that 'it's OK'. If consumers experience the price as high, they will interpret this as the contribution necessary to obtain a synergy effect. A high price may also be moderated by the awareness of the savings of time, money and hassle that would otherwise have been needed to make the purchases.

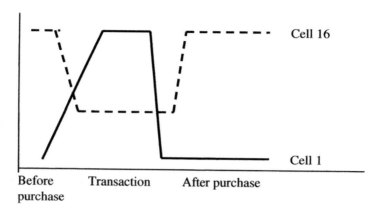

Before   Transaction   After purchase
purchase

Figure 5.1   Attention to the consumer in various decision phases per cell of the value matrix

In Cells 1 and 6 of the value matrix, marketing strongly emphasizes the customers' orientation phase before the purchase. In these cells, marketers and sales staff are primarily focused on creating a transaction. In general, they show little interest in what happens after the purchase. Many consumers feel that they are on their own once the transaction has been completed. This feeling becomes particularly strong if the product turns out not to function as expected. In Cells 1 and 6, there is little interest in the way in which the consumer handles and evaluates the product or service after the purchase. In Cell 11 and certainly in Cell 16, the emphasis is much more on the consumption phase: the actual consumption experience of the product or the service becomes the focus of attention. After all, this is the phase in which the added value is to be fully experienced. See Figure 5.1 for a graphic representation of the attention to the consumer in various decision phases per cell of the value matrix.

We will provide a brief explanation to Figure 5.1, from which it may be deduced that marketing along the diagonal (Figure 4.4) is going to change drastically. In Cell 1, there is an interest in the consumer at the moment that he or she belongs to the target audience. Then the interest increases strongly to the extent that the possible transaction comes closer. After the purchase, the interest disappears almost completely. There may be some interest in aggregate effects, such as overall customer satisfaction, but the individual customer experience is actually a non-issue. In Cell 16, an almost reverse pattern may be noted: attention is paid to the priorities that the customer has defined for him- or herself before a purchasing process exists. The phase of the purchase itself is not interesting, since the VGA can determine this on behalf of the customer (or can suggest, for example, a shortlist of three options). The phase following the purchase is considered to be truly important, since this is where the product or service should live up to the promised and expected value in the context of the other products and services purchased at present or in the past. Along the diagonal of the value matrix the awareness is growing that the consumer mostly cares about the consumption experience and a lot less about the purchase and ownership.

PSYCHOLOGICAL CONCEPTS

We want to understand which changes might occur in consumer behaviour when we follow the developments along the diagonal of the value matrix.

For that purpose, we discuss the dynamics in several psychological concepts that seem particularly relevant in this context. These subjects will be treated in a more or less random order:

- Information and information processing
- Lifestyle
- Perceived freedom
- Loyalty
- Needs and personal values
- Satisfaction and well-being
- Identity and transformation

For each of these concepts, we determine how their significance and content changes along the value diagonal. We will not discuss each individual cell in this diagonal for each concept. Instead, we restrict ourselves to a description of the general development along the value diagonal (Figure 4.4).

INFORMATION AND INFORMATION PROCESSING

An important aspect of the current consumer behaviour relates to the manner in which consumers deal with the provided information. Therefore, a relevant question is what the development as anticipated in this book would mean for the role of information and the information processing by consumers. As in the preceding paragraphs, let us also follow the value diagonal of Figure 4.4.

A characterization of Cell 1 is the communication spiral (Figure 2.3). There is an overload of information and it forces the consumer to make a selection from the huge quantity of information. The selection is decided by a large number of determinants which are related to the characteristics of the consumer, the characteristics of the information, and the characteristics of the environment in which the information is presented. The result is that the selection is often made in an arbitrary, unsubstantiated and careless fashion. The information that is then available for the purchasing decision is limited – to put it mildly. Possible consequences are dissatisfaction, disappointment, opportunity costs, and regret.

In Cell 6, handling the information is made somewhat easier for the consumer. First of all, the brand is located at a slightly higher level of abstraction than the level of the individual product characteristics. Commercial communication here pertains to the outer layers of meaning that have been added to the brand, such as the image or the reputation. Because of this, the consumer can more easily rely on simplified decision rules: 'I have purchased this before', 'This product is of a well-known brand', or 'This supplier sponsors my sports club'. Sometimes the commercial communication in this cell appears to anticipate developments later along the value diagonal: *joint advertising* may suggest a possible combination of products, services or products and services. Yet this actually still involves marketing in the style of Cells 1 and 6 since there is, as of yet, no real package creation.

The situation becomes even easier to survey, but then within a specific domain (health, work, leisure time) in Cell 11: the IA is able to make a preselection of the information that is functional for a particular consumer. This prevents information overload. In turn, the consumer notices that the information that is being provided is actually personally relevant. That makes it easier to ignore other information about the same domain sent by other suppliers.

In the transition from Cell 6 to Cell 11, the IA makes information available about how products and services are being combined by other consumers within a specific domain, or suggestions may be made in relation to combinations based on resemblance in design or possibilities for synergy. Consumer associations could make the step from testing separate products and services towards combinations and packages of products and/or services. Also, lifestyle consultants could advice customers how life goals and life plans may be realized through (combinations of) products and services.

Finally, Cell 16 restricts the information for the consumer to the functional minimum. There is no longer any need for individual suppliers to advertise: the consumer will anyway rely on his VGA, which performs an important part of the selection process.

To the extent that the VGA makes the decisions, it is not functional to provide the consumer with extensive information. The consumer who is indeed interested in certain information can also obtain this from the VGA. For example, he or she could request the VGA to make a first selection of the websites of suppliers of, for example, sports articles. Afterwards they can determine themselves which information and how much information they want to receive. Here the term 'permission marketing' applies: the consumer gives permission to a supplier to approach him/her with information.

Also the content of the information will change along the value diagonal: there is a progression from purchase-related information towards consumption and usage-related information. In the latter case, information is aimed at improving and optimizing the product use. The information may also refer to the disposal and replacement of products.

LIFESTYLE

Lifestyle is the entirety of activities, interests and opinions of people, with the corresponding products and services. In much scientific research, lifestyle is examined by determining 'afterwards' whether there are clusters (combinations) of activities, interests and opinions of consumers. Yet in our perspective, lifestyle is not so much a clustering and statement afterwards, but the result of a combination of choices that were made by consumers. In that case, lifestyle is the consequence of a choice that was consciously made beforehand. Consumers do often know what they consider to be important and what they approve or disapprove, but they may not realize that their preferences and dislikes are a component of a larger pattern called 'lifestyle'.

Uusitalo found as early as 1979 the following aspects or dimensions of lifestyle or consumption style that still seem to be relevant today:

- Material dimension: emphasis on the possession and use of goods;
- Social dimension: emphasis on social contacts with friends and family;
- Performance dimension: emphasis on career, earning money, and other achievements, for example in sports and hobbies;
- Exploration dimension: emphasis on new experiences, for example through travel, adventure, going out, new products and technology;

- Ecological dimension: emphasis on energy and environmental aspects of products and services, durability, sustainability, authenticity and use of public transport.

Some dimensions are typically opposed, such as the material and the ecological dimension. Due to these contrasts and the plurality of lifestyle possibilities that exist in affluent society, consumers are forced to make a choice. *Die Qual der Wahl* (The burden of choice) makes it impossible to engage in every activity. Therefore, people choose a limited domain of activities to participate in, such as gardening, photography, collecting, 'gaming', going out, travel or supporting a soccer team. These activities have the purpose of spending leisure time in a useful way, to belong to 'something', to be special or unique in something, or to excel in some area. People choose a lifestyle, whether or not consciously. Sometimes this occurs on the basis of a deep personal conviction such as religion (ranging from fundamentalism to liberalism), politics (liberalism, socialism, anti-capitalism) or vegetarianism. Based on this vision and conviction, a person will also accept all consequences of this choice. In other cases, the consumer wants to know upfront the advantages and disadvantages of potential lifestyles. And in yet other cases, consumers arrive more or less unintentionally (due to upbringing or social environment) at a particular lifestyle.

Actually, a lifestyle should be the expression of the own 'mission' of people, a long-term vision about their own goals and objectives. The manner in which purchase decisions are made, however, shows that this is an illusion for many consumers. Without help, they are not able to define clear long-turn goals and associated spending patterns, so support would be welcome. The VGA could help to determine what the priorities seem to be, based on the actual spending pattern. Subsequently, the consumers themselves can determine whether these apparent priorities are congruent with their real priorities. Feedback may be functional in highlighting imperfections. For example, consumers, through their VGA, may discover that they:

- use a lot of household energy in comparison with others;
- spend more money on their car than they thought;
- have lower home expenses in comparison to others;
- would do well to refinance their mortgage;
- consume more fat and sugar as compared to the average consumer;
- spend more to replace defect products in comparison to others;
- spend relatively little on repairs and relatively more in replacements;
- spend a disproportionate amount of time on activities that are not valued highly.

In relation to lifestyles, the VGA might indicate, for example, that much is spent on the material dimension and that redistribution towards, for example, the exploration dimension in general has led to greater satisfaction among similar consumers. The information or the feedback is not coercive. The consumer himself maintains complete freedom, including the freedom to follow or not to follow the recommendations.

PERCEIVED FREEDOM

The symbiosis of consumer and VGA might suggest that people will become dependent on systems, and in doing so, will lose their freedom (decentring). The VGA 'dictates' what needs to be done and the 'poor consumer slave' obeys it. Obviously this is not what we have in mind. The VGA is a purely supportive service. If it is used appropriately, it will even increase freedom. It provides appropriate possibilities and guidelines that a person might otherwise not have considered. Products are suggested that otherwise might have been ignored. Conversely, other products are not purchased that otherwise would have been bought for the wrong reasons. Consumers who are supported by their VGA know their options better and are better able to compare the pros and cons of these options. And they do not have to spend scarce resources – time and money – on activities that they do not like and find unrewarding.

In order to achieve a goal, sometimes it is necessary to limits one's own freedom temporarily. For example, to achieve a savings goal a monthly payment is needed. This obviously restricts discretionary income and financial freedom. People know their lack of willpower and are prepared to accept an obligation in order to achieve the desired goal. Thaler and Shefrin (1981) distinguish two motivations in people: the need for short-term spending (the spender) and the need to pursue long-term goals (the saver). To keep the spender within them in check, people take measures such as an automatic savings plan or obligatory repayments of loans. Temporary restrictions to freedom are therefore functional to reach a higher-order goal. In cooperation with their VGA, consumers may impose a temporary restriction of freedom on themselves in favour of a long-term goal. This does not affect consumer autonomy in the relationship with their VGA. In principle, they set their own goals and make agreements with their VGA as to the achievement of these goals. The VGA may suggest goals to the consumer, but only if specifically requested to do so.

The feeling of freedom develops due to the following factors:

- Better knowledge of the possibilities, including their feasibility and consequences.
- More personal control of choice and behaviour.
- More insight into the future possibilities.
- More purpose and ambition in life.
- Better formulation of personal goals and values.

'Perceived freedom' is a new psychological concept that may present a challenge for researchers and practitioners. Individuals probably differ in the perceived freedom that they experience, depending on their personality and the situation. If people ascribe their achievements to their own efforts (personal control) they experience a higher degree of perceived control and freedom. If they evaluate their own actions as being effective (self-efficacy; Bandura, 1986), this also leads to a higher degree of perceived control and freedom. If the number of available options from which a person can choose is large, it provides a feeling of freedom, but it may also lead to information overload which makes the choice more difficult. Time pressure has a negative relation to freedom and is obviously not perceived as a contribution to freedom. Finally, a high degree of self-confidence and belief in one's own capacities has a positive effect on the perceived control and freedom.

The consequences of perceived freedom include, for example, that people experience no (or less) frustration during setbacks and that a person has the feeling that he/she will succeed the next time. It may also lead to higher satisfaction and increased well-being. Even though some freedom of choice may be delegated to a VGA, the availability of a VGA may result in a higher level of perceived freedom. Stated differently, a lower level of freedom (the freedom to select goods and services) is exchanged for a higher level of freedom (the freedom to select activities). In fact, the VGA allows the customer to reach the level of freedom that is personally desired. The VGA does not impose restrictions on the customer in any way.

Although the individual freedom of consumers remains entirely untouched, along the value diagonal (Figure 4.4), consumers are decreasingly able to escape from the new market structure. Consumers themselves choose their lifestyle, whether or not assisted by the VGA. This occurs based on the past (traditional values and habits), what other people do (conformism, 'spot what's hot'), own future plans, judgements by others and judgements by experts. Some consumers pay a lot of attention to the opinions of others: they have a large degree of self-monitoring (Snyder and DeBono, 1985). They want to become popular by conforming to situations and to others. They deliberate about what is up-to-date and in fashion. But some other consumers pay little attention to others, go their own way and attempt to achieve their own objectives: they have a low rate of self-monitoring. They may be less attracted by the very notion of a VGA, or may ignore its advice.

Consumers themselves determine to what extent they want to deviate from the pattern that is suggested or recommended by the VGA to which they belong. Incidentally, it is possible that the VGA notes deviations from the normative choice and stores these in the database. In the future, suppliers might then take this into consideration in terms of their supply – a form of personalization of supply. The same may be true for another expression of the need for freedom: the need for variety. A VGA may 'know' to what extent a customer appreciates consumption surprises and may adapt the package to this knowledge.

In summary: in Cell 1 of the matrix an apparent freedom exists: consumers assume that they determine their choices and make expenditures purely based on their own needs, preferences, wishes and desires. This is an illusion. On the one hand, they are locked in by their own past spending. The characteristics of the possessions restrict financial spending options and freedom of action. On the other hand, a consumer is his or her own barrier due to psychological (motivational, cognitive) limitations. These limitations make consistent, rational choices almost impossible.

The apparent freedom of Cell 1 is gradually dissolved as the diagonal is followed towards Cell 16. It is replaced by an apparent lack of freedom in Cell 16. In reality, Cell 16 offers a lot of freedom because consumers no longer need to apply scarce resources towards the purchasing process that is only intended as the preparation of the consumption and usage. After all, the goal is not purchasing in itself, but using and consuming products and services (fun shopping is an exception).

The lack of freedom exists only apparently. In Cell 16, this is because consumers, who are not yet familiar with the VGA system, have the preconceived notion that they will be forced against their will to incur various unpredictable expenditures. Yet that is neither the design nor the intention of the VGA. On balance, the freedom of the consumer therefore increases as Cell 16 is approached along the value diagonal.

LOYALTY

Restriction of freedom may not only be the consequence of the circumstances or be the result of earlier decisions, but may also be the consequence of explicit choice. Consumers may choose to restrict their own freedom by entering into a more or less steady relationship with a supplier or a brand.

Loyalty involves a self-imposed restriction of freedom, because the critical aspect of loyalty is that consumers do not reconsider for each decision whether the brand that was purchased in the past, is still superior to competitive brands. The consumer is willing to make the purchase without comparison.

The vertical dimension in the value matrix (Figure 4.4) is related to the relationship continuum. As the relationship becomes stronger, loyalty increases and the inclination to switch to another supplier decreases. Along the diagonal (Cells 1, 6, 11 and 16), loyalty is stronger than along the vertical dimension (Cells 1, 5, 9 and 13). This is due to the fact that the growth of added value at the individual level is more strongly emphasized in the diagonal. Alongside the vertical dimension, the consumer must be persuaded to remain within the relationship and to demonstrate (pseudo) loyalty. Repeat purchases that occur in these cases appear to indicate a loyal customer, but are in fact related to transaction-related advantages and disadvantages. True loyalty only exists when a consumer remains with his supplier, even if a competitor (temporarily) has a better offer. Many current relationship measures may be positioned on the vertical dimension, but not on the diagonal. Marketers take measures such as savings plans (stamps or air miles) that motivate the consumer to make repeat purchases, but that do not generate the commitment as a characteristic of true loyalty.

Loyalty develops along the diagonal as follows. In Cell 1 there is no loyalty at all, either from the supplier towards the customer or from the customer towards the supplier. The one-time transaction is a transient meeting, and even if the transaction is repeated it is the result of accidental choice. The meeting remains transient. The comparison may be made with a stranger that crosses our path each day on the way to work. This is a repeated contact, but there is no relationship, let alone that there are feelings of mutual loyalty.

In Cell 6, the likelihood of loyalty increases due to the additional associations that are connected to the brand and because the supplier supports repeat purchases with focused actions. Yet true loyalty does not yet exist in most cases; it is rather a calculated cooperation, such as the cooperation of room mates or people sharing the same front door for purely financial or pragmatic reasons.

In Cell 11, the supplier not only focuses on the long term of his product or service, but also ensures that the product or service provides consumers with direct benefits. The supplier presents him/herself as customer oriented, pays more attention to the consumption phase, and shows a genuine interest in the satisfaction of the consumer. The consumer returns the favour with an increased degree of commitment towards the supplier. A mutual feeling of partnership develops.

Finally, Cell 16 is characterized by true loyalty, which is expressed not only in repeat behaviour but also in positive feelings (attitude). The consumer is not only very positive about the partnership, but has the intention of continuing it for a long period. The supplier makes an effort to look after the long-term interests of the customer, and the customer applauds this. Cell 16 presents the 'marketing marriage'. The fact that it becomes increasingly difficult to reconsider the partnership over time is not perceived as a restriction of freedom, but as a welcome consequence of decisions that were made before. And they lived happily ever after!

NEEDS AND PERSONAL VALUES

The concept of needs presents a challenge in consumer behaviour. We may assume the existence of as many types of needs as there are products and services. But even then we still do not have the certainty that needs have been fully covered. In marketing, a tendency exists to assume a need after it has become clear that consumers demonstrate an interest in a product. This leads us to assume that we can predict future demand based on the need concept. However, this is an illusion. In addition, needs are as extensible as rubber bands. Needs 'shrink' if they cannot be met (and the same applies to aspirations, wishes and desires) or if they cannot be satisfied. Needs increase or expand when more basic needs have been met. As soon as a need has been met, and the consumer has become used to the new consumption level, a more comprehensive ('higher order') need arises. Obviously this applies more to material issues than to products and services that directly lead to saturation (such as food products).

Due to the elusiveness of the need concept, it is wise to analyse at a higher level, at the level of the personal values. Needs are usually derived from values. Brands associate themselves with needs or values. It is more difficult for a brand to claim the association with a value than to connect with a need. Large brands with considerable investment potential will attempt to refer to personal values in their communication with the target audience. But before we explain the importance of needs and values for the diagonal of the value matrix, it is important first to provide a brief explanation.

Types of Values

Rokeach (1973) made a fourfold classification of values (see Table 5.1) comprising instrumental and terminal values at the individual and social level. The classification is still up-to-date and applicable. Instrumental values in themselves are not goals, but they are important means in order to achieve certain goals or end values. Instrumental values may be individual (competence such as ambition, skill, neatness and self-control) or social (morality such as honesty, responsibility, helpfulness, politeness and obedience).

Terminal or end values are goals that are worthy of pursuit in and by themselves. Terminal or end values are also individualistic (self-actualization in the form of happiness, wisdom, pleasure, a comfortable life and an exciting life) or social (social orientation such as freedom, peace, equality, friendship, beauty and safety).

Table 5.1 Value classification by Rokeach (1973)

	Instrumental values	End or terminal values
Individualistic	Competence	Self-actualization
Social	Morality	Social orientation

Terminal or end values may be important, sometimes even unattainable, life goals on which a lifestyle is oriented. End values may be religious or social in nature, such as salvation, self-actualization, happiness and peace. Instrumental values translate the lifestyle into concrete behaviour. Examples of instrumental values are: neatness, friendliness and politeness. Life goals may be instrumental in nature and may be a condition for achieving terminal goals.

Needs, instrumental values, and end values may be used to provide brands with content. Along the diagonal of the value matrix, we observe a progression in the use of needs and values to characterize brands. Cell 1 involves brands that have a direct, functional connection with concrete needs. For example, it is hot and the consumer feels like eating an ice cream. The brand claims coolness and refreshment. In Cell 6, the augmented product goes a lot further. Here, the brand attempts to make a link with instrumental values: for example friendship or neatness.

In Cell 11, where category packages are composed for which the consumers enter into a long-term relationship with a supplier, we notice that end values are being invoked. Examples are care and safety. Finally, Cell 16 is the cell where the reference to end values can best be shown to its full advantage, because the VGA has access to many possibilities and a long period to achieve a main objective as an end value.

We will provide a few more value classifications: one by Schwartz and Bilsky (1987) and the VALS-classification (*Values and Lifestyle*; Riche, 1989). We add these for two reasons. The first is that values are an important concept in the justification and presentation of the activities of the VGA. The second reason is that values are connected closely to another concept, discussed earlier, that has a central focus in Cell 16: lifestyle.

Schwarz and Bilsky (1987) provide a different value classification than Rokeach, using the dimensions of open/closed to change and self-transcendence versus self-enhancement (Table 5.2). Based on this fourfold classification, clear lifestyles may be observed.

1. 'Open self-transcendence' contains an exploratory lifestyle in which change, innovation, stimulation and adventure are central. New products and services and especially new experiences are important to this group of consumers. These consumers in effect want to make efforts to 'transcend' themselves, to become 'better', 'more unique', or 'richer in experiences'.
2. 'Open self-enhancement' includes a hedonistic lifestyle of performing and enjoying. These consumers especially want to enjoy now and not later. Their performances are focused on not falling behind and to achieve the level of prosperity that others have also achieved.
3. 'Closed self-transcendence' is a conservative, traditional lifestyle with conformism as the main theme. The achievement and maintenance of traditional norms and values is dominant in this regard.
4. 'Closed self-enhancement' is a lifestyle in which certainty, safety and power play a large role. These consumers are especially focused on strengthening their own position, and preventing and reducing risks.

Table 5.2 Value classification by Schwartz and Bilsky (1987)

	Self-transcendence	Self-enhancement
Open to change	1. Provides direction to life; stimulation	2. Hedonism, achievement
Not open to change	3. Conformism, tradition	4. Certainty, power

There are also dynamic models indicating the developments of values and lifestyles over the course of someone's life. The VALS system distinguishes eight lifestyle groups (Riche, 1989) according to three development or growth routes or orientations:

- *Principle*, using stable norms and principles.
- *Status*, focused on achieving goals and performance.
- *Action*, focused on doing things on one's own and having unique and special experiences.

The lowest group are the *strugglers* with a minimum income, who make great efforts to make ends meet. According to the VALS model, each development or growth route or orientation leads to the highest lifestyle: self-actualization.

The principal route or orientation consists of believers and fulfillers. The status route or orientation consists of the strivers and achievers. The action route or orientation consists of the makers and experiencers.

The following eight lifestyle groups are thus part of the VALS model:

- *Strugglers*; who can only make ends meet with great effort.
- *Believers*; people who believe and have trust in the help of God and others. They are inclined to a certain degree of fatalism.
- *Fulfillers*; people who pursue certainty and derive it from principles.
- *Strivers*; people who work hard to get ahead.
- *Achievers*; people who are focused on achievements at work, in hobbies and sports.

- *Makers*; people who know how to make things happen and prefer to do as much as possible on their own. 'At least then you know it's done well.'
- *Experiencers*; people who pursue unique and special experiences.
- *Actualizers*; people who have achieved a certain level of self-actualization.

A VGA will fulfil different functions for these eight groups. The possible function is indicated below for each group. This relates to the main functions. Obviously a VGA can fulfil several functions simultaneously for a group of consumers.

- For the *strugglers*, the VGA fulfils a safety-net function, comparable to social security: relief during illness, employment, searching for unemployment benefits and subsidy options.
- For the *believers*, the VGA is a tool that should be trusted and whose recommendations will be followed if sufficient trust exists.
- For the *fulfillers*, the VGA can provide certainty and an anchor function.
- For the *strivers*, the VGA is a practical service tool that provides directions on getting ahead and achievement.
- For the *makers*, the VGA provides operational instructions regarding how something may best be done.
- For the *experiencers*, the VGA provides possibilities to gain unique and special experiences.
- For the *actualizers*, the VGA is a tool to increase well-being and happiness, and also to fulfil a number of other functions such as financial and medical services.

Some lifestyle classifications assume that people will use the same values in all areas of life, that is that they will always be open or closed, and always focused on self-transcendence or self-enhancement. The VALS classification assumes a development along three routes with the end value and goal of self-actualization. Yet this does not always have to be true. People may be innovative in one domain (work) and conservative in another (family). In that case, values are domain-specific (Van Raaij and Verhallen, 1994). Domain-specific values may serve as a stepping stone towards end values. We need to indicate how we imagine domain-specific values for each of the examples of the domains such as work, household chores, hobbies, vacation and use of leisure time.

Individual companies and organizations will want to connect their products' or services' image to these values but realize that this goal is hard to reach for a single product or service. Because a VGA systematically bundles products and services that each only partially can refer to a value, the VGA is in a much better position to achieve a credible and firm association. The VGA will appeal to a value (self-actualization?) at the highest level in order to live up to its own status.

Needs, functions and values are interrelated. They can be placed in *meaning structures* and *value maps* are quite applicable in this regard (see Figure 5.2). A meaning structure consists of three levels: product characteristics, benefits and values hierarchy (such a meaning structure was first suggested by Reynolds and Gutman, 1984). Tangible characteristics of products and services lead to product benefits, advantages and consequences for the users. These benefits and consequences are desirable and useful in the context of the values and lifestyle of users. For individual products, it may be important to know through which functions their characteristics lead to values. It is possible that two different brands within one single product category, based on the same characteristics, arrive at different end values through different routes through the hierarchy. For example, one brand of margarine claims that the low amount of fat (characteristic) leads to a slim figure (function) and therefore physical beauty (value). Another brand of margarine states that the low amount of fat (characteristic) ensures that the user will feel fit (function) and will look forward to a long, carefree, healthy life (value).

Different goals are associated with the three levels of the hierarchy. These goals correspond to the successive cells of the value diagonal. In Cell 1, consumers have information goals in relation to the characteristics of products and services. In Cell 6, the communication is still mainly focused on functions and benefits (possession and usage goals), although efforts are already being made to address values and lifestyles. The latter succeed better and in a more credible way in Cell 11, and especially in Cell 16. In this cell, the VGA will be able also to provide information regarding product characteristics, but such information is actually hardly interesting at this level, let alone necessary. Here, it is more functional to refer to the highest level in the hierarchy. Ultimately, the highest goals remain the end values of satisfaction, happiness or well-being. But even the meaning of this concept will differ across the steps of the value diagonal, as we will argue below.

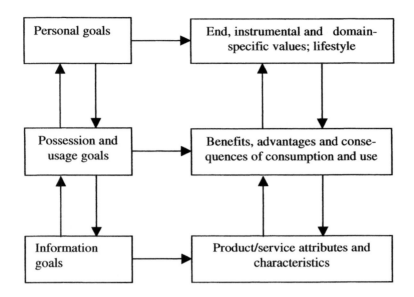

Figure 5.2 Hierarchy of values and goals

SATISFACTION AND WELL-BEING

In Cell 1, organizations often derive the satisfaction of their customers from the organization's own evaluation of the physical quality of the sold product or the objective characteristics of the service provided. There is no real interest in the satisfaction of users, especially since in Cell 1 there is no interest in repeat purchases or loyalty.

In Cell 6, satisfaction is important, but is often interpreted at the level of product characteristics and benefits. The marketing department may get the market research to administer a questionnaire to customers with questions such as 'To what extent are you satisfied with our opening times?' (characteristic), '...with our price level?' (characteristic), '...with the freshness of our products?' (characteristic). However, even if all scores are positive, such a result does not necessarily mean that customers will return. In this regard we may once again refer to the distinction between satisfiers and dissatisfiers (Herzberg, Mausner and Snyderman, 1959). A positive score on characteristics that are dissatisfiers holds no guarantee at all that customers will exhibit repeat behaviour or that they will develop any kind of loyalty. Satisfaction reactions in this situation are more elicited than spontaneous.

Therefore, it is the research that stimulates an explicit consideration of the quality of characteristics rather than the characteristics themselves. The satisfaction evaluation feels somewhat artificial. By using this kind of research, an organization appears to be condemning itself to a long stay in Cell 6.

If a company wants to make the transition to Cell 11, it would do well to also take along the functions of the characteristics and any references to values. For the supplier, satisfaction in the form of a positive reaction to a question in a survey is not sufficient. The supplier wants to know for certain that the obtained score reflects the real satisfaction of the customer. If the satisfaction is not sufficient, all stops are pulled out to improve the supply. Although satisfaction in itself does not have to be a sufficient reason to develop loyalty, it is possible for dissatisfaction with a product or service to cause loyalty to cease. In Cell 11, loyalty is vitally important to the supplier, and therefore it is one of the central points for management, together with satisfaction.

In Cell 16, satisfaction is no longer a good concept to describe the experience of the consumer. Satisfaction is applicable to individual products and services and perhaps, in Cell 11, also to the combination of various products or services within the same domain (the domain package). But when the domain packages are combined into meta-packages, a more important and larger part of the daily life of the consumer is serviced by the offered supply. The concept of 'well-being' is better suited for this level. After all, the intention of the VGA is not to maximize satisfaction with the individual products and services, but to make a positive contribution to the well-being of the connected consumers.

Therefore, we observe two shifts occurring along the value diagonal in the opinion about satisfaction. The first is that the experience of consumers becomes more of a central focus point in comparison with the product characteristics. The second is that satisfaction will encompass a large domain. This means that the evaluation of separate products and services becomes less important, and the evaluation about the impact of the total more relevant. The VGA, after all, is responsible for the collective contribution that products and services provide to the consumer's experience of well-being. Product or service advantages, therefore, are not evaluated as isolated aspects, but are evaluated as part of the total package.

In summary: satisfaction develops from a concrete level towards an abstract level through the following steps:

- Cell 1: Evoked positive evaluation of the absence of dissatisfiers (necessary characteristics)

- Cell 6: Evoked positive evaluation of the presence of satisfiers (benefits).
- Cell 11: True, spontaneous satisfaction about experiences (benefits and values)
- Cell 16: Experience of well-being: (combination of) end values.

For many companies, consumer evaluation of product attributes and benefits is still the central focus. But in Cell 16, satisfaction with products is replaced by consumer well-being in terms of certainty, safety, harmony and other important values. It is the role of the VGA to safeguard the well-being of the individual consumer. In addition, the VGA may create the conditions and opportunities for maintaining and improving well-being, which is the most important reason for the VGA's existence.

The maintenance and improvement of well-being and happiness occur in a market environment in which new products and services are continually being offered. The VGA can keep track of which new products and services make the current products or services out of date or sub-optimal. The system can also give instructions regarding the replacement of components, the maintenance and the disposal of products. Such a system already exists, albeit in modest form, for cars. It automatically warns the driver if a car needs a service overhaul. This may be done through an indicator in the car itself, but then the information is limited to that specific car and the market situation is not involved. It is also interesting to the owner to know when it would be a good time to exchange the current car for another one. A VGA might have access to the necessary data (about the owner, his/her financial situation, his/her priorities, his/her evaluations of cars) to make an optimal proposal. The proposal might go as far as giving a recommendation to exchange the current car in March of next year at a specific dealer against a Volvo S60 with such and such characteristics and accessories, and to finance this car in the following manner. A consumer who has gained a few good experiences with the relevant proposals, may eventually even be prepared to let the VGA handle the order, the negotiations and the delivery of the car.

There are several ways in which products in the possession of the consumer may become obsolete: technical, economic and psychological obsolescence of products.

- *Technical obsolescence* includes wear and tear and defects that cannot be repaired, which leads to replacement of a product. If the repair costs are higher than the current value of the product, then a product is both technically and economically obsolete.

- *Economic obsolescence* includes a less efficient use due to obsolete functionalities and too high an energy consumption. The product is then replaced to obtain more up-to-date functionalities and lower energy consumption. Examples are high efficiency heaters and PCs. These products are replaced when a new 'generation' comes onto the market with clear functional advantages.
- *Psychological obsolescence* includes outdated fashion and design that no longer fits with the current times or with the current values and lifestyle of owners. For example, clothing is discarded and replaced especially due to psychological obsolescence and less due to technical or economic obsolescence. Consumers differ with regard to their 'fashion sensitivity' – a characteristic that can be taken into account by the VGA.

In the developments outlined here, the VGA will use timely replacement to save the consumer from technical and economic obsolescence of components (products, but perhaps also services) in the package that is offered. Psychological obsolescence may also be considered, although that phenomenon does not apply to all products. For domains such as clothing this will certainly be the case; for some other less visible products and services probably less or not at all. There are products and services that are only used in the private situation and that are invisible to others, such as the washing machine, the laundry dryer and the assistance of a doctor. For such products and services, psychological obsolescence does not play a role (or hardly). There are also products and services that are primarily used in public situations and that are highly visible to others, such as clothing, hi-fi equipment and restaurants. In those cases, psychological obsolescence may indeed play a role.

In Cells 1 and 6, obsolescence involves only one single product. In Cells 11 and 16, obsolescence is a more complex phenomenon. In those situations, either components of the package (domain or meta) may be obsolete, or the entire package. A well-functioning VGA will always pay attention to the weakest link in the whole package. Which link should be replaced first to make the whole chain function better? In Cells 11 and 16 this might mean that an individual product is replaced, although the consumer had no complaints about this product by itself.

IDENTITY AND TRANSFORMATION

The symbiosis of the consumer and the VGA implies decision-making at a higher level than for separate products and services. Will everything then be perfect? Will people no longer make mistakes and will they only make optimal decisions together with their VGAs? New deficiencies (*biases*) that may appear can also be corrected again with an advanced VGA. A VGA should be insensitive to these biases and should process the information in a 'neutral', unbiased manner.

Our own identity will for some part be located in the VGA that is available to us, just like a manager can be effective with good secretarial support. Therefore, disaster will strike if our VGA leaves us, is defective or no longer functions well. This is many times worse than a crashed hard disk of your PC in the current situation. Some people already feel seriously deprived when their family car is in the garage for a day for repairs or maintenance. So it will be all the worse when the VGA is 'down' and not operational. The customer would feel seriously handicapped.

A recent development in personnel management ('people management') is to focus less on the correction of less favourable characteristics of people, and to focus instead on supporting and strengthening the good characteristics of employees. The principle of people management is to allow people to do especially those things that they are good at, because these are probably also the things that they do best. This motivates them. The same principle is likely to apply, and even more clearly so, to consumers. VGAs are able to take over less interesting tasks from consumers, such as financial matters and taxes, so that they can concentrate on those things that they enjoy most, for example playing with their children and spending time on their hobbies. To the extent that this is indeed the case, the demarcation lines between work, hobby and leisure time will become less sharp over time.

Personal Growth

The emphasis on objectives and 'making something of your life' will strengthen the dominance of personal growth and development. In fact, in the situation of Cell 16 people are already being asked early on in their lives (at school and while in college) to develop objectives and a scenario for the rest of their life. Or they are presented with scenarios from which they may choose one. In any case, they will be confronted with questions and decisions about what they want to accomplish. Which training do you want to take? Which skills do you want to learn? Which professions seem interesting to you? Which lifestyle, sports and hobbies do you want to choose? Possibly even partner choice and the choice whether to have children may not be excluded from this advice process, since these issues also have an important impact on the achievement of life goals and personal growth. People are also more directly confronted with the concept of achievement: to strive for some major goal in life. A fatalistic or indifferent attitude is strongly discouraged by this process. People are stimulated to have a long-term perspective. The VGA will help to reduce inter-individual differences with regard to the period of time for which ambitions are set.

VGAs can help to promote personal growth and development. But they cannot impose personal growth and development on people who are not interested or who lack a long-term perspective. Teachers and lifestyle coaches may be able to play an important role in this regard. Compare the self-actualization stage in the needs hierarchy by Maslow (1954) (see Figure 2.7). We need to add that we are only referring to the top levels of this hierarchy, since the lower levels have been satisfied already. What we actually need is a further distinction within the top level.

Maslow's hierarchy worked well for developing economies. Now that most of the more basic needs have been satisfied through the way in which society has developed, new needs are developing. It is an important challenge to close the gap between Maslow's needs and the values of Rokeach, Schwarz and Bilsky. This is becoming more important with the introduction of VGAs.

The top level values in the Maslow hierarchy and these levels in general are described by Pieters and Van Raaij (1988). With the aid of a VGA, it should be possible to achieve the following top values better or more effectively.

- *Self-actualization*: this is a need to make a good use of one's own talents and capacities in order to realize values. The VGA can help to better apply one's own talents and capacities in terms of completing tasks and solving problems.
- *Self-expression*: this is a need to express oneself and to be able to express thoughts and feelings that are understood and appreciated by others. The VGA can function as 'ghost writer' by generating and selecting facts and arguments that may be used for this purpose. Yet self-expression will still need to be done by the person himself/herself.
- *Need for variety, excitement, and stimulation*: the fulfilment of this need reduces boredom with a current situation. Berlyne (1963) argues that people pursue an optimal level of stimulation. If the current stimulation level is below the optimal level, then exploratory behaviour develops to gain new experiences that will increase the stimulation level. Obviously, avoidance behaviour may occur when the stimulation level is higher than the optimal level. The VGA can determine the current and desired level of stimulation and provide direction to the desired change.
- *Need for beauty and experiences*: this is a partly cognitive, partly emotional need for a 'beautiful' and attractive environment and

design. The VGA can consider this as a criterion in the selection of choice alternatives and the combination of package components (for example, the mutual 'fit' between fashion items).

- *Need for understanding and insight*: This is a cognitive need for understanding, insight and arrangement in order to know the causes of phenomena (better) and to obtain a higher degree of control over the environment. An advanced VGA can help to make connections between phenomena and developments and help to create new insights in this way.

CONCLUSION

Due to changes in the market environment, not only suppliers but also consumers will start to behave differently. We expect that the behavioural change will occur gradually, but it points in a clear direction: consumers will be more focused on the consumption itself and less on the process of purchase and preparation for consumption. The attention will shift from the appreciation of a single, isolated product characteristic towards the experience of well-being in relation to the supply of products and services that is tailored to the individual consumer. ICT is a tool that may be applied to achieve a goal and cannot function as an unguided missile. In previous chapters it was argued that the goal consisted of the combination of two dimensions (the product or package dimension and relationship duration). In this chapter we have determined the implications of the path towards Cell 16 in terms of the goals, needs, values, lifestyle, perceived freedom, loyalty, satisfaction, well-being and information processing by consumers. In Chapter 6, we will make an inventory of implications of this for markets and marketing. Subsequently (in Chapter 7) the focus will be on the question of what all this may mean at the level of society.

6. Implications for Markets and Marketing

SUMMARY

In this chapter, we discuss the consequences for marketing of the expected developments that were described in the previous chapters. This chapter is structured on the basis of the levels that can be distinguished within marketing: the vision (the goal), the strategy (the path to the goal), the tactics (the use of instruments) and, finally, the operations (the execution of those instruments). This is a hierarchy: changes in the marketing vision are expressed in the strategy, which in turn is translated into tactical and operational measures. The previous chapters may be seen as a preamble to the marketing vision.

At the strategic level, we will observe how organizations may assume different positions in the value matrix and how they may move through this matrix. At the tactical level, we will discuss the consequences of the changed strategy for the use of the traditional elements of the marketing mix. This will also include critical comments regarding the use of these instruments in current marketing. In this chapter a comparison is made with Customer Relationship Management (CRM) for the relationship dimension of the value matrix.

INTRODUCTION

This chapter explores implications for marketing and research. The first question that needs to be answered is whether the reasoning presented in this book will turn out to be tenable in the long run. We only have a scenario labelled as 'Cell 16'. What is its likelihood and how much value should be assigned to it? Our only argument is that the scenario originates from the combination of different current developments, that there are signals in the market that point into the indicated direction, that a vast majority of marketing strategists react positively to the idea, and that, in fact, several organizations did decide to follow the strategic route toward a VGA status.

One of these organizations is a large-scale wholesaler. One organization is a very large party in the Dutch health care sector, and VGA initiatives are undertaken in the area of finance and travel. Company names cannot be mentioned yet due to confidentiality agreements. Of course, these arguments and initiatives do not guarantee validity of the presented arguments. Nor do they guarantee future success. But they give us sufficient confidence to present our vision about the potential implications for markets in general, for marketing, and for marketing research.

In the previous chapters we explained how, in our expectation, the distinction between the different market sectors will start to disappear and how the antagonistic nature of the market situation will become weaker. At the same time, society will become more business-like, because societal phenomena and processes increasingly manifest themselves like transactions. For example, societal themes such as solidarity and charity are viewed as part of exchange processes. More and more, helping others seems to become some cost–benefit trade-off. We may also observe an increase of commerce in traditionally non-profit sectors, such as education, sports and health care. A simultaneous, opposite trend is that the market is developing a social aspect, for example by supporting Third World projects. Market parties are no longer part of a pure zero-sum game, in which a favourable result for one party implies an unfavourable result for the other party. The win–win situation no longer counts as a special form of business relationship that should be especially pursued and that should only be mentioned if successful. The exception is becoming the rule. Marketing is being significantly transformed. Even its definition is undergoing considerable changes. Several decades ago, marketing was the somewhat chic, American-sounding term for the application of sales techniques. After that, it referred to the orchestration and operationalization of various instruments at the tactical and operational levels. Then, it moved to the more sophisticated level of strategy. In the near future, marketing will become associated with supporting people in their never-ending attempt to increase personal well-being. Marketing sure has come a long way from sales techniques.

Basically, it shows that the focus of marketing shifts from the moment of purchase, through the pre-purchase phase to the consumption or usage phase. Stated differently, the emphasis in marketing changed from monetary result, to buying process, to consumption effect. This means that consumption, as the primary focus of the customer, now will become the primary focus of marketing. Marketing made quite a detour before it eventually returned to the customer.

SYNERGETIC MARKETING

Which market situation is likely to develop? The basic idea is that the market structure will adapt to the new function of marketing. The new function of marketing is based upon the notion that knowledge of the customer is the most critical asset of a company or a non-profit organization. (To avoid possible confusion: we mean the customer knowledge of marketers, not the product and service knowledge of customers.)

If customer knowledge is crucial, the distinction between profit and non-profit becomes less sharp, and even the distinction between suppliers and customers slowly disappears. Customers, in their role as suppliers of information, can be viewed as producers. Vice versa, suppliers adopt the role of customers (of the same information). Goods, services and money are not the only elements of exchange. Now, en route to Cell 16, information needs to be added as a decisive, super ordinate element.

So in the market there is a continuous exchange of money, time, efforts, goods, services and information to help optimize the combined result. Increasingly, parties are and perceive themselves as directly responsible for the results obtained by the other party. If some party withdraws from the system, he or she not only discards the disadvantages, but also (or even more so) the advantages. However, the customer who wants to benefit from the added value of the VGA system will be more than willing to contribute in the form of money, effort and information.

With the increase of the flow of information, parties are better informed of each other and can take each other's interests better into account. Parties will start to experience and demonstrate mutual responsibility. In principle, responsibility has no pre-set boundaries. The ultimate responsibility neither stops at a geographic border, the end of a phase in the production or consumption process, nor at the end of an era or with a generation. Responsibility also does not restrict itself to achieving trivial effects, but it will extend to the realization of the goals customers consider to be important. As suppliers will not be able to achieve this purely by themselves, cooperation with other suppliers is important for adding value. This can be done either 'horizontally' (package formation), 'vertically' (relationship formation), or 'diagonally', integrating relationship formation and package formation. In this chain, all parties are responsible for the result of their particular contribution. Their output is the input of the next link. Complementarity is the key. The quality of the total chain and the total package is dependent upon the performance of the individual links and contributors. Market parties will claim that responsibilities are the reason for their existence and will also demand that other parties take their own responsibility seriously. And so a self-supporting and self-propelling system develops.

Although marketing no longer appears in its old shape, traditional elements and instruments are still available. We indicated before that these instruments are swallowed by the respective spirals (the innovation spiral, the communication spiral, distribution spiral and price spiral). As a reminder: the innovation spiral means that although products and services do indeed improve over time, the opportunities for inventing breakthroughs is more limited than the suppliers' need for surplus value. Suppliers copy each other's improvements and innovations; product life cycles (recovery times) shorten drastically. Suppliers' interest in further improvement declines. Spurious innovation drives out true innovation. The introduction of new products reduces the invisibility of existing products. It is like planting additional trees in an already dense forest. Also here, 'more' is not necessarily 'better'. The communication spiral is not able to absorb the effect of the innovation spiral. More communication results in less being communicated. Here, more of the same may even lead to a negative result, such as customer boredom and irritation. Distribution eventually comes up empty-handed; also, more attempts at having contact with customers eventually results in contact-averse customers. Ultimately price remains the only arena for competition. But here the same rule applies: the larger the price competition, the smaller the price differences, and the smaller the profits and the room for competition.

The spirals lead to a situation where everything is the same for everyone. Supply becomes a homogeneous mass, a *commodity*. Even if some suppliers want to avoid being sucked into the grey standard centre of the market, they may no longer have the resources to do this. Supply variety starts to fade. Who said that low prices are a blessing to customers? Over the long term, customers are better off paying higher prices if the profits are ploughed back into supply improvements and innovations. Higher prices lead to higher differentiation and, potentially, a better fit between supply and customer demand. But it is not clear how this should be achieved. Anyhow, speeding up the spirals makes no sense. Therefore, we suggest that the nature of the game be changed. An alternative game should allow for a continuous improvement of the supply–demand fit. In principle, there seems ample room for continuous improvement. Take, for example, the food area, where we can observe and anticipate the following steps in the development of marketing (steps 5, 6, and 7 are not taken yet on a larger scale):

1. The sale (push) of ingredients.
2. The sale of pre-mixes.
3. The marketing of ready-made dishes.

4.   The preparation of meals.
5.   The management of nutritional value.
6.   The effort to match the food to individual circumstances.
7.   The introduction of an integrated system that supports the individual customer to be maximally satisfied with the food supply, which takes into account his or her personal preferences and specific physical, social and physical circumstances.

But the situation has not yet progressed that far. And even if it had, the question would still be whether this type of improvement presents the final solution. In the current market situation, the spirals are still turning, being wound up like watch springs. They become more difficult to unwind. Marketing instruments gradually become obsolete. Added value is evaporating. Variety in consumption becomes the new focus. But the fate of variety is predictable: it will become so standard that it will lose its function.

The marketing spiral makes ever-smaller rotations around the black hole of decreasing added value. We argued that this trap may be avoided by 'synergetic marketing'. Synergy in this term has two different meanings. It refers to the alignment of products and services (products and product/services and services) vis-à-vis each other. It also refers to the alignment of the sets of customer needs and the total product/service package. And it applies to the match of the short-term and longer-term customer interests.

What would synergetic marketing mean in terms of marketing policy? The answer to this question needs to distinguish between four levels: marketing vision, strategy, tactics and execution. Each of these will be dealt with in the following paragraphs. The marketing vision represents the general context for the strategy, tactics and execution (operations).

MARKETING VISION

The marketing vision is the general starting point, the philosophy (or the 'hang-up' or prejudice) of the decision maker. This level pertains to the substantiated expectation of the decision maker in relation to the most important factors that determine marketing success. It determines the criteria on the basis of which strategic decisions are defined. For example, if a company has a strong product orientation, value criteria will focus on the objective quality or technological innovation of the product or the service. If a company is strongly customer-oriented, it will focus on criteria related to the customer perceptions, satisfaction and complaints. Different marketing visions or orientations result in different marketing policy decisions.

At the level of the marketing vision, we expect that the true insight into customers will strongly increase. More and more, marketing decisions will take the psychology of customer behaviour into account. It will absolutely no longer be sufficient to merely know customer socio-demographic characteristics and the nature of their purchases. It will become necessary to determine *why* (or *why not*) they behave in the manner that the supplier expects or hopes for. Customer focus will be sharpened into a customer behaviour focus.

The difference is that with a focus on customer behaviour attention will be given to the causes of behaviour. With a behaviour focus, the marketer is focused on truly understanding the customer. A behavioural approach takes into account that customers often do not act rationally, and acknowledges that a deep insight into the origin of their actions helps to optimize supply. Economic psychology, the psychology that considers decisions in economic and market situations, can help to clarify how and why people process information, make considerations and decisions, select and handle products and services, become satisfied or dissatisfied, and do or do not engage in repeat purchases or express complaints. A better insight into the human possibilities and limitations shines a new light onto current marketing activities, and also shows which behavioural aspects require particular marketing support.

Technological overkill is impossible with a behaviour focus. Perhaps a behaviour-focused organization allows less room for sheer creativity than in a product-focused organization. But there will be less overkill, lower costs, and a higher likelihood of successful products. So far, innovations have been predominantly technology driven. It is time that customer behaviour is welcomed as an innovation driver as well.

Insights into customer behaviour may help suppliers to obtain a better insight into how customers evaluate products. In general, the marketer assumes a high rationality of the customer. This leads to an overestimation of product/service appreciation, information absorption, and customer decision-making quality. Marketers consistently overestimate the degree to which the customer is motivated, or has the capacity and the opportunity to behave as expected or desired by the marketer (Poiesz, 1999).

In this context it is important to note that a VGA originates from a stronger behaviour focus and a more realistic perspective on the customer. The VGA is even a central tool for the development of a behaviour focus. It is able to protect the customer to a certain degree against his/her own biases, inconsistencies and irrationalities. In turn, the VGA can protect the supplier against the consequences of these deviations from the expected behaviour. Therefore, the VGA serves both customer and service provider at the same time.

From a behavioural standpoint, the distinction between customer, purchaser, industrial purchaser, and user is artificial. If the final criteria are the advantages (benefits) that are obtained by using the product, there is no reason for making a distinction between types of purchasers and customers, nor between types of goods (fast-moving consumer goods (FMCG), services and industrial products). Instead, we should focus on the benefits and the realization of values that customers derive from consumption. This was already known in the 1960s with the benefit segmentation approach by Haley (1968). Yet at that point in time the idea was not generally accepted.

An important aspect of the company vision is the profit orientation. Contemporary companies focus primarily on short-term profit and on compensating investors. We expect this to change in two ways. (1) There will be more attention to long-term profit, and (2) profit will be seen as the result of the cooperation between the company, its partners and the customers. All parties are involved and provide an input to the end result. This means that they perceive that they have a joint responsibility, which reduces dissatisfaction and complaints (Van Raaij and Pruyn, 1998). The traditional distinction between shareholderes and stakeholders will disappear. The customer co-operative association will reappear, but in a stronger version than we have seen before. This means that customers will probably also be shareholders, and will invest more interests in a company than present-day customers. Profit then is no longer linked to a single party, but may be seen as the result of the cooperation between suppliers and customers. Profit will be re-invested into this cooperation.

The concept of profit will also change. Originally, profit was considered a type of exploitation index. The more a company was able to 'squeeze' out of its customers, the higher the profit. When the concept of 'added value' was introduced, profit was seen as a tool for creating added value over the long term. In the developments outlined here, profit is viewed as a temporary financial reserve available for customers at a later point in time. Here it will be made available in the form of increased value/ specific benefits. At the micro level, this means that the customer and supplier/VGA will consider each other as partners. At the meso level, it implies a shift in power from the stakeholders to the customers/members. And at the macro level, it may even mean the combination of the traditionally opposed ideologies of capitalism and socialism. A VGA stands for socialism in a capitalist mould.

The antagonism between supplier and customer makes way for cooperation, for a long-term, truly win–win situation for both parties.

The alternative profit notion would hold a solution for the well-known problem of the conflict between short-term and long-term company results. Investors call for short-term results; customers want short-term and long-term results. Company strategists are stuck in the middle. However, if the

roles of customers and investors merge, there is no room for any other conflict than a personal conflict of interests, which can only be solved by the
individual customers/investors themselves (possibly supported by their
VGA). Thus, in a VGA system, where the roles of shareholder and customer are combined in the same persons, financial shareholder pressure is
relieved. The emphasis on short-term or long-term effects may even provide
a basis for the positioning of a VGA.

In summary, the developments that we anticipate will lead to seven implications at the level of the marketing vision:

1. Marketing is a spiral of spirals. If a company does not want to get
   caught up in this, it will need to consider a marketing strategy that does
   not boil down to more of the same. A fundamentally different way of
   thinking is required.
2. The other way of thinking cannot be captured in one single dimension.
   Marketing has become so complex that it is necessary to consider various developments simultaneously: package formation, relationship
   formation and application of ICT to the very combination of the first
   two.
3. Added value should remain unchanged as the central, leading theme of
   marketing policy.
4. In the search for new added value, a behaviour focus is an important
   starting point.
5. Within a behaviour focus, the awareness should grow that the prevail-
   ing model of the customer needs to be revised. The company should
   take into account a customer who is less motivated, less capable, has
   less time available and finds himself in less favourable purchasing and
   consumption circumstances than is often assumed by the marketer.
6. A different function for marketing requires a redefinition of roles. The
   classical antagonism between suppliers and customers ceases to exist.
7. The previous point implies that profit will obtain a different place and
   significance. Profit in marketing that is characterized by antagonism
   and that is focused on the short term is fundamentally different from
   profit within a partnership that is oriented towards the long term. The
   VGA adopts the latter notion.

MARKETING STRATEGY

The strategic level considers long-term marketing objectives. We argued for
a strategic approach that goes beyond merely creating long-term relation-

ships. At present, relationships are often managed with the help of electronic information systems referred to as Customer Relationship Management (CRM) systems. With CRM, customer data are stored in relational databases. CRM helps managers in assessing the frequency, recency and monetary value of the purchase behaviour of customers, and in adapting marketing activities to purchase patterns. In spite of its obvious advantages, CRM is often associated with four problems or limitations:

1. No matter how customer-oriented CRM may appear to be, it is still strongly oriented towards the advantage of the owner and manager of the customer data. The supplier still has the central focus, not the customer. 'Marketer Relationship Management' therefore would have been an equally appropriate title.
2. CRM is primarily used as a tactical tool to stimulate sales rather than as a strategic asset. The use of customer data is primarily focused on segmentation and the selection of target segments, on finding prospects (new customers) based on profiles of current customers, and on the selection of names and addresses for specific marketing actions.
3. The third problem is that it creates possibilities for abusing personal data. The violation of privacy not only jeopardizes the relationship between customers and a particular company. It also damages trust of customers, their willingness to share information, and long-term relationships in general.
4. Finally, CRM in itself does not follow the value diagonal, but only the relationship dimension. Therefore, CRM is only a partial step in the direction of a true customer focus.

Branding

As we have already argued in the previous chapters, we expect that a shake-out will occur among the currently existing brands. To a large extent, the VGA will take over the primary function that brands occupy in current markets: to be a beacon representing certainty, continuity and positive value associations. In this sense, the VGA may also be regarded as a brand. It has the potential to develop into a 'meta-brand' – a brand that subsumes other brands. A meta-brand is based upon such a level of trust from customers that they almost 'blindly' accept the assortment and the information from the VGA. The stronger the VGA brand, the less important the reputation of the individual brands that are presented and represented by the VGA. This development leads to the rise of a limited number of meta-brands, which are positioned closely to the goals and end values of the customer. More strongly than most of the currently existing brands, they are associated with (instrumental and end) values of a high level of abstraction such as safety, security or adventure.

Meta-brands will become a reliable identification and anchor point for customers in the overloaded economy of information, choice options, brands, products and services. The meta-brand offers structure, overview and something to hold on to in this overload situation. Producer brands will continue to exist and will be used primarily in a business-to-business context. Meta-*branders* will operate as *buyer agencies* for their customers and end users.

Many current large brands have the potential to remain leading brands and to become a VGA, but this is not automatically the case. It is important to possess a database with customer data. The owner of the database is in effect the owner of the brand.

Over time, traditional brands will become the background for the new brands, unless they are able to develop and exploit a database with customer data at the domain level. In that way they can maintain contact with customers, not just on behalf of one single product, but for a combination of products and services, across different domains. The meta-brands optimize the supply of goods, services and information for each customer.

For established, large brands this means that the competition may come from an unknown and unexpected direction. In Cell 11, the Automobile Association (AA) could become a competitor to insurance companies in terms of travel and damage insurances. In Cell 16, the AA could even expand its service to other domains. As a VGA it could, using an expansive database, create an integration between domains such as leisure activities, holiday trips, education (*life-long learning*), insurance and other financial products. Obviously, the AA does not need to produce these products and services by itself. Instead, it serves as a coordinator, who stays in close contact with individual customers and with potential suppliers. The associated care providers might develop a competing brand in relation to the existing care insurers. Customers' associations could in principle develop into important customer brands based on their reliable image (but in doing so they would lose their independence and oppositional role). Banks would not just handle the financial domain, but might also link up with other domains, such as housing and work. Credit card companies such as Master Card, Visa and American Express might also be able to do this. American Express already offers its members financing, hotel and restaurant reservations, car rental, business trips and luxury vacations. The foundation of the new brand is the functionality of the combination of products, services and information and the synergy that is experienced by the individual customer. This shows again that the mere existence of a database is not decisive in itself. The essential component is the added value and synergy that can be made visible, noticeable and understandable for customers.

Organizations that already enjoy a certain trust from the customers have the potential to raise their brand to a VGA level. Market leaders would have a head start if they developed an ambition in this direction. The AA was already mentioned because this organization enjoys a large degree of trust by its members (it is not restricted by the suspicion of a commercial intent). Other organizations such as energy providers, telecom companies, customers' associations, housing corporations, (medical) care institutions and privatized government institutions may have the same advantage. Non-profit organizations could in principle become a clear competitor of their commercial counterpoints such as banks and insurance companies. International retail chains such as The Body Shop, IKEA, H&M and Zara, could use the trust that they have developed among customers to develop a reliable and credible meta-brand. Often, these chains already sell products that do not belong in the regular assortment. At the same time, we should note that they do not simultaneously address the relationship dimension in a way that is necessary for following the diagonal in the value matrix.

Because of their database, agencies for temporary employment such as Randstad have a unique opportunity to develop into a VGA and to claim a part of the non-labour market. They are already expanding their concept of the labour market by including career counselling and career planning in the package. This could be further expanded in the direction of insurance, financing, moving (mobility), and house rentals. An expansion towards leisure activities would certainly not be unthinkable and would probably be perceived by the customers as a logical extension.

The examples clarify that once the boundaries of the traditional lines of business, chains and suppliers are put up for discussion, a large number of attractive possibilities arise. A supplier could be a VGA itself, provide an exclusive contribution to a specific VGA, serve several VGAs, or reach the customer independently. One party becomes the leader of the network and of the 'face' (the brand) towards the customers. Whoever takes and maintains the initiative in this market develops a clear head start. Other parties are then forced into the function of business-to-business supplier of a few products and services, without having direct contacts with the end users.

Meta-brands that develop a long-term relationship with their customers show a great degree of stability because they have a steady customer franchise, which also means steady sales. We expect that markets will be dominated by a limited number of meta-brands. Brands that do not have this status will find it increasingly difficult to hold their position in the market. It may sound dramatic, but once a company loses a customer to a VGA, this customer is highly unlikely to be regained. Switching to a VGA is much easier than switching from a VGA. The continuous emphasis on added value, synergy effects, long-term results and individual attention all ensure that the power in the market gravitates towards VGAs. These are likely to 'divide' the market into value areas. They do not violate competition rules, as the advantages for the customer are evident.

Historically, this would be an interesting development. Once, competition was considered necessary for market self-correction. By comparing price–value ratios, customers favour the best purchase option, and unattractive options are deleted from the market supply. In the new market structure described here, self-correction is built in the relationship between supplier and customer. The critical market mechanism is formed by the information exchange between supplier and customer, rather than by the customers' comparisons among suppliers. Thus, the desired effect is reached in a different way. Competition, which seemed to be the unique instrument for market self-correction, loses its exclusive function. One might even argue that competition is only an indirect route to customer value and that in a VGA-based market, customer interests are safeguarded in a more effective and efficient way.

The status of the VGA is not only associated with power, but also with responsibility. It develops from the responsibility for the technical quality and the price of products and services, to the responsibility for the value that the customer actually experiences during consumption. Historically, this is a logical extension. Traditional economists argued that value is created through the production of goods (the physiocrats even limited this to the production in agriculture and cattle breeding). Traditional marketers argued that value is not created in the production, but in the exchange of goods and services. However, also the exchange itself no longer seems to guarantee value. Now the position of value is shifting towards the actual consumption of goods and services. In the latter view, value is only created when the user experiences the advantages (benefits) of the product or service and is satisfied with it. This applies in principle not just to one single product or service, but for an interconnected assortment of products and services. The initial product care transforms into customer care, the care for the satisfaction and the well-being of the customer. Accordingly, the attention of marketing will shift from the transaction (sell/buy) to consumption. Marketing activities and responsibilities will change to adapt to this shift in function. Customer experience is key. See also Pine and Gilmore (1999) on the experience economy. A consumption focus provides new marketing opportunities, particularly if combined with the notion of meta-brands. These brands have the opportunity to create their own experience universe around the products–services assortment, a universe in which customers like to be.

For example, Disneyland advertises the 'magic' that people experience when they visit the Disney park.

It is too early to anticipate what the next stage will be in the reasoning about customer value. But some speculation seems allowed. Possibly the next focus will be on customer growth and transformation. Consumption, in essence, may be limited to a short-term activity. Products, services and information may also help people to manage their life more effectively and efficiently beyond the mere activity of consumption, and to be more focused on long-term, societal, international and environmental effects in relation to personal needs, ambitions, values and interests. Big Brother is peeking around the corner here, but the critical point of difference is that the VGA is based upon the interests of the individual person and not upon the interests of a power-oriented other party.

In VGA-based marketing, complementarity and synergy are the new key words. The crucial question is how complementarity and synergy should be determined. The current marketing notions that are most closely related are line extension and brand extension. With a line extension, an existing brand adds a new variety to its brand, for example a new flavour, colour or size. A brand extension uses the existing brand for products that do not belong to the original assortment. Camel presents, in addition to cigarettes, fashion and shoes. Both examples indicate that it is possible to move the product domain and the brand domain relatively independently of each other. An important condition in this regard is that the customer experiences the extension as being a logical one. If Camel also offered baby food, the extension would probably not be understood by customers and perhaps would also not be appreciated. The examples indicate that, within certain limits (that are determined by customer), a brand can lead its own life and may develop into an institution. This also brings us to the notion that it is not necessary to limit the VGA brand to its original product category. For example, a railway system can offer leisure activities. Sony can organize trips to the opera in Vienna. Obviously, a stable brand that has been built up consistently over the years, and that is strongly tied to customer values, has more room to manoeuvre than a young brand that only refers to product characteristics.

The question of when and how a brand starts to expand itself in the direction of a VGA cannot be answered definitively. The best we can do here is to indicate a few options. The actual development depends on the organization's ambition and on the current position of the brand in the market. A possible starting point is the brand itself. A supplier with a highly valued brand might develop or purchase a database. Another possible starting point is a cooperation between two parties that is focused on complementarity.

An existing database may also provide the start of a VGA. Organizations for temporary employment, for example, may have a greater strategic opportunity than they currently realize. They should abandon their preoccupation with labour, and determine for what other purposes their own database might be functional. For such a party it would not be easy to try to develop a strong brand on its own, owing to the costs and the time necessary for development. Cooperation with an existing brand of a complementary product is a strategic option.

VGAs may be seen as crystallization points in the market. It is not clear where they start, but when they start, they have the potential to expand rapidly. We expect that the *first-mover advantage* plays a special role in the development of VGAs. Once cooperative efforts have been created in an early stage of development, it later becomes more difficult to break them apart. The cumulative effect of a developing cooperation means that it is difficult for the parties to withdraw from the construction that has been developed. The sunk costs and the switching costs are high. Because the cooperation is, in principle, focused on developing long-term relationships with the customer, the partners commit themselves to a long-term time frame. The complementarity that needs to be realized requires that various cross-connections are being developed. Suppliers that do not have the status of VGA and that do not belong to a VGA network occupy a risky position. VGA networks will have a tendency to grow organically and pick up a substantial market share. The remaining niches will continue to decrease. For these niches, contact with customers will become increasingly difficult, as customers are primarily oriented towards their VGA. The VGA is unlikely to recommend unknown products from niches. This may require niche players to identify themselves both to end customers and VGAs.

An important starting point continues to be that it is not the supplier who determines the complementarity, but the customer. If the customer is not convinced of the added value of a complementarity, it will not be offered. Due to the importance of strategic decisions, the observation and appreciation of complementarity by customers is highly relevant. As the network of suppliers behind the VGA expands, complementarity becomes a characteristic that develops from a search characteristic to an experience characteristic and finally to a credence characteristic (Nelson, 1970, 1974).

A search characteristic is a characteristic that may be evaluated by the customer based on available information, for instance a coffee mug. An experience characteristic relates to a characteristic that cannot be evaluated beforehand, but only after the usage, for instance medical treatment. Finally, a credence characteristic indicates an aspect that customers are no longer able to judge on their own, not even after the usage, but they trust that the supply is good. An example of a credence good is 'green electricity'.

In Cell 1 of the value diagonal, search characteristics are dominant. The closer we come to Cell 16, the more search characteristics decrease in favour of credence characteristics. In Cell 16, customers are no longer able to judge the quality of the complex supply, and they have to rely on their trust in the VGA.

In summary, seven general strategic marketing implications may be noted:

1. It is becoming increasingly important for organizations to determine where they are located within the value matrix and which course they want to take within this matrix (the 'migration path').
2. For any party that has ambitions in the direction of Cell 16, the possession of a database is an extremely important condition for being able to pursue the value diagonal.
3. A party with a substantial database may turn into an attractive partner or a dangerous competitor, even if the party does not operate within the same market.
4. Increasingly, choices will be made on the basis of trust. Trust, in turn, is based upon the cumulation of consistently positive experiences. If trust is still limited due to lack of customer experience, reputation may serve as a substitute.
5. The combination of a favourable reputation and a database presents an excellent starting position for a new VGA.
6. The design and start of a VGA are very important. Right from the start the VGA should be based on the added value of the complementarity as experienced by customers. The start is important for suppliers, since the cross-connections in a network that has already been formed around a VGA present a barrier to new entrants. Competition may be fierce between parties that, apparently, both start off in the direction of a VGA within the same market domain as the *winner-takes-all* principle is likely to apply.
7. The added value as experienced by the customer is the key criterion in all these activities.

MARKETING TACTICS

The tactical level describes the use of the instruments of the marketing mix for the purpose of reaching the strategic goal. Decisions regarding marketing instruments relate to the short term and medium term.

We describe several implications of the expected developments for the use of traditional marketing instruments. It should be clear that we cannot provide a detailed elaboration. Therefore, we will briefly discuss each of the following subjects:

- Products and services: quality and innovation
- Communication policy
- Price policy
- Distribution policy

Products and Services

The added value of products and services is no longer exclusively located in their continuous improvement. The question is whether investments should be made in a further improvement of the characteristics of the current product or service (with the risk of overkill), or in complementarity with other products and services. The focus will no longer be on technical or professional quality, but on contextual quality, the quality within the context of existing possessions, future plans and responsibilities.

There are several types of innovation. There are the breakthroughs that we cannot easily imagine or anticipate taking place: sometimes, they just seem to originate from nowhere. Yet, such innovations occur with some frequency. Examples are the Internet and possibly, in the near future, the linking of computer processors to human brains. In addition, there are the more gradual innovations which imply meaningful changes of existing goods and services. The first type occurs too infrequently to serve as a basis for marketing policy, and is only possible through systematic investments (and some creativity and luck). The second type relates to gradual adjustments that are often no longer sufficient to create a consumer's experience of added value. But there is ample room for innovation in relation to the complementarity between products and services (or products and products and services and services).

Rogers (1983) distinguished between discontinuous innovations, dynamically continuous innovations, and continuous innovations. Discontinuous innovations involve new products and services that require a significant adjustment of a consumption pattern or lifestyle (the introduction of hydrogen motors in cars). Dynamically continuous innovations involve a rather substantial improvement of a product or service that, in itself, affects customer behaviour to some extent (the introduction of DVD players). Continuous innovations are not really innovations, but gradual, rather insignificant product or service adaptations that have no impact on customer behaviour (DVD players with a new design).

The same qualification may be applied to packages or combinations of products and services. Some attempts at forming packages are hardly noted by customers. Some financial products that serve as each other's extension may be combined in a single product. Other packages affect customer behaviour. An insurance company may team up with a particular car repair chain or a medical insurance company may cooperate with particular hospitals or care organizations. An example of a discontinuous, innovative package is the joining of a care organization and a hotel chain to provide luxury facilities to recovering patients. It may be expected that packages are more likely than individual products and services to affect customers' lifestyles. After all, packages may be formed in order to reduce the hassle that customers experience, and are constructed to generate increased well-being. Customers' consumption patterns and life styles may change because of a reduction of time, effort and money spent on the purchase process.

The VGA may have to help customers to understand the particular function of packages. The larger the package, the more difficult it will be for the customer to identify its particular benefits. Thus, it may be expected that marketing will shift attention from the quality of product characteristics to the quality of relationships and integration of products (and services) and their impact on customer well-being. As indicated earlier, this may be supported by branding the VGA and by referring to general values.

The total supply of products and services will be better matched to the individual customer. This is partly based on the interaction with that customer. It enables suppliers to produce in a more focused fashion. The enormous costs that are made to experiment with new product introductions, to build inventories and to cover financial risks can be significantly reduced. Periodic sales to get rid of excess stock are no longer necessary, simply because there is no excess stock. Waste is sharply reduced. Money, time and energy that were originally invested – with high risk – in *trial and error* activities, marketing and commercial communication can be used for supply individualization, system upgrades and customer interaction. Instruments that indirectly contribute to value creation will be replaced by instruments and processes that directly create value.

Complementarity and integration are the criticial terms. With respect to what package aspects can it be achieved? In principle, the opportunities are endless. Here we will present possible examples relating to quality, price, functionality, timing and usage situations.

Quality

The first example is the matching of the quality levels of products that are functionally related. For example, there is no point in purchasing an expensive hi-fi installation with a cheap speaker set. Depending on the type of user, the customer would be better off purchasing a somewhat cheaper installation and upgrading the speakers, thus creating a more harmonious package. The term 'quality alignment' may be used to describe the principle.

Price

The price or cost advantage of a package is clear: it avoids the overlap that would require a customer to pay more than is necessary. For example, a customer already has health insurance through his or her insurer. Therefore, he/she does not need to be covered again for the same costs through travel insurance, even though these are generally included in this type of insurance. The price of the travel insurance may thus be lowered. If we think of a package that not only integrates products and services at a particular moment in time but also over time, it it clear that the potential advantage of a package is considerable. Penny-wise-pound-foolish spending not only occurs with respect to individual purchases, but also (or especially) with regard to combinations that develop over time. A better insight into the interrelationships of benefits and costs would help the customer to increase the experienced value significantly.

Functionality

Here we can think of the degree to which the functions of different products and services match to support each other. This is sometimes referred to as compatibility, although this word is more exclusively used to describe technical fit (compatibility of equipment, for example, between PC, telephone, fax and handheld computer). But the concept may be extended to products that do not need to function simultaneously. Suppose, for example, that two members of a household both need transportation. By choosing a certain combination of cars it is possible to arrive at a maximum of functions (sport, family car, long trips, bulk transportation). A 'mobility package' might even combine public transportation and private transportation (including rental cars). At an even more general level, mobility and communication might form a package. If we need to communicate with people, is it necessary to see them face to face, to have a telephone contact with video, or just plain telephone? Do we assume too easily, because of existing routines and conventions, that only one type of communication applies?

Timing

The purchase of a new product is matched in time with the purchase of another product. A recommendation is made to delay the purchase of a new sofa until the curtains need replacement, which (according to the VGA) are almost at the end of their technical life span. By waiting half a year with large home maintenance, it becomes possible to have it done at the same time as four other homes in the same neighbourhood (which may lead to considerable cost savings).

Usage situations

Recommendations are possible with regard to the actual usage of products and services that are already acquired. Patients are recommended to increase, slow down, or delay the intake of particular pharmaceutical products given their physical condition at a particular moment in time. Consumers obtain feedback as to the amount of detergent used for washing clothes (over-dosage is typical). They are warned that the combined use of two cleaning products may produce intoxicating effects. Given the available cupboard space at home, a consumer is advised to buy the medium size container of product X instead of the extra large container. Given the personal preferences of the consumer, the cost in terms of money is traded off against the cost of space.

Communication Strategy

Information transfer will continue to play an important role in the interaction of supply and demand. The current quantity and format of information is ludicrous compared with what appears to be possible in the future: fine-tuned individualized information presented at the functional moment and at the right location. The current communication hysteria is dismantled into an interaction that is tailored towards each specific goal, individual and context. At present, customers first need to become aware of data and then need to determine whether it is information for them. If it is, they need to determine how much of it they wish to receive. A newspaper is a medium that contains many times more information than the reader selects for processing. The same applies for magazines, TV, the Internet, and actually for all other types of media. Information overload does cost us a lot of time. Apparently, while learning is impossible without information, information may also hamper learning. Of course, incidental learning (as opposed to intentional learning) may occur, but this type of learning is predominantly beyond the control of senders, and provides no solid basis for marketing policy.

Communication in present-day marketing refers to product and service benefits and direct financial costs. However, other costs such as time costs are becoming more important. If more emphasis is placed upon overall value experienced by consumers, it may be expected that information relating to these other costs (including time costs, irritation costs, physical and mental energy costs, and opportunity costs) will be integrated more in the decision to purchase and consume. Because of the increasing complexity of the decision, support will be needed. A VGA is capable of providing this. A VGA can weigh the costs on an individual basis, depending upon the personal budgets for each of the resources. For example, a VGA may give time costs more weight than financial costs in purchase trade-offs for a consumer with a high income and a strict time schedule, and it may communicate and advise accordingly.

Technologies such as hand-held computers and satellite-supported positioning and navigation systems will help in the future to present information at the right place at the right moment in the right format to the right person. No more, no less.

Although the phrase 'integrated communication' is often referred to at present, it will only be a true reality in the future. Integration of communication will take place by matching media in such a way that the information need of an individual recipient connects exactly with the information supply, regardless of the number of suppliers and the number of media that provide input for this purpose. To put it more simply: both *information overload* and *underload* are avoided. It is impossible to obtain an accurate and complete picture of the various media that will be available on the market in a few years, thus no sensible estimate can be made of what their integration may look like. In this context the miniaturization of electronic equipment is interesting as it increases the possibilities for technical integration. Experiments are already being conducted on the integration of media with other customer items such as houses, refrigerators, care and even clothing (Van Raaij, 2000). Technological possibilities for identity recognition are rapidly expanding, which means that the individualized contact with the customer no longer needs to be connected to a certain location or to the initiative of the customer.

We do not support the optimistic belief of some suppliers that new technologies will enable them to reach customers in an almost unlimited fashion. Anyone who attempts to imagine the situation that would develop in such a scenario has to come to the conclusion that it would be untenable. Systematic communication overkill (for example spam) leads to communication ineffectiveness and customer irritation.

The new media actually provide customers with more possibilities to take the initiative. But the VGA can anticipate the initiative and provide the customer with leads, to be taken up by customers. Much current shopping behaviour has the purpose of visually inspecting the merchandise. With an increase of media for visual communication, the possibility for evaluating products at a distance is growing. For example, in order to find a new carpet that needs to match the current interior, it will no longer be necessary to visit various furnishing stores, let alone visit them in different cities or shopping centres. The VGA, familiar with the current interior design and the personal tastes, presents a first selection that may be viewed on a screen. Printing the image allows for a direct comparison with the current interior, or a simulation can be made of the living room with the new carpet. If desired, the customer may also leave the choice to the VGA, with the option of returning the merchandise.

Pricing Strategy

What determines the price of a product, service or package? In current marketing practice, price is a somewhat limited concept by the exclusive focus on the financial costs relating to the purchase of one specific product. The price does not refer to the costs associated with using the product, maintaining and discarding it. Neither is there any mention of the costs, in terms of time and effort required for getting the new product started: 'The price of this PC is € 2000; average installation time: one business day; irritation index of manual: 70/100'. In a broader sense, costs also represent what the customer has to deny him- or herself in order to make a certain purchase. The true price, therefore, consists of the costs in terms of money, time, effort, and the opportunity costs. Opportunity costs arise because by the purchase of one product the opportunity to buy another product is forgone. We expect that customers will be decreasingly interested in the financial price but more so in the actual life-time costs and the other costs of the product. At present, these costs cannot be integrally evaluated. Due to their own mental limitations, and the fact that price is only communicated with the most limited definition, people are forced to interpret 'price' as being exclusively financial. The other costs that play a role do so only implicitly, which makes their impact on the evaluation unclear, unsystematic and therefore non-rational.

The VGA helps to take the integral costs into account during the evaluation of a product, service or package. We expect that the traditional product-specific financial prices will be considered to be irrelevant by customers, since they can no longer judge them in the broader context of product/service packages. The only basis for evaluating the cost component is the trust in the VGA.

Leasing constructions demonstrate the growing popularity of having a party other than the customer deal with the indirect costs of consumption. For this reason, leasing is a concept that more directly relates to the VGA concept than payments per transaction. If a benefit can only be experienced in the broader context of available products and services, the same applies to price. This reduces price of a single product or service to a meaningless aspect. What is cheap at face value (an isolated purchase of a distinct product or service at a particular point in time) may be expensive in the total set and over time.

Distribution Strategy

We expect that a clearer distinction will develop between functional and fun shopping. Functional shopping will decrease, while fun shoppingwill increase. The VGA will play a more explicit role in functional shopping: information supply, recommendation for purchase, implementing mandated actions and looking after the delivery process. Customers will increasingly delegate to the VGA the shopping activities that they consider to be boring and uninteresting, that they find difficult to do themselves, and for which they feel to have too little time.

Services will also increasingly be booked through or by the VGA, such as the gardener, chimney sweep, window cleaner, cleaning service, and laundry in and around the home, and more general services such as insurances, cultural events, education and vacation planning.

Some experiments have been conducted already with home delivery of groceries. Although not all of these experiments were successful, it does not mean that the idea of a new marketing system is not feasible. Apart from the fact that failing experiments can also be observed in present-day marketing, there seems to be a particular reason why innovative ideas have a hard time being successful: new marketing ideas are marketed with old marketing instruments. For example, the communication of home delivery of groceries put a special emphasis on the extra financial price of the service, while ignoring the advantages that the customer might experience. These advantages relate to savings for the customer in terms of money (car costs, parking costs, babysitting costs and so on), effort and time (travel time, shopping time, waiting-at-the-checkout time, loading and unloading). New concepts only have a chance to succeed with new marketing approaches.

The VGA should be able to organize the logistics of the delivery of groceries and other necessary purchases in a more efficient manner than customers are now doing themselves. In the whole value chain, the logistics are taken care of at a highly professional level, thus reducing the price to be paid by the consumer. However, as soon as products leave the retailer, logistics are a mess. The logistical process engaged in by a consumer is often disproportionate in relation to the purchased items. In other words, acquisition costs are often disproportionate in comparison with product price. Also the societal costs of the current logistical system are high. Instead of one single party (like a VGA) arranging the delivery of purchases in a systematic and cost-effective manner for a group of customers, customers arrange their own purchases individually. They take their individual cars to travel to the stores, often spend more time shopping than budgeting, and require elaborate facilities including traffic infrastructure and parking facilities. Scarce resources may be depleted at a higher rate than that at which consumers' purchase-related values increase.

A lot could be saved if distribution were better organized in time and space. The Internet plays an important role in this respect, and this role is likely to become more important in the near future. On the other hand, this might mean that a number of current stores and store concepts are no longer needed. If the customer has the opportunity to delegate functional shopping to the VGA, stores for functional shopping are no longer required. The answer might be to rebuild these stores into fun shopping locations or to combine stores into attractive shopping and entertainment centres. Consider the design of the modern shopping malls in Minneapolis (USA) and Edmonton (Canada), which include attractive experiences in restaurants, playgrounds and amusement parks. The attractiveness of a shopping centre depends on the 'assortment' of shops and the attractiveness of individual shops. As with products and services, the customer needs to be able to derive an added value from going to a (fun) shopping centre.

It is obvious that the Internet will become the medium of choice for the VGA. Through this medium, transactions, information exchanges and distribution between VGA and customer will be arranged.

MARKETING IMPLEMENTATION

Marketing implementation relates to the specific design, interpretation and execution of the elements of the marketing mix (marketing instruments), as determined by the decisions that are focused on the short term. How valid is it to present any implementation suggestions if the general future marketing scenario to which they relate is still a matter of discussion itself? There is a risk of premature recommendations.

However, implementation considerations may also contribute to the assessment of the feasibility of the ideas presented in this book. So we will present our suggestions with due prudence. Incidentally, while they are meant to elaborate the idea of the VGA, they may apply to present-day marketing as well.

CONTENTS OF THE VGA

CRM (Customer Relationship Management) can be seen as a type of relationship management that is the precursor of the VGA. In what respects does the VGA concept differ from the CRM? In order to answer this question, we first have to provide a description of CRM.

CRM databases generally maintain the following personal data:

- Socio-demographic and personal characteristics of customers such as address, age, gender, income, educational level, and family composition.
- Possession of durable goods, type of house, rental/owner-occupied dwelling, car, subscriptions to newspapers and magazines. Purchase behaviour with regard to services.
- Purchasing history, recency and frequency of purchases, monetary value of past purchases, payment method and payment discipline.

Although the ambition of CRM is in the direction of a management support system, in reality it often serves merely as a sales tool. The main reason is that the same management that required a CRM system does not know what to do with it. It is too often assumed that the mere availability of a lot of data will provide the insights required for effective management. Reality has shown that this is an illusion and that data are only relevant if they can be transformed into strategically and tactically relevant information.

So while a VGA cannot exist without a CRM-like data system, the availability of such a system does not imply strategic relevance, let alone a VGA position. The VGA contains the same data as reported above, but is supplemented with the following data, especially in the beginning, when the VGA still has to get acquainted with their customers:

- The information sources and media used frequently by the customer.
- Customer search behaviour on the Internet: through which links and routes does the customer arrive at the desired information?
- Psychological phenomena such as autonomy (arriving at answers and solutions independently or quickly turning on the VGA), risk acceptance or risk aversion (or preference for certainty), values, lifestyle, culture and involvement/interest of customer with respect to social issues such as safety, environment, volunteer work, and so on.

- Variable customer wishes and preferences in regard to various products, services and domains, including customer's need for variation.
- Desires, plans and goals for the long term.
- Evaluations of consumption experiences with specific products and services (and later product packages). These are especially important for fine-tuning future offers to the consumer. Overall satisfaction with VGA performance.

The VGA maintains customer data in order to be able to serve the customer better. Based on this data, the VGA can get to know the customer better and serve him or her better over time. A VGA learns from the interaction with the customer in the following ways:

- Explicit instructions by the users.
- Imitation of the customer, for example how customers search on the Internet: direction, intensity, sequence and time spent on sites and components.
- Observation and imitation of other customers in similar situations.
- Receiving positive and negative reactions (feedback) of users to the information, advice and orders provided by the VGA.
- Observation of consumption experiences and (dis)satisfaction.
- Use of heuristics (abbreviated choice processes) to collect and check information quickly and effectively.
- Development and adjustment of the interface, style, frequency and intensity of the interaction with the user, in such a manner that it helps to develop trust and cooperation.

The CRM system not only stores the relevant data, but makes it possible to analyse interdependencies, for example with the help of multivariate analyses and neural networks. It is this possibility that provides a unique knowledge base to the VGA. It allows for a better understanding of an individual customer over the course of time and it allows for comparisons between individual consumers and consumer groups. For example, an individual consumer X may be advised to purchase a particular service on the basis of the positive experience among a group of consumers who have a similar profile to consumer X.

As was underlined earlier, a VGA develops over time. The VGA needs to learn from customers, and the customer needs to get used to the possibilities and effects of the system. There needs to be a natural fit or match between the customer and the VGA. The VGA needs to grow towards this fit and prove its services in that way. A VGA will mainly be evaluated along the following dimensions:

1. Credibility: based on expertise, relevance (validity) and reliability of information and advice provided to customers.
2. Expert knowledge: the knowledge and expertise of the VGA. Does the VGA have access to timely and well-analysed information? In accordance with the set-up of the VGA, a VGA may hire or buy expertise from outside sources.
3. Relevance: the suitability and applicability of the information and advice provided. Relevance is the match of the advice with the preferences, plans and life goals of the customer.
4. Reliability: based on the honesty and impartiality of the VGA. Does the VGA really work in the interest of its customers, and not in the interest of some other commercial party?
5. Attractiveness of the design and style of the VGA. Form, style and branding (brand policy) play a role in the success of a VGA.
6. Symbolism, cultural and social significance of the VGA. The VGA can, as the representative of a large number of customers, provide input into the social debate about timely issues, such as mobility, environment, tax rates and political issues. The Automobile Association already does this on behalf of its members, albeit without consulting its members directly. Obviously, this social function can only be implemented if and when the VGA has acquired a certain size, expertise and reputation.

Product Strategy

We already stated that the attention of marketing may be expected to shift from the pre-purchase stage and the purchasing stage itself to the – often lengthy – consumption and usage stage. In the latter, customers are supported in the optimal use of products and services, in the maintenance of their products, and in the combination of products and services. It is astonishing that in current marketing so much attention is devoted to the purchasing stage only, while this is a relatively short and unimportant stage from the perspective of the customer. It reflects the infamous preoccupation of sales staff and service providers with the transaction as the moment in which the company's own advantages should be demonstrated, and not with the actual benefits and advantages that the product or service deliver to the user. This preoccupation is even expressed in the way a number of products have been designed. Sometimes, these appear to have been developed to please the ego of the producer rather than to optimize the buyer's consumption experience. Consider, for example, technologically high-grade products that contain so many functions that the actual usage suffers. Support for the consumption is actually discouraged by providing difficult manuals. The mere fact that some manuals are complete books should be a cause of alarm for product designers. Producers should force themselves to determine how customers are dealing with their products and the corresponding manuals, before these products are released on the market. Producers should respond to questions regarding ergonomics and usefulness. Products and services should adapt to customers, not vice versa.

Communication Strategy

The VGA is tailored to the individual customer. It should serve large groups of customers at the same time and yet give all customers the impression of being served individually. This impression may be encouraged by delivering fast and direct feedback, by personalizing the VGA and personalizing the communication – the technique that is also used in direct communication. Nearness may be suggested through the application of the GPS (Global Positioning System). Customers who are near a store from which they need to collect something will receive an SMS message from their VGA giving the relevant information.

Price Strategy

With regard to price, we do not share the notion of relationship marketing that relies on bribing or luring of customers into a long-term relationship. The relationship must be the result of the value experienced and not the result of short-term give-aways or gadgets that only serve as a compensation for lack of real value. Giving discounts to customers for returning to the same store or the same brand indicates that other possibilities for delivering added value have been exhausted. In essence, with a discount, a provider pleads guilty to sub-optimal performance. In the value matrix referred to earlier, discounts, loyalty programmes, bonus miles and so on all reflect a deviation for the value diagonal. Why give away money, if the consumer basically prefers more value over saving money?

Distribution Strategy

It is too early to discuss the operational consequences of the expected developments. The only clear issue now is that shopping itself is an activity that in the near future will come under more pressure due to the development of alternative shopping and distribution concepts. It seems that the more attractive a store, store chain, or shopping centre, the larger the likelihood that the customer will continue to visit. Stores that are focused on daily consumption and household maintenance goods are entering a danger zone. It appears that in the near future, merely modernizing store design will no longer be an effective means for maintaining its attractiveness.

CUSTOMER RESEARCH

We need to consider future developments, possible strategies, the future use of marketing instruments and their concrete implementation. We can attempt to answer a number of questions based on our own knowledge, experience and insights. Yet we know that these do not always indicate the appropriate direction and that we even run the risk of being misguided. Therefore, a supplement is needed with the input of the leading actor: the customer. Customer research is an important tool to arrive at insights into the actual backgrounds of behaviour, assuming of course that this research is carried out according to professional standards.

Customer research undergoes a change in both status and appearance along the value diagonal. In Cell 1 of the value matrix, formal customer research is not relevant; it is only 'wasted money'. The only form of 'customer research' is like the routine question asked by the waiter in a highway restaurant: 'Was it OK?' A negative answer would probably produce a surprised look and a shrug as, in Cell 1, the answer does not really matter. In Cell 6, research is important but is still very much related to product perceptions and brand evaluations. Adaptive conjunct analysis (ACA) can be used to develop evaluation criteria – and therefore preferences – from the choices made by customers. If the number of choices that have actually been made is too small, an option is to present fictitious choices in order to derive customers' choice criteria and priorities.

Research on the position of products and brands within a customer lifestyle is relatively rare. The same is true for research on the associations between products and brands on the one hand and values on the other. Relationship-oriented research is closely related to CRM activities. Brand loyalty is a typical research theme in Cell 6. Research into line extensions and brand extensions also takes place in this cell, but this is more due to tactical than strategic reasons.

In Cell 11, the emphasis on strategic research increases. Attention is paid to the fit between products and services within the same domain. Customer research may indicate whether the trust that the customer has built up with a brand might be stretched too far if the brand is expanded to new products or services. In this cell, lifestyle research also becomes more important.

Finally, in Cell 16, research on lifestyle and values is essential. As indicated before, lifestyle may be determined by determining behaviour (activities), interests and opinions. The measurement of interests and opinions is often less reliable because in questionnaires customers are able to present themselves as different and 'better' than they really are. The behavioural measurement is the most reliable, because the actual behaviour and devotion of time to activities is closer to consumption and may often be determined by observation and registration. The VGA system covers all three types of data, so that the validity of the information may be checked.

Research in this cell relates to the more basic considerations that customers make. How do they balance money, time and effort against each other? What priorities do they assign to various life domains such as living, working, leisure time, care and education? To what extent are they willing to accept risks? It will be clear that these kinds of questions cannot just be presented to customers directly, as fundamental trade-offs are often implicit. The experiences and reactions of individual customers, which are stored in a database, can help to clarify which general objectives these customers are pursuing.

In Cell 16, research also focuses on the question of which elements should be added to the package in order to expand the service provision as effectively and efficiently as possible. Note that the size of the package has no *a priori* limit and can continue to expand, depending upon individual customers' preferences.

There is also another distinction among the types of research that occur along the diagonal. Research in Cell 1, to the extent that it even occurs, is ad hoc and purely problem-oriented. For example, customers have stopped buying a particular product; why is that? In Cell 6, research is often incidental, not just inspired by acute problems but also by market strategic and tactical questions. In Cell 11, research is a more structural operation. The intensive interaction with customers in Cell 16 means that research is going on continuously. Therefore, the word 'research' does not seem to apply any more. Here, research is not a separate management support activity. Continuous information exchange is critical to the marketing concept in this cell.

Finally, there is a third difference between the types of research across the cells of the value diagonal. 'Research' in Cell 1 occurs in the form of direct or telephone contact between supplier and customer. In Cell 6, research takes place in a more formalized manner, using research methods and instruments that have been developed for that particular purpose. Because Cells 11 and 16 are more dependent upon ICT support, it seems obvious that the type of research will adjust to the new technical possibilities. It is therefore interesting to provide a brief overview of the various forms of digital research.

Which forms of online digital customer research already exist or will be developed in the near future? Each of these may help clarify the individual customer's priorities and preferences:

1. Online, personalized questionnaires that are presented via email or the Internet to ad hoc cross-section samples or to customer panels.
2. Online focus groups: a group discussion via the Internet with anonymity of participants and equal opportunities for participation since there is no or less dominance by certain people in the group.
3. Online interviewing: without disturbing non-verbal 'cues' such as body language and facial expressions (although it may be argued that such cues sometimes also contribute to a valid interpretation of the reaction).
4. Online experiments via the Internet, for example advertising reactions research, evaluation research, measuring reaction times for (pop-up) buttons, intersitials, websites and webpages.
5. Online scientific game research such as ultimatum games, prisoner's dilemmas, and bargaining.
6. Online simulation, virtual reality, for example of shops, shopping centres, furnishings, traffic situations and choice of potential hair styles.
7. Observation of customer searching behaviour ('surfing') and purchasing behaviour on the Internet through the analysis of click streams and log files.
8. Analysis of online registration data, such as cash register scanning in shops, data regarding the reach and use of media and household purchasing data.

Note that if carrying out research on points 7 and 8 it is not necessary to collect new customer data. Customer data are already registered and only need to be analysed. It is important to note that, initially, research was initiated by the supplier. Now, it develops into an exchange of information in which both parties may have the initiative in giving information. In the near future, the balance may shift to the initiative of the customer who will provide information even without having been requested to do so.

Online research has several advantages compared to traditional forms of research: it can use international panels, it guarantees anonymity of the participants (expressed in a higher external validity), larger samples may be drawn and the diversity of samples is larger. Online research can easily zero in on the customers of a certain service or the customers associated with a particular VGA.

The VGAs in symbiosis with customers function at a higher level than customers by themselves. Then:

- Both parties may provide new data;
- Both parties may take the initiative to further action;
- Both parties may check the results for validity and relevance; and
- Both parties may make decisions.

The very notion of the VGA leads us to expect that the dominance of the VGA in the relationship will increase over time, although the customer ultimately decides about the nature of the balance.

In this chapter, it has become clear that the border between market effects and social effects is often difficult to draw. In the following chapter we will discuss the social and cultural effects that we anticipate for VGA marketing.

7. Social and Cultural Effects

SUMMARY

In the relation between supply and demand, an important role is played by the government, consumer organizations, and non-profit organizations as well. The government even plays a double role: the delivery of public services and the regulation and protection of general interests, health and safety of consumers. In the harmonious, non-antagonistic cooperation between VGA and consumer, there is no longer any room for the traditional role of consumer protectors such as the government and consumer associations. In addition, non-profit organizations are starting to adopt marketing principles and practices and are, therefore, increasingly starting to behave like commercial organizations.

In this chapter, the advantages and disadvantages of the VGA will be discussed. The VGA has an impact on the culture, politics and society. New communities may be created through the VGA. Ultimately, the VGA may function as a personal life manager that optimizes the allocation of the resources money, time and effort for a person or a family. For many people, the most scarce of these three resources is the available time.

INTRODUCTION

The developments as outlined in the previous chapters are not restricted to the interaction between consumer and supplier or between the demand and supply side of the market. There are also social and cultural effects. It may be expected that the functioning of the market will have an influence on social structures and processes and on the way in which people arrange their lives individually and together with others. In this chapter, we will therefore determine what the social and cultural consequences may be of the way in which the interaction between the supply and demand sides is developing. In this regard we first discuss the role of various social parties that play their own, specific role, such as the government, consumer organizations and non-profit organizations.

In Chapter 4 (Figures 4.3 and 4.4) we introduced the value matrix and the value diagonal. Cell 16 was proposed as the point at which the interests of suppliers and consumers optimally converge. We also substantiated why the trend in the direction of Cell 16 is an obvious and likely development. In the present chapter, we once again address this cell to obtain an impression of social effects that may be associated. Obviously, we are not able to refer to empirical evidence, as the future does not present hard data. Instead, we will once again resort to the tools of scenario analysis and deductive reasoning.

When comparing the cells of the matrix diagonal, it may be noted that the situations of Cells 1 and 16 are complete opposites. In Cell 1, there is a supplier, a customer, a product or service, and a price. The consumer makes a consideration from a limited number of alternatives based on a limited number of apparent characteristics. At the point of purchase, the customer receives the selected product or service and the supplier receives the agreed price. Marketing activities may mask the simplicity of the purchase, but in fact the situation involves a simple, straightforward transaction that is limited in time, scope and impact.

The situation is quite different for Cell 16. Although there is a single direct supplier, it is unclear how the various components of the supply have been matched to each other, and what the relationship to the price is. After all, it no longer involves simple transactions but a complex, continuous, apparently fluid stream of products and services that is not restricted in time, of which the scope (the reach of the number of products and services in the package) is, in principle, infinite and of which the impact on the individual consumer is potentially very large. The customer effect in Cell 1 is limited to satisfaction with certain product characteristics, and the customer effect in Cell 16 is related to a more general level of well-being.

In addition to suppliers of products and services, several other parties (will) claim responsibility for consumer satisfaction or, more generally, well-being. These parties include, apart from the VGA, the government, consumer organizations and non-profit organizations. These parties have complementary functions in the current market with regard to the protection of the safety and health of consumers and the promotion of consumer satisfaction and well-being. We will address these parties consecutively, along with the potential implications of the developments for the market and marketing.

GOVERNMENT

The question regarding the future market position of the government is difficult to answer because the government performs multiple roles. The government itself is supplier of (collective) goods, provisions and services for the promotion of collective well-being. It also has a stimulating or re-straining and controlling task in relation to the functioning of the market. The government stimulates or restricts the free market mechanism in the interest of citizens. It may stimulate by providing subsidies, or it may restrict by the selective use of, for example, taxes, duties, and zoning or geo-graphical planning. In addition, the government may check market function-ing, counteract improper competition, protect against fraudulent practices, discourage the use of harmful products, and limit undesirable social effects of certain forms of consumption, such as smoking. This complex, almost paradoxical combination of tasks creates a tension that has been reduced over the past decades. Traditional governmental services and provisions such as public transport, education, health care, mail and maintenance of public spaces have been increasingly transferred to the market sector where these services have the opportunity to develop a more favourable price–quality relationship.

Obviously the government still has the responsibility for tracking and fighting excesses that may lead to the disproportionate advantage or disad-vantage of certain individuals or groups in society. This responsibility fits with the pattern of functions that only a democratically elected party such as the government can settle. In doing so, the government is in effect focusing on its *core business* and is withdrawing from a market environment that in principle is quite capable of functioning autonomously.

Yet this does not answer the question of what the core business of the government is, since it is in effect an ideological question that is rooted in a view of human nature. In various Western societies a social model was pursued in the 1960s and 1970s that took care of its citizens 'from the cradle to the grave'. The concept was that the government should protect its citi-zens against economic and financial risks in a labour and market environ-ment that was focused on exploitation. The government considered itself to be responsible for security and development opportunities. Yet this system eventually turned out to suffer from an underestimation of human ambitions and self-sufficiency and an overestimation of the solidarity of citizens, which led to the development of inefficiency and disproportionate use/abuse of services and benefits. The lack of an internal correction mechanism and an external *benchmark* prevented the quality of the system from being ad-dressed. Privatization of a number of governmental responsibilities brought the relevant services and service provision into a commercial context, which resulted in the optimizing of the process due to the discipline of competition and internal comparisons. Governments withdrew and continue to withdraw, although slowly and often only partially, from areas that can be left to the private sector. Over time, it turns out that an increasing number of traditional government tasks are candidates for privatization. Only a few tasks appear to fall to the government exclusively and by principle, such as tasks associated with the use of weapons (army and police), maintaining law and order (justice), international relations, and income distribution (taxation and social security). Privatization and deregulation therefore mean that the political choice of the citizen is increasingly being replaced by the purchasing decision – whether delegated or not – of the customer.

The free market principle means that a competitive environment creates the best conditions to enable a choice from options that are attuned as much as possible to individuals' needs. In addition, the free market provides as many variations of products and services as are operationally and economically possible, because individual desires show a large degree of diversity.

This has the consequence that consumers are now capable of deciding about products, services and provisions that in the past were only available indirectly and through a delayed process of political choice. Freedom in relation to the retirement age, for example, implies personal choice. Until recently, this freedom did not exist or had to be 'extorted' via parliament. Through privatization and deregulation, government decisions with respect to the collective sphere are now increasingly being transformed into consumer decisions on their individual interests.

Although citizens in democratic societies can vote for and choose a parliament that serves the general consumer interests to a greater extent, there are clear differences between the political and the market system, and the roles of citizens and customers/consumers:

- Political choices are at most indirect because politicians indicate intentions of which the practical implementation is still uncertain. A government must be formed based on the number of votes, and it is unclear to what extent the politicians' original intentions will survive the process of coalition and policy formation. A citizen who uses environmental protection as an important argument for his or her political voting behaviour, is not guaranteed that the environment policy will have a dominant place in the coalition agreement, even when the person he or she voted for is included in the government. After all, a coalition agreement is the result of a compromise with other parties and priorities. On the other hand, a consumer can directly include in his purchasing decision the degree to which a product burdens the environment.

- In the same manner, consumer choices involve individual concrete effects in the short term while political voting behaviour involves a collective effect in the long term, which makes the latter effect more uncertain.
- A third difference relates to the degree in which the supply is tailored towards the individual. In the political domain there is little or no room for differentiation and segmentation of the market. A bridge across a river is either built or not, and cannot be built for just a segment of the population. This is in contrast to the market in which differentiation and segmentation are the justification for the existence of many suppliers. A political choice therefore is much less able to serve the interest of individual consumers than the consumer choice.

Although privatization and deregulation mean that the government has less control over the functioning of the market, this same market ensures through its own mechanisms minimization of disadvantages and maximization of advantages. Therefore, anyone who considers the interest of citizens and consumers to be very important should prefer a restriction of the role of the government in the market. The primary market-specific task of the government is to guarantee the functioning of the free market mechanism.

The value matrix anticipates that the free-market mechanism functions optimally in Cell 16 (Figure 4.4). It is in the interest of citizens/consumers that the services and provisions that were originally offered by the government as a market party are integrated into the system through the free market. In Cell 16 there is less need for a government that protects consumers against deceptive marketing practices and undesired products and services, because suppliers will be focused in an honest manner on generating long-term advantages for customers and on preventing unfavourable effects. For example, it is not in the interest of the VGA, nor in the interest of long-term oriented suppliers to present products to consumers that have a disproportionate health risk. Therefore, the role of the government as arbiter and controller may be reduced to a minimum in Cell 16. Other parties are taking over the protection and promotion of the general well-being, whereby well-being includes a broader definition than consumer satisfaction. Consumer satisfaction is limited to a specific product or a specific service, is related to the short term and only refers to the person of the consumer that evaluates the product or the service. Well-being includes the package of goods and services in their interdependent connection as it leads to positive effects over the short term and the long term, not just at an individual level, but also at the collective and societal level.

CONSUMER ORGANIZATIONS

While the government in the current market is focused on the protection of general consumer interests, consumer organizations play an important supplementary role in the protection and promotion of consumer satisfaction in separate market segments such as food products, household appliances, electronic appliances, cosmetics, mobility and telephone. Consumer organizations focus on the goal of protecting the consumer from inferior products, unwise decisions and misleading/deceptive marketing practices. Yet with the changing character of marketing, it may be expected that the role and function of consumer organizations will also change.

Consumers have less of a need to be 'protected' when the interest of the consumer has also become the interest of the supplier. The intermediary function of a consumer organization will no longer be needed when the supply and the demand side are no longer antagonistic, but belong to 'the same camp'. In Cell 16, an individual supplier will be focused on providing a product or a service that represents an added value over the long term in the consumption package. The checking will be done by the supplier himself, by the VGA and by the other suppliers, in the recognition that the quality of the total supply depends on the weakest part of the total. Therefore, suppliers will pay more attention than they did in the past to the quality of the products and services that are being offered as a complement to their own products or services. Suppliers will become more mutually dependent and will pay increasingly attention to the quality of complementary products and services. This quality is partly determined by the integration of their contributions.

Because individual products and services no longer determine the total quality, the selection and quality control are increasingly being taken over by other parties. Quality will be determined over the long run and the short run. This means that consumer organizations will lose their traditional checking function. Product comparisons are no longer relevant because products no longer need to be evaluated in isolation. A product may score relatively low on certain characteristics, but precisely those characteristics might mean that the product is an excellent match for a set of other products and services or for a package that the consumer already owns. Misleading marketing activities have no place in a market in which parties are oriented to long-term relationships. Consumers will increasingly be asked to provide direct feedback regarding their experience with the supply, which provides the supplier with an opportunity for timely corrections. In addition, consumers will inform their suppliers or VGA about (supplementary) needs and desires. Due to the more direct and intensive interaction between demand

and supply, the importance of the informative function of consumer organizations is strongly reduced. In making purchasing decisions, consumers will have less of a need to be assisted by consumer organizations since the VGA can accomplish this faster, pre-emptively, better and in a more individualized manner. Therefore, a strategic reorientation is needed for consumer organizations.

NOT-FOR-PROFIT ORGANIZATIONS

Not-for-profit organizations typically serve a general social purpose or devote themselves to the promotion of the interest of certain groups of consumers. Consider schools, universities, hospitals, theatres and museums. The addition 'not-for-profit' is a relative term in various respects. In the first place, these organizations also require financial reserves and investment resources. Due to the trend towards privatization and deregulation, non-profit organizations are faced with a reduction of subsidies provided by the state. Secondly, not-for-profit organizations are increasingly realizing that they are also dealing with consumers or customers (instead of patients, visitors, students, pupils) who can make choices, which means that these suppliers are in a competitive environment. In the third place, in recent years the quality of the management of these organizations has increased significantly, which means that also in this respect the distinction with commercial organizations is getting smaller.

These trends are increasingly forcing not-for-profit organizations to maintain a type of operational management that is similar to a commercial organization. In contrast to the fairly recent past, non-profit organizations are also now using strategic planning and they are developing their own marketing activities.

A special type of not-for-profit organization is the charity institution. It is focused on a 'good cause' such as cancer research or environmental protection. The issues mentioned above with respect to non-profit organizations in general, also apply to these institutions. They in fact also find themselves in a competitive environment and the marketing activities that they use to promote their goal and to collect money are hardly distinguishable from commercial companies in nature, intensity and professionalism. The Heart Association competes with the Kidney Association, the Red Cross, Amnesty International, Unicef, Greenpeace and Oxfam for the donations of citizens. VGAs may 'adopt' a charity if the members of the VGA agree on its social relevance. The VGA may then donate a proportion of its turnover to that specific charity.

We predict here that products and services of not-for-profit organizations, including charities, will follow a similar development line as predicted for commercial products and services. In Cell 16, various products, services and provisions will be combined regardless of the type of organization from which they originated. This means that the size of the package of goods and services that is assembled on behalf of individual consumers will increase significantly. This package consists of all those issues for which people, in their role as consumer, may (or have to) make decisions or may (or have to) make choices. The strict separation that could be made in the past between the various traditional parties in the market disappears the closer we get to Cell 16. Increasingly, traditional government supply, and products and services of non-profit organizations, are being placed in a commercial setting, and commercial companies are focusing more on the public interest and take longer-term societal consequences into account. Companies offer products that consumers can use to support social purposes, thus displaying their social responsibility. For example, consumers now have the opportunity to switch to energy that has been produced in a sustainable way ('green electricity'). Ethics is on its way to become a topical theme in the commercial sector. Increasingly, commercial organizations refer to general social values in their communication and presentation.

So, non-profit organizations are presenting themselves in a commercial fashion, and commercial organizations are supporting 'good' causes via sponsoring, and are showing their societal involvement. The distinction between various types of market parties is disappearing or becoming less relevant. After all, the consumer is primarily interested in the total supply, not in the nature of individual suppliers.

In summary, traditional market-specific antagonisms will fade away or disappear. The sharp distinction between the supply and demand side will soften, the distinction between profit and non-profit will become irrelevant, the disproportionate emphasis on short-term effects will give way to a clearer balance between the short term and the long term, and the differences between individual, social and societal effects will be attenuated.

For suppliers, the exclusive focus on the end product will be replaced by the full chain concept, with attention being paid to the specific contribution of the individual links to the total value chain. The question is to what extent each link contributes positively to the end result, and to what extent each link produces negative effects that only become visible at the last link or at the end of the value chain. Although certain products are harmless in the short term, they may produce negative consequences in the long run. Due to a changed view of responsibility, suppliers do not simply 'pass the buck' for the harmful effect on to the next link in the chain. The harmful effect is already made visible at the relevant link. For example, the production of tobacco products might occur in a very environmentally friendly manner in the pertinent link, and therefore it would not cause any disproportionate negative effects in the short run. Yet the long-term effects for consumers at the end of the chain mean that the responsibility for the health problems and health costs is shifted to the health care, the insurance companies and thus to the collective of premium-paying citizens.

The chain concept makes it clear that the costs of the treatment of tobacco products should, in fact, be allocated to the link that is responsible for these products. This means that the long-term costs are included in the price of the product at purchase. The polluter should pay. In a market system where products are interpreted as independent units, it is possible to ignore unfavourable long-term and social effects and focus, instead, on individual advantages in the short term only. In a market system that is focused on optimizing interconnected complementation of products and services of a widely varying nature, it will be inevitable to address the significance and therefore also the full costs of the market supply. In this regard it will be clear which party carries the responsibility for a component of the chain. Parties will hold themselves and each other to this responsibility and will no longer be able to hide behind a non-transparent market. This principle also makes explicit that the customer/consumer himself or herself has a responsibility for short- and long-term personal and societal effects. At present, ignorance still can be used as an excuse for particular decisions and behaviours. In the near future, this will be more difficult.

This brings us to the significance of marketing developments for what is considered to be important socially and what is crucial for the manner in which people behave as citizen in their environment.

In the second part of this chapter we will make an inventory of the social–cultural implications. We will not restrict ourselves to market-specific effects and consumer behaviour.

CULTURAL ASPECTS

It may be clear that it is not the intent here to provide an introduction to the phenomenon of culture, or to present a broad description of market cultures, but to make an estimate of the social–cultural changes that may be the result of the predicted marketing developments. 'Culture' is a difficult concept that is often used as an umbrella term for issues that we cannot name concretely. It may be intepreted as the equivalent of 'norms and values' and 'general style of living' (or 'general style of acting' in non-consumer contexts). Because we expect that people's norms, values and general style of living will change as a result of the predicted developments, we cannot avoid the topic. See also Chapter 5, which focuses more specifically on the behaviour and the lifestyle of consumers.

We take culture here as the totality of knowledge, rules, norms, values, material objects and conduct or behaviour that is characteristic of a certain group. Culture may be defined at various levels. For example, the concept of culture may apply to a relatively small group of people (a subculture), to the culture of a society (the French culture) or even to the Western culture. Over the course of history, people that belong to the same group develop more or less stereotypical behaviours, and they arrange their environment in a way that characterizes them, which makes them different from people of other groups or societies. Within the individual groups/societies, people become so habituated to the (results of) their behaviour and that of others, that they often only notice their own culture when it is directly confronted with another culture. In a certain sense there is also a market culture: in the Western world this consists of a collection of silent agreements, conduct that is taken for granted, communication, (consumptive) habits and patterns and typical objects and symbols. Culture also refers to general social values, rules, knowledge and institutions.

To a large extent culture depends upon people's behaviour. Three charac-teristics of the VGA have the potential to influence behaviour significantly:

1. *The extent of engagement of the VGA*
   A person may decide for himself or herself to what extent tasks and re-sponsibilities are transferred to the VGA. This may, in principle, vary from not at all (the person keeps the initiative to himself or herself) to completely (the initiative is delegated to the VGA).

2. *The nature of the role of the VGA*
   There are various possibilities in this regard. For example, the VGA might play the role of informer, or be the party that clarifies the alter-natives between which choices need to be made. In a third possible role, the VGA may receive the command to create a shortlist of these options or, as an advisor, to indicate the preferable alternative or de-fault. Finally, the VGA may make the decision by itself and arrange the transaction.

3. *The number and nature of the decision domains*
   Finally, the function of the VGA may vary, depending on the number of areas or domains that are agreed upon by the customer. For exam-ple, it is possible to engage the VGA only for issues relating to living, or only for use of leisure time. In a more expanded version, living, working, leisure time, health, sports and financial planning may be in-tegrated.

Based on these aspects, the extremes on the VGA continuum are known: total autonomy of the customer versus total autonomy (as permitted by the customer) of the VGA. Even though these extremes will not take place in reality, for reasons of clarity they should be specified so that the boundaries are known.

People will be able to choose for themselves to what degree they want to engage in the interaction with the VGA. Therefore there will be no automatic engagement of the VGA, or of an obligation to use it. The choice regarding whether or not to engage the VGA, or to use it more or less – or perhaps even several VGAs – depends on the outcome of the comparison of advantages and disadvantages. The outcome determines the extent to which the VGA affects the general style of living. Here we present a brief inventory of both advantages and disadvantages, and will provide some comments on the latter.

ADVANTAGES OF THE VGA

The following advantages of using a VGA may be observed.

Time Savings

The VGA is able to save a great deal of time that otherwise would need to be spent on collecting information, making decisions, checking, executing administrative tasks and shopping behaviour. For example, the VGA is able to complete tax returns to a great extent. An important amount of time is spent answering the question how time should be used. Just the reading of a magazine, for example, may be subdivided into time that is devoted to the search and selection of what should be read and the time actually reading. If the selection time can be reduced, the person could devote more time to those things that are truly interesting to him or her. This example may be expanded to a range of other activities.

Provide an Overview

People are not able to have an overall view of their entire life. This applies both to life taken over time, but also to a combination of activities at any given time. To the extent that this is a source of concern ('What am I overlooking?'; 'Am I forgetting something important?'), the VGA is capable of reducing this concern.

Signalling Function

The VGA may have an agenda-setting function and notify the person of an impending event or a development that requires a (re)action. In the current market it is also possible to purchase incidental notification services, such as a wake-up service, a notice that a passport or driving licence is about to expire, the alert that an insurance term is ending, or a bank that warns that a decision is required with respect to an investment fund. Yet it is necessary to devote a lot of energy to planning and keeping up with those issues that require an investment of energy or attention. The VGA can function as a continuous, active and initiating agenda. Together with the second function, the VGA is able to prevent unpleasant surprises. *Big Brother is watching me*, but not in the sense of observing or spying, but in the sense of taking care of. Big Brother is *watching over me*.

Increase in Comfort

People have a preference for or dislike of the execution of certain tasks, quite aside from the time that they are required to devote to these tasks. For example, some people enjoy the process of maintaining an administrative system completely and correctly. On the other hand, there are also people who loathe doing administrative duties. Some people interpret being en-gaged with investments as a game that can be played during leisure time, while others see investments as a burden that they prefer to keep at a great distance. The VGA may be used for the execution of less desirable or unin-teresting tasks. Activities that a person dislikes may be transferred to the VGA. Obviously this applies more to tasks that are associated with handling data or information and less for physical activities, although the VGA may also play an indirect role in that respect. Someone who dislikes gardening can delegate this to the VGA, which subsequently searches a party that could perform this service, obviously taking into account information that is already known about the garden and its owner (size of the garden, ease of maintenance, available budget, intensity and type of use of the garden). In principle, the VGA could even give instructions to match the garden more with the personal wishes of the owner. This again depends on the priorities of this owner, but a well-informed VGA also has access to the relevant information in this regard.

The VGA has knowledge about the wishes of many different consumers at different locations. This creates the basis for a distribution system that can arrange, in a logistically optimal fashion, for the purchase to be deliv-ered to a certain location within the desired timeframe. In this context it is interesting to compare two different imaginary situations: in situation 1, 100 consumers all wish to purchase, within a timeframe of two weeks, the same product which they can find at ten different shops within a reasonable distance. In this situation, these consumers all arrange the purchase and the transport of the relevant product by themselves. On average these 100 consumers spend 5 euros on transportation and parking costs, and one hour on travel and shopping time. This is a total of 500 euros and 100 hours. In situation 2, the VGA determines the optimal route that a truck should drive to deliver the relevant product (together with other products) to the right locations. The average transportation costs per product are then dramatically decreased and the time savings for the consumers are significant. The money and time that has been saved can be devoted to other, more preferable activities. In this manner, the VGA is able to make a considerable contribution to the comfort of the consumer.

Taking over Responsibilities

As the previous example has already clarified, the VGA may take over responsibilities and even do this in such a way that the resulting decisions will fit more consistently into the overall picture of preferences of the person than that person would have been able to do himself/herself. Because the information-absorbing function of the VGA is in principle unlimited (technological progress makes storage of extremely large databases possible and affordable), it is possible for the VGA to use information regarding nutritional habits in order to make suggestions regarding adjustments in those patterns or to make medicines available. The 'food-VGA' may in this regard contact the 'medical VGA' (if permitted by the concerning person, of course).

Representation of Interest

To the extent that the VGA plays a more important role in a certain domain, it will be able to represent the interest of the relevant person, whether as individual or as a member of the collective. For example, a VGA negotiate the price, may argue the need for products and services, call for innovations, or may make individual or collective interests visible for parties who make (political) decisions. When the VGA represents a large number of persons from the target audience of a market party, it may represent the persons and lobby to obtain a specific result for them.

Social Effects

A VGA will develop for itself a set of products and services that demonstrate an interconnected complementation. This means that the target audiences of these products and services in fact will not be too different from each other. This creates the possibility of group formation around a VGA, also because of the own identity and positioning that the VGA will start to claim in the market. In this regard, the VGA acquires the characteristics of a brand. Because the VGA has the natural tendency to expand itself, the importance of the brand and the corresponding symbols (brand name, logo, house style) become progressively more important. If the VGA is able to clarify which position it is claiming on the market and is able to follow through on that claim, the conditions have been met for the VGA to obtain the status of a brand. The stronger the brand, the more people in the relevant target audience will be inclined to identify with the brand, and the more the target audiences will converge into one single group. Due to the large significance that a VGA may gain, people in the target audience will experience a strong connection with the brand. Internal affinity is likely to be stimulated among the connected people. The VGA will obtain the status of a club or association in which the participants feel like members. Therefore, it may be better to speak of 'members' of a VGA rather than 'consumers', 'customers' or 'citizens'.

Representation and Negotiation

The VGA may exert political pressure, to the point where the consumer/citizen as member of the VGA community no longer perceives a distinction between the VGA and a political party. Because citizens often only have a faint idea about the correspondence between personal priorities and programmes of political parties, it is not unthinkable that some citizens might be willing to either delegate their vote to their VGA (or even vote for it!).

In other words, the VGA is capable of assuming the care from cradle to grave, but in another fashion than was expected several decades ago within the political system. The functions or advantages of the VGA are likely to appeal to many people. But this does not change the fact that there are also disadvantages that may have to be dealt with. We discuss them here and add to each disadvantage a brief comment.

OBJECTIONS AGAINST VGAs

A number of objections against and disadvantages of the VGA may be mentioned.

Giving up (Part of) the Own Autonomy

By using a VGA to take over one's own initiatives, decisions and actions, the person gives up part of his autonomy to the VGA (*decentring*). He or she no longer knows precisely what will happen and why, losing their grip on the process that is going on. People exist by the grace of their autonomy, and by taking away their autonomy, their existence will be violated.

This argument might be valid, if the number and the nature of the activities that people undertake in their life, were fixed. Yet human activities demonstrate an unlimited variety and flexibility. This means that any hiatus that develops in the behavioural repertoire when some activity is ceased, is immediately replaced with another, more attractive activity. So the reduction in autonomy is in itself not a problem; but it would be a problem if no other, more attractive activity could take its place. Practically translated this means: why would someone want to continue completing their own tax returns for the protection of their autonomy, when this activity competes with activities that are more attractive to that person, such as playing tennis, reading or walking? Or why would someone want to protect their autonomy if this is expressed in tasks that the person prefers to avoid? Our grandparents did not have less autonomy when they were using servants to do their household work.

Autonomy may be equated with freedom. Some people feel that their freedom would be restricted if their purchase decisions were delegated to the VGA. If the freedom within the domain of purchasing is the critical freedom for a person, there is no rule indicating that it should be given up. On the other hand, if the mere act of acquiring goods and services has become the prime way to express our freedom, then what has happened to us?

Increasing Predictability

By using information from the personal past and feedback regarding recent experiences, the supply for a consumer may move towards an average or limited set of products and services that eventually will not change any more. Knowing beforehand that everything will be arranged according to the own preferences, reduces the tension. This makes the experience shallower, as there will be neither disappointments nor positive surprises. If a consumer has once given a specific author or composer a very positive judgement, the VGA will concentrate on the books and music of this particular author/composer. The same applies to clothing styles, vacation destinations and modes of transport. New experiences, experiments and surprises seem to be excluded in this way, while unexpected new experiences often provide an important source of satisfaction and enjoyment.

On the other hand, it can be argued that consumers themselves choose the extent of variation or one-sidedness. They are not required to engage the VGA, they can engage the VGA selectively, and the VGA can be asked to operate temporarily. The consumer determines on which domains the VGA will be active for him or her. Within these domains the consumer may indicate to what extent there should be room for innovation, variation and deviations from the beaten track. The consumer can indicate when boredom sets in. The ratio between known and unknown, or between predicted and unpredicted, may be determined beforehand. The very feedback that is so important in the consumer–VGA relationship will also prevent tedium and monotony from developing. After all, if a consumer shows a gradual reduction of satisfaction, the VGA will have to take the initiative to stop and reverse this development. In this sense, a VGA may be viewed as a self-correcting phenomenon.

Dependence

By connecting to a VGA, the consumer develops a certain dependence and feeling of constraint which increases with a growing engagement of the VGA. Switching costs could become very high since building up a new relationship with another VGA would take a lot of time and effort. In that case, a person becomes the VGA's hostage.

It is to be expected that the development of a relationship with a VGA is a kind of one-way street. The way back will be very difficult. It is easy to keep expanding the collaboration with the VGA in a step-by-step fashion. The relationship with the VGA is like a swamp: the more vehemently one tries to get out, the more difficult it becomes to escape.

Although the dependence does include a restriction of the room to move – a person cannot briefly join another VGA – dependence can be seen as the price paid for enjoying the advantages. The burden is on the VGA to clearly prove that the dependence or continuity has an added value as compared to a temporary relationship. Compare a marriage: dependence does occur, but the advantages of the mutual dependence are balanced against the disadvantages of more or less enforced continuity plus the switching costs. Additionally, the instrument of feedback will prove to be powerful enough to find the right balance between freedom and dependency.

Restriction of Privacy

A familiar discussion at present concerns the question regarding to what extent the privacy of a person should be protected. The VGA is based on usage of person-specific data. The more a person is prepared to communicate about himself or herself, the higher the quality of the supply will be due to a more optimal attuning of the personal characteristics, history, ambitions, needs and wishes that were communicated to the VGA.

In this context it is important to make a distinction between person-specific data and data that are associated with personal sensitivity. If legal agreements can be made about the manner in which the individual data is used, the consumer him/herself can determine which information he or she wants to provide for which objectives. It can be formally agreed (contract) that the data given to the VGA are used to make purchase- and consumption-related decisions only, and are not to be given or sold to other parties. Privacy concerns are usually related to data misused by 'third parties'.

A matter that is not solved nor dealt with here, is the question of data ownership. This is a legal issue that may have important consequences for VGA development. It is important to note that the VGA not only serves to integrate the individual customer's data. It also serves to select and organize providers in relation to the individual's data. This function of the VGA cannot be removed because it is intricately associated with one particular VGA only. So there is no such thing as a consumer simply picking up his or her database and switching to another VGA.

Uncontrollability

The complexity of the connections has reached such a high level that it is almost impossible for the consumer/customer/citizen to determine whether the information selected by the VGA, the advice provided or the decisions made are truly better than other decisions. Quality becomes an obscure detail, also because it has to be determined for each individual person. Therefore it is impossible to determine whether the VGA has indeed charted the best course or arranged the alternative that is the most suitable for his/her situation.

Although this is an important argument, the same situation, in fact, exists in the present market. Consumers are often no longer able to judge the quality of the products and services that are being offered. This applies not only to the purchase, but also during and after the usage. Who can evaluate the quality of a DVD recorder beforehand? Who is able to determine whether an accountant has done a good job? It is usually an illusion to think that consumers are able to use product information to choose in a well-considered manner the alternative that is optimal for them. This applies not just to complex products and services, but also to daily items such as groceries. Which consumers know how well their purchased food package is matched with the own lifestyle and what the consequences are of unwise choices? Of course, this argument may not be used as a licence for the VGA. It should be able to provide substantiated advice and to make decisions, even if the consumer is not able to understand or appreciate the arguments.

The objection clarifies that a VGA has to pay attention to building trust in the way in which decisions are developed. An important consideration that should be incorporated into this process is that the consumer is not at the mercy of the whims of a VGA for a number of years. The feedback that it provides should contain sufficient guarantee that the VGA does not systematically miss the boat. It is likely that an external, independent checking institution may be used for recommendations relating to the long term (a new role for consumer organizations?).

In Summary

Both advantages and disadvantages exist to the expected developments. Although the disadvantages require substantial attention, they may to a large part be neutralized. The number and importance of the advantages appear greater than the disadvantages. Additionally, the technological developments that are required for the advantages to materialize can hardly be stopped or slowed through political or social discussions. Over time, culture and society tend to adapt to technological progress, not vice versa.

Therefore, we expect that the development and linkage of extensive databases that pursue individualized service provision can, at most, be delayed and made difficult, but they cannot be stopped. This is not an expression of a preference by the authors, but of the general experience that, on the political–social level, laws and rules in the end typically adjust to what appears to be technologically and socially feasible, as long as the advantages for some do not bring disproportionate disadvantages for others.

VGAs AND THE ROLE OF TECHNOLOGY

With respect to the market developments, we allowed ourselves to make statements that relate to the next term of approximately five years. The social and cultural developments predicted here require a longer period. We employ a term of approximately a decade to indicate that we are not referring to the distant future. Some changes may perhaps appear a little far-fetched, but we deduce these from the issues we have proposed so far. In estimating the validity of predictions, it should be noted that a decade ago it appeared inconceivable that barely ten years later mobile telephony would have such a high penetration. Around 1990, very few people considered it possible that an individual holiday maker in the year 2000 would be able to call his family from a foreign mountain top to provide an update on the view and the weather. Of course this does not say anything about the validity of our predictions (which can only be judged ten years from now), but recent history teaches us that in estimating the effects of technological developments, we should not be too modest.

Technology will facilitate and stimulation information exchange between the person and his/her VGA. Part of the information provided to the VGA will be the result of the deliberate intention to do so by the concerning person. Another part will find its way to the VGA automatically, for example through bar codes, satellite, person-specific chips, through the use of person-specific media such as the telephone, and through equipment that indicates that it needs repair, is worn out, or requires an update.

Because of new technologies, it will become easier to monitor individual people and to provide on-the-spot advice or instructions. For example, people will receive personal information about issues related to their well-being. With the help of the grocery list or the groceries ordered it can be determined whether the cholesterol norm is being exceeded, whether a vitamin supplement is required, whether the environment is being burdened disproportionately, and whether the number of calories matches the individual activity pattern.

A similar example may be presented for the prescription and intake of medicines. In the near future it will be possible to execute simple medical tests at home or to have one's physical condition checked by subcutaneous sensors, of which the results may be passed on to the VGA automatically, which in turn determines if measures are needed, and if so, which ones. Because the pharmacy database will be integrated into the VGA by then, the VGA can check for undesired interactions with medicines that the person already takes. It can provide medicines directly and without having been requested to do so. Or it can make an appointment with medical support. From one point of view, this seems patronizing and rejectable, but there is a lot to say for it from the perspective of prevention. Again: it will not be an obligation, but whoever rejects the service is consciously choosing health risks that otherwise might be avoided. The result is also that the intermediary function of the pharmacist will become more restricted.

In a broader context, it is expected that parties that derived their function from the exclusive access to certain information, will need to transfer that function to the VGA when the information obtains an added value in

191

combination with other information. This means that the added value of traditional intermediary functions largely disappears. There will only be a future for intermediary functions if another, exclusive added value can be defined for it.

CONSUMER CLUBS

It is possible, in our view, for different VGAs to develop more or less simultaneously, but independently from one another. VGAs are likely to specialize in various combinations of products and services that will differ in composition, quality and price. Due to their dominance and visual presence, VGAs may attract people that together form social groups or social layers. Consumers join other consumers with similar interests, opinions, activities, values and lifestyle as expressed by their VGA. The VGA becomes a lifestyle consultant for its members. VGA clubs may also serve as a social network and may become quite visible, because the proud participants want to demonstrate their membership. People no longer have a great variety of different products/brands for different situations to show their status. Rather, they may identify themselves in a simple, consistent way, for example by a VGA name, VGA logo, or VGA credit card.

However, an objection may be raised here as well. With too many products from one single brand, consumers may actually develop a feeling of constraint and feel like a prisoner of the brand. Naomi Klein (1999) represents the anti-corporate movement in the United States, a protest movement against the dominating influence of large companies on consumers. The French brand for skis, Rossignol, consciously uses a second brand in the ski market to avoid market dominance. Do we all want to listen to Virgin CDs in a Virgin plane? And do we all want to live in the Disney city Celebration (Florida) so we can watch Disney movies and read Disney books there? There is a critical difference between a 'Klein brand' and a VGA. A conventional lock-in originates from one-sided supplier interests, and a lock-in by the VGA results from deliberate customer choice. The VGA may serve as a meta-brand for the consumer by taking over the function of individual brands, just as a supermarket may take over the function of national brands. The VGA represents many suppliers for whom it is no longer relevant to present themselves individually to their target audiences. The VGA determines what is needed for whom, and therefore, the only thing that counts is the relationship between the producer and the VGA. The VGA develops into a meta-brand with all the corresponding characteristics, symbols, expressions, rituals and events.

VGAs may develop around luxury and standard products and services. Their positioning may range from exclusivity, status and prestige to 'value for money'. Compare an exclusive golf club with a discount store. Compare Club Med with a simple holiday park. VGAs may even become digital political parties and position themselves on a left–right dimension, or on an ideological versus pragmatic dimension. In some VGAs, social and environmental considerations may play a role, such as relieving problems in Third World countries. Other VGAs are primarily focused on the individual advantages for its members, regardless of the social consequences. This may result in a new form of social classification, market segmentation or stratification.

People/members want to identify with their VGA. In doing so, they communicate who they are (want to be). This becomes easier because the VGA relates to many different products and services. People who want to differentiate themselves now, have to do so with a large collection of different brands that collectively indicate a certain status. Without these brands the difference disappears. Meta-brands offer the possibility of identifying oneself in all circumstances and at all moments. In addition, meta-brands are a far stronger instrument for personal identification than a variety of individual brands combined.

At present, consumers still show a broad assortment of brands: Nike, Boss, Porsche, Sony, Philips, Parker, Rado, and so on. These will be subordinated or even hidden behind the name and symbolism that the VGA will adopt. The VGA is strongly oriented towards the continuation and expansion of the relationship with individual members and towards the creation of a membership database that is as large as possible. After all, the more members, the larger the negotiation power towards suppliers. The fact that the members have very diverse consumptive preferences is no barrier at all to the continuation of the VGA.

In the VGA, there is no room for a third party such as an owner or a collective of shareholders. The members are the shareholders and they share, in one way or another, in the profit. The board of the VGA determines how much profit can be distributed and how and when, and the members are the beneficiaries. This strengthens the bond between the VGA and its members and ensures that a member, as consumer, prefers to spend through the own VGA. The relationship thus becomes stronger, more durable, and more intense. The consumer has become a hostage, but has consciously chosen that fate. They still have the freedom to break off the relationship, that is there is no contractual obligation, but the consumer will refuse this due to the evident advantages and the limited number of disadvantages.

Internet Communities

It is likely that VGAs will communicate with their members via email, SMS, MMS and the Internet. Power companies already communicate with their user about their actual and expected energy consumption. Power companies also provide their users with advice on how to reduce their energy consumption. Computer and software suppliers alert their users to updates of programs and protection against dangerous viruses. This service provision is easily expandable into *alert services*, notification of new possibilities and warnings during sub-optimal situations.

Consumers will accept these *alert services* only from service providers and (meta) brands that they trust and to whom they have given permission to send them such messages. The marketing demonstrated by the VGA goes a lot further than 'permission marketing', however. We might call it 'acceptance marketing' or 'cooperation marketing'.

Many Internet communities already exist in specific domains or with specific themes. These communities originated with, and were developed by consumers. Internet communities (operating often internationally) could be the beginning of consumer VGA clubs. The current Internet communities may be divided into the following groups:

- Communities that are based on hobbies and interests, such as Virtual Gardens, Antique Cars, and other communities around a hobby or interest.
- Communities based on transactions and collective purchasing in relation to a specific product class: for example Virtual Vineyards. Often membership is required. This looks like a consumer purchasing cooperative.
- Communities based on representing interests: Silicone Survivors, a protest movement against the 'deadly' breast implants of Dow Corning and other producers. (This is a clear example of an 'old-fashioned' strong opposition of producer and consumer.)
- Communities based on exploration and relaxation, for instance focused on sex, games or cartoons.

Note that these communities have a rather small base of interest. The VGA is likely to cover broader and more domains than these Internet communities.

THE VGA AS A PERSONAL LIFE MANAGER

Basically, the notion of the VGA presumes that people prefer to optimize long-term goals, transform these into mutually consistent decisions, and implement them in a serial pattern of effective, efficient and coordinated actions. In fact, if we stretch the notion of the VGA as a purchase intermediary, we arrive at the notion of a life plan. This plan may combine personal ambitions, personal capabilities and personal circumstances. It may be adapted along the route as growth takes place and new circumstances develop. Life planning is a new concept for most people. For a variety of reasons, many lack clear goals, muddle through, and take only small incremental steps. Often, their decisions reflect past experiences rather than future goals, resulting in living life on a day-to-day basis. Of course, people should be completely free to adopt long-term goals or live on a (more?) relaxed day-to-day basis. However, to the extent that they would prefer some life planning, they should be facilitated – for example by a VGA.

Life planning would address, for example, the following aspects:

1. A long-term ambition or perspective.
2. The motivation to achieve these objectives.
3. Abstract thinking in scenario ('what if') terms.
4. A broad field of vision, extending beyond the traditional and obvious possibilities.
5. Personal capabilities and perceived *personal control*, the conviction that goals can be achieved through personal effort. This is the opposite of fatalism, the feeling that 'others' and the circumstances determine someone's fate (external control).

Career choice advice and career counselling have been well-accepted concepts for a long time. Probably something similar could be developed for life planning.

So the VGA will gradually expand its own function over time to the point where it is not limited to the market domain. This is because the distinction between what is relevant to consumers and what is relevant to citizens, often cannot be made very well. In the second place, the package concept only applies when more domains are covered by the system. As the number of domains increases, it becomes less accurate to speak of a VGA as merely a customer-supporting facility. A VGA may not focus exclusively on purchases and consumption of products and services. After all, achieving consumptive objectives also requires a match with activities relating to different responsibilities including generating income, and these, in turn, need to be matched with desires related to the use of leisure time.

Over time, the VGA pulls information towards itself about various domains. The synergy that is created by the combination may subsequently be used to derive information and recommendations that are tailored towards the individual. In any case, at that point the designation of VGA no longer covers the width of the support that is being offered. Therefore, a VGA may develop into a personal life manager.

Here we will briefly discuss the VGA that has developed into such a function. We do not predict if, how and when such a VGA would come into existence. We merely describe the concept that might develop as an extension of the purchase and consumption-related VGA concept discussed thus far.

EMPHASIS ON WELL-BEING

The VGA places an emphasis on the experience of general happiness and well-being. The goal is to maximize the *life-time well-being*. By this we mean the average sum, over time, of positive and negative experiences. Sometimes negative experiences are needed to avoid even more negative experiences or to actually gain more positive experiences. This means that it may be necessary to allow certain negative experiences to occur. The simplest example is a subcutaneous injection (for many people a somewhat negative experience) intended to avoid the more negative experience of illness. Accepting a disadvantage in the present may result in a proportionately large advantage in the future. Consider an investment with a large expected return later. It is the function of the VGA to achieve as positive a balance as possible between positive and negative experiences over time, taking into account the life expectancy, positive opportunities and negative risks. Although this is a universal pursuit of humans that is not time-specific, the achievement of a positive balance will be sharpened due to the options that the VGA may offer.

Resource Allocation Support

The gradual transition of the VGA concept may best be explained by an expenditures hierarchy. This hierarchy indicates how small, less important spending aspects combine to form larger, more important expenditures. Conversely, it indicates how the large-expenditure categories may be subdivided into smaller categories and units. An expenditures hierarchy may best be imagined as an (inverted) tree diagram in which each branch splits into even smaller branches until the level at which further branching is no longer possible nor useful. At the lowest level we find the individual characteristics of products and services. The next level represents brands. At the next higher level, cars belong to the category of transport or mobility. At this level we should no longer refer to 'expenditures', but to 'allocations'. At the most general level, three basic resources may be allocated: money, time and energy (own effort).

In their role as consumers, people make decisions within and about these levels: about product characteristics, or about types of products or brands. The decisions that are made about more general categories are often implicit. It rarely occurs that someone decides for his own household which percentage of income should be devoted to each expenditure category in a certain period. Even fewer people will make explicit decisions about the allocation of the general resources money, time and energy, in order to achieve important life goals. So, the higher the level of expenditures/allocations, the more implicitly the decision will be made (while, in fact, higher level decisions are more important in their effects). The paradox is that the more important and impactful the decision is, the less it is experienced as such. Here the VGA may help out.

The VGA can offer insights into the way in which considerations are apparently being made between the more global allocation categories. Feedback can help people to determine for themselves what they want to achieve and how they want to do it. The VGA is then able to point to deviations between the apparent allocations and the allocations that would correspond to major personal objectives. The VGA may also provide relevant recommendations as needed. These recommendations may subsequently lead to adjustments in allocations or to changes in ambitions and objectives.

In human decisions, the future is usually weighted less than the present. There is less information about the future, it is impossible to determine the future based on current knowledge, and the future weighs less heavily than the present from a psychological perspective. Yet a decision in the present may influence a person's future well-being. The VGA clarifies the consequences of current decisions for future situations and will lead to a stronger position of the future in everyday decisions.

The VGA may also indicate what someone is giving up or should be giving up in the current pattern of expenditures and allocations. If current expenditures and allocations mean that objective A turns out to be receiving a high priority, the VGA can clarify the opportunity costs (missed opportunities) with respect to objectives B, C and D. People are often less satisfied with a selected objective if they feel that the other objectives are attractive as well. They experience regret. The VGA may provide the arguments related to why the selected objective is the most attractive one.

The Broker Function

The VGA is aware of various objectives of various people in their specific situations. Because these people are not aware of each other's objectives, possessions and desires, they are unable to determine where they can help each other, or where collective activities or possessions might provide a mutual benefit. Imagine three people who live in the same neighbourhood. Each of them wants to use a high-pressure cleaner from time to time. In the current situation, the lack of communication is responsible for the fact that each person possesses a high-pressure cleaner. Suppose that none of these three people care about ownership of the cleaner. They just care about the possibility to use it from time to time. The VGA is then capable of advising collective purchase, or another form of mutual collaboration (borrowing/leasing).

The same argument applies to services, of course. By using the available information to check which houses in a neighbourhood need some paintwork, the VGA could, on behalf of the owners, make a deal with a painting company. The VGA can also help to make common interests visible of people who do not know each other. In this regard the VGA is not just a consumptive but also a social broker or intermediary (again, privacy is key; no action is taken without permission of the concerning person).

By result, society may be much more transparent, leading to other ways of organizing major activities. For example, a full-time relationship with a specific employer seems less probable in the future. Employers and steady employment may be replaced by temporary clients and contracts. The VGA arranges the link between the demand and supply and makes agreements about the continuity and intensity of work, obviously in agreement with already known individual preferences. This possibility is supported by technological developments that facilitate tele-working. The VGA will then serve as a temporary employment office that focuses on a more efficient use of ambitions, talents and preferences of 'freelancers'.

Social Control by the VGA

Suppliers and consumers are now largely anonymous to each other. The many business (and business-like) relationships in society and the reduced mutual solidarity may lead to a high level of alienation. Alienation, lack of mutual interest and lack of social control are factors that facilitate rule-breaking and possibly even crime. There is a threat that a social situation will develop in which solidarity cannot easily be found, and egocentric, if not parasitic, behaviour becomes more and more widespread.

A person who wants to be associated with a VGA gives up part of his privacy by making extensive personal data available. These data accumulate over time. In such a system, fraudulent behaviour will be identified much earlier than in a system where each transaction takes place as a distinct event and no individual data are stored. A VGA that is able to follow an insurance claim pattern of a particular person over many years may easily detect fraud. This makes fraudulent behaviour less likely. In addition, members of a community will be less inclined to bring damage to fellow members or to unjustly limit the profit that is to be divided among them.

In order to protect its own position and functioning, a VGA may refuse a new member. During their membership, some members may make a negative contribution to the result (read: the well-being of the other members). If this is the result of calamities such as illness and death, the VGA functions as a safety net and provides insurance based on solidarity. If the negative result is the consequence of fraud, parasite behaviour or consciously taken disproportionate risks, a member may be expelled or receive a reduced profit share. Incidentally, expulsion means that the built-up knowledge disappears, that advice is no longer available, and that the switch to another VGA will be very difficult.

Whoever disturbs the well-being of others will have to carry the responsibility for that behaviour and will have to accept the consequences of being excluded from the community, of no longer having access to information tailored to the person, of no longer being able to profit from economies of scale, of no longer being able to present themselves as a respected member, and so on. If someone commits fraud and is caught, he or she risks becoming a pariah. The *bona fide* members are prepared to surrender a part of their privacy in exchange for the certainty of fair play and mutual control. People who have nothing to hide and trust the VGA have no need to invoke privacy protection. Although *Big Brother* is looking over one's shoulder, this is not done selectively. Everyone in the system is subjected to the same controls and agrees to that situation beforehand.

If someone takes large risks and therefore may cause high costs for the system, he or she may also be fined with a reduction in the profit distribution. It is interesting to determine how the monitor functions. We can think of a few examples. It is possible to monitor by satellite how fast a specific car is moving. Information about this may be stored in the database. A member that commits speeding and other traffic violations, may receive a warning from the VGA. If a member actually causes damage as a result of risky behaviour, he or she may be held personally responsible. The VGA may also create rules that members are expected to follow, for example: expulsion from the VGA when drinking and driving.

Thus, the system is based on clarity, fairness and solidarity. In effect, this represents traditional, ideological values that once upon a time people thought could be enforced through political–ideological systems. It has become apparent that these systems were not based on realistic assumptions. It seems somewhat cynical that the reasoning presented here suggests that only the capitalistic ideological system may eventually lead to these values, albeit via a detour of the VGA.

WELL-BEING: LIFE EFFECTIVENESS AND EFFICIENCY

The pursuit of well-being through life management may be seen as the maximization of life effectiveness and life efficiency. Life effectiveness or life efficacy refers to achieving personal goals and ambitions. Life efficiency relates to the costs and benefits. The better efficiency has been arranged, the easier it is to realize effectiveness. Although we realize that we are encroaching on the philosophical domain, we dare to make a few statements here.

Until now, it has not actually been possible to state that people are able to arrange their lives in a well thought out manner. The number of potential objectives is very large and internally competitive. Human ambitions eventually tend to adjust to limited possibilities, but in fact people would wish for much more than can be realized in a single lifetime. This implies choices. The more efficient choices are, the better personal goals can be achieved. But for many people it is true that not all goals can be achieved. Resources such as time, money and energy may be insufficient. Therefore, it is necessary to make considerations and decisions with respect to these basic resources. Although the internal balancing between money, time and energy for the achievement of personal goals is a crucial issue, little is known about the process by which trade-offs take place An occasional researcher has studied the issue (Wąsowicz-Kiryło, 2000), but there is no systematic knowledge regarding this crucial area.

We plead here for a larger social and scientific interest in the way in which basic allocations and trade-offs between money, time and energy are being made. It is impossible here to take an advance on the insights that might develop from such research. It is clear that money, time and energy are partly exchangeable. People can buy time and save energy by outsourcing tasks for payment. We will briefly discuss each of the three, while paying attention to the developments that occur in that area. In addition, in Figure 7.1 we present a summary of the various substitutions that may take place.

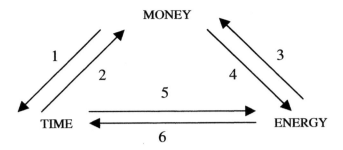

Figure 7.1 Possible substitutions between time, money and energy/effort

For sake of clarity, we present an example for each possible substitution:

1. Hire a servant to save time
2. Do-it-yourself to save money
3. Spend effort to earn money
4. Hire a service to save energy/effort
5. Spend more time to save effort (work slowly)
6. Spend more effort to save time (work hard)

With respect to the allocations at the highest level (related to money, time and energy or effort), it may be noted that these are partly determined by personal choices, but are also partly determined by constraints: restraining pre-conditions. We can use this as a basis to point out different groups in the society, people who possess structurally different degrees of freedom in the use of money, time and energy for the realization of personal objectives. On the one side of the continuum the *haves* are located, and on the other side the *have-nots*. In this context, the *haves* are those people who have such a sizeable budget at their disposal in terms of money, time and energy that they are not restricted in their budgeting for the achievement of their objectives. They are able to achieve their goal by allocating money, or time, or energy, or by using a combination of those factors. An example is the young, healthy heir of an early-deceased millionaire. He has a lot of money, a lot of time, and energy in abundance. The *have-nots* are at the other end of the spectrum. They are not able to realize their ambitions because they have insufficient money and insufficient time and energy. For example, the mother on social security who spends most of her 24 hours managing a household with four children. Has no money, no time and is always tired.

In between both extremes, there are interesting groups of people who have access to more of one allocation resource than another, but who are in principle able to spend more from one category to compensate for the lack in another category. Retired people who are financially comfortable have a lot of time at their disposal, but may lack the energy to undertake all sorts of activities. They replace adventuresome, but tiring travelling by a taking a relaxed cruise. They delegate the planning of the trip to others, as well as the transport to the airport and the toiling with suitcases, and are well prepared to pay extra for these services.

The manager who has sufficient money and sufficient energy but a shortage of time, will arrive at other considerations and contemplations. He may perhaps be inclined to spend his money to save or even create time. Youngsters who have relatively large amounts of time and energy will use time and energy (and less money) to achieve a goal. The budgets are partly determined by the size of the 'stock'. These groups are, in principle, able to adjust budgets through allocation decisions. The question of whether this is possible, and if so, how, is often approached intuitively. Almost nothing is known about the most basic considerations that people make. And the oddity is that people do not realize which considerations they make themselves with respect to money, time and effort, let alone that it is clear how these are allocated across the present and the future. Actually we are considering a complex allocation of resources across a six-cell matrix, of which the one entrance relates to the resources and the other entrance makes the distinction between the present and the future. See Table 7.1.

In the ideal case, people would have to determine the budgets in each of the six cells, after they had determined their various life goals, in such a way that the available total budget would not be exceeded. This is a very complex decision. The question of whether people consider the allocation of money, time and energy, is already odd in itself. Incidentally, this leads to deviations of rational behaviour that have been described by Scitovsky (1976). He indicated that illusions exist with respect to the three resources. These illusions cannot be combined with a rational starting point. Below we will cite and interpret his observations freely.

Table 7.1 An allocation matrix for money, time and energy/effort

	Present	Future
Money	1	2
Time	3	4
Energy, effort	5	6

Money Illusion

In the most objective and strictest sense of the word, money is an exchange resource, but people assign their own value to it. This leads to the situation that they are not very capable of dealing with the objective value of money. For example, they continue saving, even if they have no specific purpose for it. They even save at the end of the period that relates to their life expectancy, like a nest-egg.

During inflation, people experience their money decreasing in value, yet they continue saving to compensate for the loss. If the loss in value is compensated in income by the authorities at the end of a labour period (the 'inflation correction'), people incorrectly see this as an increase of income and therefore as an increase of spending possibilities. In this way, inflation is actually being stimulated by inflation correction. People want more money, even when they have so much money that they do not know how to spend it. Here we want to extend the money illusion into the illusion that money itself guarantees happiness. A shortage of money limits the experience of happiness, but an excess of money creates concerns about how to handle it.

Illusion of Time

People ask for more free time, but when they have it at their disposal, they do not succeed in finding a satisfying way to spend it. People spend the evening in front of the television set, even though this leads to negative feeling afterwards. In an objective sense, time is a constant factor of which the units are equal amongst each other. Yet from a psychological perspective, time is not a constant, which means that in some situations time has more, and in some situations less, personal value. People more easily accept activities and thus time obligations for the future than for the present. Future time seems to be discounted, whereas present time seems to be valued more highly. Another strange phenomenon is that people want a higher compensation for a delay of payment than they want to pay for having the payment earlier.

Illusion of Effort

People take the car to work so they do not have to spend extra effort, and in the evening they work on their home trainer or go to the fitness centre to exercise. People indicate that they are tired after spending energy on less attractive activities, while they feel stimulated after spending the same amount of energy in more rewarding activities such as sports. Some people have a nervous breakdown if they have to spend too much energy in a short time; others become overworked if, during that same time, they cannot spend enough energy.

While these illusions in themselves are sensational, they create an almost comical effect when combined. People spend money to save time and spend time to save money. They spend energy to save time and they spend time to relax. They spend money to avoid spending energy and spend energy to make more money. In addition, these effects almost always occur simultaneously, not just between people and over time, but even with the same person and within a short timeframe.

The budgeting of resources that is crucial for the achievement of important personal life goals turns out to be a chaotic process into which there is still little insight. This results not only in a restriction of life efficiency, but also in a restriction of life effectiveness. Due to systematic and arbitrary deviations of rationality during the application of resources, people do not succeed in achieving their life goals. In other words, people block their own well-being. This disadvantage is reduced by the fact that most people are not aware of this issue. But it does provide an opportunity to help people to arrange their lives more efficiently and effectively.

The VGA may fulfil an important function in this regard. The first function is to point out inconsistencies to people. This will help them to become aware of deviations of rationality which they can use as a basis for implementing changes. A second function is to make concrete suggestions with respect to budget adjustment.

> Given the current pattern of activities and the health situation of the past month, it is necessary to add half an hour of extra movement per day for the next two weeks and to spend more time outdoors. You will find walking routes that have been selected for you on the website and two teeing-off times have been reserved on the golf course. You are playing with Peter Johnson. You do not know him, but apart from golf, you share horse riding and Mayan culture as common areas of interest. The appointments have been entered into your calendar already. Do you prefer something else? Please let us know.

Big Brother is not only watching you, but also watching over you if (and to the extent that) you wish it.

APPRECIATION OF TIME

In a system where the considerations are being made visible, it turns out that not only budgets but also stocks are limited. 'Units' of money, time and energy can only be spent once. Because units of money and energy can in principle be replenished, people will realize that time is the only truly scarce resource. This may be expected to have a positive influence on the subjective value that people assign to time. Time develops itself in the experience of people as the most precious good. Time cannot be stored, saved or preserved for later. At most it can be bought or exchanged against other resources, with the understanding that this is only possible in relation to units of time, not or only in a limited way in relation to the total amount of time. The other two resources will be used more to generate time. Let us therefore consider time once more, but this time by paying attention to its future significance.

Due to the greater emphasis on well-being, more attention will be paid to the ultimate criterion: the (mathematical) product of quantity and quality of time, in other words of life span and happiness. Time needs to be managed and evaluated with the help of criteria that have been determined individually but that fall within the limitations of the interest of the group. *Time management* is not the right phrase for this, since this term is used in a short-term interpretation. Time management as we mean it here is management over the course of time, even a lifetime.

It may be expected that the current and future generations will differ significantly in their experience of time. There are various reasons for this. Photo and video images are very realistic these days and show people who are no longer alive. Several decades ago people had static or otherwise jerky, vague and non-coloured images that suggested that the documented people and situations were recorded long ago. That same suggestion of time difference no longer applies. Historical images present themselves in a very realistic way to us. People who no longer live seem to communicate with us via the media in a way that is no different from people who are still alive.

In the second place, due to societal and political developments, people are forced to consider the financing of the later stages of their lives, their retirement plans and pensions. At a relatively young age people are expected to be concerned with their own future. The old age phase is becoming more concrete and therefore also becomes a psychological reality.

In the third place, time pressure in the faster society has increased to such an extent that time has become a more prominent *commodity*. Everyone is 'busy', which in effect means that there is a lack of time. The stock has remained the same, but more activities and events need to be done within the same amount of time. On a continuous basis new tools intended to save time are introduced on the market, but their only effect is that more is done in the available time, rather than less in the same time. The introduction of the word processor is an example. Texts now do not need to be first written, then typed and finally corrected. Technology has made it possible to integrate these activities and save time. Yet the surplus is not being reserved for activities that increase well-being, but for increasing productivity, as if the investment in future well-being is more important than well-being itself. This is not meant to suggest that working cannot be part of well-being, but that the balance tends to favour work systematically. If productivity is the instrument to a goal, the instrument seems to have gained dominance over that goal. Therefore it is an illusion to think that technological developments will lead to further time savings. But also because of the increasing time pressure, the value of time is increasing, which means that the increase in productivity will come to a logical limit. The introduction of the concept of *quality time*, reserving time on the calendar for relaxation, can be seen as a signal that the limit is approaching, that the scarcity of time is becoming visible, that the value of time is increasing, and that it is being handled more consciously.

Money counts strongly as the equivalent of possessions. We expect, in connection with the previously discussed issues, that money will play a more important role as a tool for obtaining time and for optimizing the use of time. Possessions will decrease in significance. Owing to the economic growth in the Western world, the scarcity of possessions and the function of possessions as a status-increasing tool is declining. This has reduced the value of possessions, not just in an absolute sense, but also in a relative sense in relation to the other two scarcities. Because the Western consumer can fulfil many wishes, needs shift towards the direction of services that may save time and energy and that have functions that cannot be satisfied by material goods. If this means that time and energy become available, then these can be spent on activities from which consumers derive a greater satisfaction.

Recent marketing approaches and new financing options make it clear to the customer that ownership of products is not necessary for a positive consumption experience. Consumption experiences may even be hindered by an 'overdose' of owned possessions. After all, there are also disadvantages associated with it. Possessions have to be acquired, paid for, maintained, repaired, administered, insured, finished, replaced and/or thrown away. This requires money, time and energy that, by consequence, is not available for the consumption experience itself. Frequent innovations lead to a rapid obsolescence of existing possessions. Long-lasting possessions may lead to boredom, especially for persons who are oriented towards undergoing as many different, stimulating experiences as possible. Whoever does not own, but borrows, rents or leases durables is able to keep using the most recent provisions with all the corresponding advantages. Possessions may limit the match to specific usage goals and usage situations. A convertible car is fun in summertime but not so functional in winter. As a result of the growth of options for temporary possessions and through financial constructions, products that originally were status-related are becoming available for a broader public. This weakens the association between possessions and status. The primary focus is no longer on owning it, but on the experience and perception that the product or service is able to generate. Pine and Gilmore (1999) called this the 'experience economy'. We expect therefore that, increasingly, money will be used to acquire the experience itself, which is not the same as the experience through possessions.

The conclusion here is that time is the ultimate criterion, that money is increasingly used on behalf of time and the experience of time, and that energy is the tool for optimizing the ratio of time and money. The obvious complication is that spending energy also requires time.

It is therefore still unclear how the interconnected considerations actually take place, although it is clear that these are important for the quality of life. People on their own are not able to make these considerations without insight into their own priorities and expenditures. When the VGA provides this insight, people may arrange their lives differently. This goes much further than changing purchase patterns. The transformation, the substantive reorientation that we are referring to, will be expressed not just at the individual level, but also at the social and cultural levels.

8. Epilogue

INTRODUCTION

The scenario offered in this book is not based on empirical facts, which is typical of scenarios. There is no scientific basis for the system that was proposed. Yet we have attempted to present an approach that is internally consistent and coherent. Also, it is an extrapolation of the combination of market trends that may be observed at present. The presented scenario may best be interpreted as a dressed-up hypothesis. It is not our intent to sit back and wait to see whether the hypothesis will be confirmed. Instead, the function of the scenario is to identify early warning signals that indicate the nature of the development. We should be alert to these signals. We have the impression that they can already be observed – otherwise we would not have written this book. What is more, without any arrogance, we dare to say that earlier publications have resulted in concrete attempts by a number of profit and non-profit companies to initiate VGA-oriented strategies. Confidentiality agreements do not permit us to reveal the companies concerned. These companies insist on having established some VGA status before their strategic ambitions are made public. This sounds surprising as most companies are not so secretive about their strategies. However, a VGA strategy differs in several respects from other strategies: it can be established quickly (organizing partners is relatively quick and easy as compared to setting up new production lines), it means a stronger bond with customers and a new type of competition that differs in three ways from traditional market competition. First, a VGA status implies non-switching customers (you win them or you lose them – forever). Second, competition may not be confined to traditional market boundaries. A bank may compete with a hotel chain, a mobility provider, and with a real estate developer. Organizing supply rather than producing supply becomes the core competence, together with insight knowledge of customers. Third, copying the competitor is no longer feasible. The way supply is organized in a VGA system, based on customer insights, simply cannot be copied.

The ultimate competence that will make or break market power is the understanding of individual customers. It is not possible to understand individual customers on the basis of their demographic characteristics, nor on the basis of their purchase pattern. Customer understanding is not limited to one domain and is not restricted to one period either. Customer understanding is to be taken as a continuous process that extends and deepens over time. This is the only means to a long-lasting powerful position in the market. Any other approach or instrument is second best.

Kim and Mauborgne (2005) argued that competition could be evaded by searching for the so-called 'blue ocean' – a market domain that is not governed by market and marketing conventions. One of the most prevalent conventions may be that customer value is created as a direct result of market supply. This convention urges market suppliers to produce goods and services with the hope and expectation of meeting customer demand (Figure 8.1).

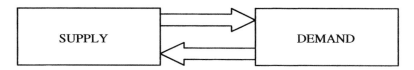

Figure 8.1 Value created by market supply

Another model, slightly different in appearance, but significantly different in meaning, addresses a systematic flaw in this relationship, which results in ineffective and inefficient gaps between supply and demand or between a supplier and a customer. Markets should be governed by a model that empasizes an indirect relationship between supply and demand. The relationship is mediated by customer understanding as the core concept in marketing (Figure 8.2).

Figure 8.2 Value created by supply and understanding the customer

This figure stresses the need for understanding customers before supply is designed, produced and marketed. It is important to note that customer understanding is to be taken in the broadest possible meaning and should not be restricted to the product or service level. As a simple example: a consumer may not 'need' a cosmetics product, but recognition by peers.

On the one hand, this position is not really new. On the other hand, we may note that the number of systematic attempts to develop customer understanding as the core of business strategy is very, very limited. All too often, customer understanding is a matter of marketer intuition. There is no problem with intuition per se, but people overrely on it, resulting in a wide array of marketing successes and failures.

The function of this book is to stimulate the discussion about future marketing and about the consequences of marketing developments for customers and customer behaviour, both in business-to-consumer and business-to-business markets. Company strategies are often related to the medium term and not to the period of about five years that has been used here as a starting point. Even though the far away future is a long shot, the discussion about long-term scenarios may be quite relevant. It forces us to consider trends that can be extrapolated from past and present experiences, and to consider developments that may unfold in a highly unstable manner. A warning is due here: it happens too often that we determine how a single, specific development might be important for our own company, while it is more likely that its fate is determined by several developments taking place simultaneously. The reality of dynamic markets should invite us to consider combinations and interactions of developments instead of adopting a comfortable, narrow focus.

A discussion about the long term helps us to 'reason in reverse' regarding the strategic goals that we have posed for the medium term. If we take the long-term future as a starting point, we have to go to the 'past' ('backcasting') to arrive at the medium-term future. These kinds of exercises are somewhat artificial. Yet they are necessary in a time where change may be the most typical characteristic.

We observe that the question regarding the future development of customer behaviour is not one that occupies a central place in science. Science naturally has a preoccupation with hard facts. The present weighs more heavily than the future. Scientists are assessed and appreciated for publishing about the results of scientific research. Scientific journals place a great emphasis on data. As reflections on future developments do not produce any data, they encounter a high threshold for scientific publication. This restrains many scientists from paying attention to the question of what future markets and future customer behaviour will look like. While science should be expected to produce innovative ideas, its results are rather conservative.

Many questions remain to be addressed; too many for this book. We will select the most pertinent questions and attempt to address these briefly in the final pages.

1. How far-fetched is all of this?
2. Could people finally make rational decisions with the help of the VGA?
3. Will people actually allow such an infringement on their lives to occur?
4. Could databases be abused?
5. Will we become happier? Is Utopia within reach?

HOW FAR-FETCHED IS ALL OF THIS?

No absolute answer is possible to this question. We dare to state that we have not intentionally searched for eccentric ideas. We see this book as deriving from the combination of the most important developments that markets have undergone in the past few years. We do not exclude any trend breaks and we do not know whether the developments, even if they are as we predict, will present themselves more quickly or more slowly. The developments might also go in different directions. In that case we have read the stars wrongly and charted an incorrect course.

There are a few arguments that we want to address in order to answer the question posed here in a different way. Perhaps Cell 16 may seem far-fetched, but is it not true that innovative ideas have amazed us almost continuously over the past few decades? Technology has continued to surpass our thinking about future technological developments. We see this as an important incentive to get ahead of the facts that are available at present.

COULD PEOPLE FINALLY MAKE RATIONAL DECISIONS WITH THE HELP OF THE VGA?

Over time, rationality will increasingly be approached, not according to the quality of our own mental functioning, but based on the combination of information provided by the consumer, the database system that contains this information together with historical information about the consumer, and the software that integrates the various inputs into a consumption proposal.

The transition from an irrational or a-rational customer towards a more rational system is not abrupt, but requires years of learning. It cannot be determined whether the end result is rational. The only thing that can be determined is whether the decisions and expenditures are connected with the priorities of the individual customer. Whether these priorities themselves are rational is a normative question that cannot be answered with a simple 'yes' or 'no'.

WILL PEOPLE ALLOW SUCH AN INFRINGEMENT ON THEIR LIVES TO OCCUR?

This question has been addressed before, but should be considered once again, because there are not only market effects, but also social and cultural effects. We are convinced that consumers will get used to major supporting systems as a logical extension of service provided. Most people react almost by definition with a wait-and-see approach and are often resistant to new developments, but are more than happy to adopt them later when they have proven beneficial to others.

Only a small proportion of the population is strongly oriented towards innovations and is prepared to act as innovators or pioneers (Rogers, 1983). The others will wait, sometimes even cynically so. After several years it often turns out that the relevant innovation has such a high degree of penetration and positive evaluation, that people can no longer imagine life without it.

Consumers might object that decisions that they now make themselves, will be taken away from them, as if they are being put into guardianship! We can only react to this by pointing to the way in which products and services have developed themselves over the years. They have gradually taken over more and more decisions and actions from consumers. The thermostat of the central heating determines when the boiler will burn higher or lower; the thermostat even 'knows' our weekly schedule at what time we get up and go to bed. We replaced the squeezing of oranges with orange juice from a carton. Sensors regulate the turning on and off of the light and we no longer even need to operate the sunblinds. Household appliances take over tedious, uncomfortable, time-consuming and tiring activities. It is possible to use commercial parties to take care of our travel, wake us up, sort our messages, present us with cooking recipes, and warn us that certain documents are expiring. Our cars remind us spontaneously that they need to be serviced. We are even supported in finding the most efficient route to our destinations by automatic systems. So, in fact, if we see freedom as the liberty to do things we actually do not want to do, then freedom has been severely restricted and will be restricted even more. But freedom may also be taken as the opportunity to make a choice out of the large variety of activities worth undertaking, without having to spend time, energy and resources on obligatory tasks.

What remains is the philosophical question of free will. Free will is a blessing, but what are the costs? Freedom may imply responsibilities, tasks and burdens that could be avoided. Freedom does not necessarily mean that all possible decisions are subject to a person's will. Freedom may also include the will to delegate. Freedom may even be an illusion, because we are less free than we think (Wegner, 2002). We interpret our behaviour as a consequence of our 'free' decisions, and ignore most unconscious and situational factors as determinants of our behaviour.

There is an almost unlimited number of examples that indicate that consumers hand over tasks, burdens and responsibilities to technological systems. Consumers embrace new products and services that increase the comfort, reduce the physical and mental costs, and take away the burden of spending scarce resources. It does not seem probable that this trend will reverse in the future.

COULD DATABASES BE ABUSED?

The simple, straighforward answer to this question is: 'yes'. There are many examples showing that databases may be sold or given access to for purely commercial reasons. On the other hand, there are so many positive possibilities to use the databases that abuse is not directly obvious. Furthermore, the party that might want to abuse the database, for example to obtain extra contacts with consumers, would give itself away in doing so. Evident abuse has a negative boomerang effect that cannot be corrected.

The database as referred to here is, essentially, a tool for the consumer to have a more easy access to relevant information, to process the information as well as possible, to obtain advice based on this information, and to delegate tasks to the VGA. The supplier is no longer merely engaged in 'make and sell' (as in Cell 1), but in 'understand and respond'. For this, a database is a critical instrument. As a database is the heart of the VGA, it will not jeopardize its own existence and position by abusing it. Abuse or a use other than desired by the consumer can be prevented by making explicit agreements with individual consumers about the manner in which the data may be used.

WILL WE BECOME HAPPIER? UTOPIA WITHIN REACH?

How better could we conclude the book than by saying 'yes, if' or 'no, unless'. And this is indeed what we do. But we are somewhat more specific. The system as we have proposed it will contribute to human well-being.

Imperfections in allocations, wrong decisions and incorrect considerations are being made visible, corrected, taken away, made impossible, or delegated. Decisions of people will move more in line with their own priorities. In this regard it would be a positive contribution to well-being.

On the other hand, there is the disappointing phenomenon of the so-called 'hedonic treadmill'. People display the phenomenon that they develop new needs as soon as the previous needs have been satisfied. Therefore there always remains a difference between what we want and what we have or can do. This limits our experience of well-being. We call it the preference shift (Van Praag et al., 1979). Preference shift is an individual effect that develops over time due to habituation to a higher level of need satisfaction. The more people are satisfied in their wishes and desires, the more they increase their demands in terms of quality and well-being. New, higher reference points and standards develop for comparison and for (dis)satisfaction. What used to be a luxury has become a commodity a few years later. What used to be 'extra' eventually becomes 'normal'. Consumers quickly get used to an improved product or an improved service provision. Furthermore, they compare themselves with others who are a little better off than they are, and they wish to reach that situation. This phenomenon also has no limits, because in reaching a new social situation, it is always possible to find some others who are still a little better off. This limits the experience of well-being as well. This is called the reference shift (Van Praag et al., 1979). Reference shift occurs when, after satisfaction of existing needs, consumers start comparing themselves with other consumers.

The desired situation therefore appears to be quite elastic. Well-being, as it has been said in the literature, is more a consequence of personality than of the comparison between desired and actual situations. After all, the desired situation has a tendency to continuously shift upwards. Under the influence of this comparison, new needs and preferences develop.

This raises the question, what is the purpose of all this and where will it stop? Obviously, it stops at the point where and when individual happiness is reached. Yet, as happiness is a momentary and relative situation, it can only be obtained through the experience of a positive change. So, perhaps, happiness is not the ultimate criterion. Possibly we should pursue something dynamic like excitement or surprise (something that the VGA could also provide).

The foregoing may have far-reaching implications for consumer behaviour. More knowledge and research is needed to assess possible relationships between VGAs and consumers. To what extent is the consumer free and autonomous or how much is he or she being directed (manipulated)? To what extent are consumers being 'spoiled' and made dependent on a VGA (learned helplessness, Seligman, 1975)? Will a new form of dependence on systems develop, such as patients becoming dependent on the hospital (hospitalization)? To what extent will the consumer still be responsible for decisions that the VGA has made for him or her? And will the higher goals of self-actualization and happiness actually be achieved or will the hedonistic treadmill keep turning?

Our viewpoint is simple: although happiness will perhaps continue to be unattainable, the mere activity of trying to reach it is relevant and interesting enough in itself. The pursuit of happiness may provide more gratification than the result. And it is in this pursuit that the new marketing may prove to be a big help.

References

Aaker, D.A. (1991), *Managing Brand Equity*, New York: The Free Press.

Alderfer, C.P. (1972), *Existence, Relatedness and Growth*, New York: The Free Press.

Antonides, G. and W.F. van Raaij (1998), *Consumer Behavior. A European Perspective*, Chichester, UK: John Wiley.

Arkes, H.R. and C. Blumer (1985), 'The psychology of sunk cost', *Organizational Behavior and Human Decision Processes*, **35**, 124–40.

Arndt, J. (1976), 'Reflections on research in consumer behavior', *Advances in Consumer Research*, **3**, 213–21.

Atkinson, J.W. (1964), *An Introduction to Motivation*, Princeton, NJ: Van Nostrand.

Bandura, A. (1986), *Social Foundations of Thought and Action. A Social Cognitive Theory*, Englewood Cliffs, NJ: Prentice-Hall.

Beltman, R., E. Peelen and P. Walewijn (2000), *CRM: De Klant Centraal*, Alphen aan den Rijn, The Netherlands: Samsom.

Berlyne, D.E. (1963), 'Motivational problems raised by exploratory and epistemic behavior', in S. Koch (ed.), *Psychology: a Study of a Science*, Part 5, New York: McGraw-Hill, pp. 284–364.

Bicchieri, C., R. Jeffrey, B. Skyrms and P. Danielson (1998), 'The dynamics of norms', *Ethics*, **108**, 828–29.

Blattberg, R., G. Getz and A. Thomas (2001), *Customer Equity,* Boston, MA: Harvard Business School Press.

Brandenburger, A.M. and B.J. Nalebuff (1996), *Co-opetition*, Doubleday.

Breedveld, K. and A. Van den Broek (2001), *Trends in de Tijd*, The Hague, The Netherlands: Social and Cultural Planning Bureau.

Buchanan, R. and C. Gilles (1990), 'Value managed relationship: The key to customer retention and profitability', *European Management Journal*, **8**, 523–6.

Diener, E. and R.E. Lucas (1999), 'Personality and subjective well-being', in D. Kahneman, E. Diener and N. Schwartz (eds), *Well-being: The Foundations of Hedonic Psychology*, New York: Russell Sage Foundation, pp. 213–29.

Dwyer, F.R., P.H. Schurr and S. Oh (1987), 'Developing buyer–seller relationships', *Journal of Marketing*, **51**, 11–27.

Gredal, K. (1966), 'Purchasing behaviour in households', in M. Kjær-

Hansen (ed.), *Readings in Danish Theory of Marketing*, Copenhagen: Einar Harcks Forlag, pp. 84–100.

Gupta, G. and D.R. Lehmann (2005), *Managing Customers as Assets*, Philadelphia, PA: Wharton School Publishing.

Haley, R.I. (1968), 'Benefit segmentation', *Journal of Marketing*, **32**, 30–35.

Herzberg, F., B. Mausner and B. Snyderman (1959), *The Motivation to Work*, New York: John Wiley (second edition).

Jacoby, J. (1977), 'Information overload and decision quality: Some contested issues.' *Journal of Marketing Research*, **14**, 569–73.

Jacoby, J. (1984), 'Perspectives on information overload', *Journal of Consumer Research*, **10**, 432–36.

Jacoby, J., D.E. Speller and C.A. Kohn (1974), 'Brand choice behavior as a function of information load', *Journal of Marketing Research*, **11**, 63–9.

Kahneman, D. and A. Tversky (1974), 'Judgment under uncertainty: heuristics and biases', *Science*, **185**, 1124–31.

Keiningham, T.L., T.G. Vavra, L. Aksoy and H. Wallard (2005), *Loyalty Myths*, New York: John Wiley.

Kim, W.C. and R. Mauborgne (2005), *Blue Ocean Strategy*, Boston, MA: Harvard Business School Press.

Klein, N. (1999), *No Logo*, New York: Picador.

Langer, E.J. (1982), 'The illusion of control', in D. Kahneman, P. Slovic and A. Tversky (eds), *Judgement under Uncertainty: Heuristics and Biases*, New York: Cambridge University Press, pp. 231–8.

McCracken, G. (1986), 'Culture and consumption: A theoretical account of the structure and movement of the cultural meaning of consumer goods', *Journal of Consumer Research*, **13**, 71–84.

Maslow, A.H. (1954), *Motivation and Personality*, New York: Harper & Row.

Naert, P. and B. Coppieters (eds) (2000), *Globalisering. Zegen en Vloek*, Tielt, Belgium: Lannoo/Scriptum.

Nelson, P. (1970), 'Information and consumer behavior', *Journal of Political Economy*, **78**, 311–29.

Nelson, P. (1974), 'Advertising as information', *Journal of Political Economy*, **81**, 729–54.

Olshavsky, R.W. and D.H. Granbois (1979), 'Consumer decision making. Fact or fiction?', *Journal of Consumer Research*, **6**, 93–100.

Oskamp, S. (1965), 'Overconfidence in case-study judgments', *Journal of Consulting Psychology*, **29**, 261–5.

Paas, L.J. (1998), 'Mokken scaling characteristic sets and acquisition patterns of durable and financial products', *Journal of Economic Psychology*, **19**, 353–76.

Paas, L.J. and A.A.A. Kuijlen (2001), 'Towards a general definition of customer relationship management', *Journal of Database Marketing*, **9**, 51.

Pieters, R.G.M. and W.F. Van Raaij (1988), *Reclamewerking*, Houten, The Netherlands: Stenfert Kroese.

Pine II, B.J. (1993), *Mass Customization: The New Frontier in Business Competition*, Boston: Harvard Business School Press.

Pine II, B.J. and J.H. Gilmore (1999), *The Experience Economy. Work is Theatre & Every Business a Stage*, Boston: Harvard Business School Press.

Pine II, B.J., D. Peppers and M. Rogers (1995), 'Do you want to keep your customers forever?', *Harvard Business Review*, March–April, 103–14.

Plasmeijer, P. (1999), *The Influence of the Internet on Prepurchase External Search for Financial Services*, Rotterdam, The Netherlands: Erasmus University (dissertation).

Poiesz, Th.B.C. (1999), *Gedragsmanagement. Waarom mensen zich (niet) gedragen*, Wormer: Inmerc.

Poiesz, Th.B.C. (1996), 'Relatiemarketing en de dynamiek van het "psychologisch contract"' *Themadossier Relatiemarketing*, Platform '95.

Poiesz, Th.B.C. and R. Frambach (1999), 'Marketing onderworpen aan een SWOT-analyse; een visie op haar ontwikkeling en toekomst,' in R. Frambach and Th.B.C. Poiesz (eds), *Trends in Marketing*, Alphen aan den Rijn, The Netherlands: Samsom.

Poiesz, Th.B.C., J. De Heer and W.F. van Raaij (2001), 'Consumer research implications of marketing and ICT developments', *European Advances in Consumer Research*, **5**, 66–72.

Porter, M. and E.O. Teisberg (2006), *Redefining Health Care. Creating Positive-Sum Competition to Deliver Value*, Cambridge, MA: Harvard Business School Press.

Rangan, V.S. and B. Shapiro (1994), *Business Marketing Strategies*, New York: McGraw-Hill.

Ratchford, B.T. (1980), 'The value of information for selected appliances', *Journal of Marketing Research*, **17**, 14–25.

Reichheld, F.F. (2001), *The Loyalty Effect: The Hidden Force behind Growth, Profit, and Lasting Value,* Boston, MA: Harvard Business School Press.

Reynolds, T.J. and J. Gutman (1984), 'Advertising is image management', *Journal of Advertising Research*, **24**, 27–36.

Richie, M.F. (1989), 'Vals-2', *American Demographics*, July, p. 25.

Rogers, E.M. (1983), *Diffusion of Innovations*, New York: The Free Press.

Rokeach, M. (1973), *The Nature of Human Values*, New York: The Free

Press.

Russo, J.E. and P.J.H. Schoemaker (1992), 'Managing overconfidence', *Sloan Management Review*, **33**(2), 7–17.

Rust, R.T., V.A. Zeithaml and K.N. Lemon (2000), *Driving Customer Equity: How Customer Lifetime Value is Reshaping Corporate Strategy*, New York: The Free Press.

Schwartz, B. (2004), *The Paradox of Choice. Why More is Less*, New York: HarperCollins.

Schwartz, S.H. and W. Bilsky (1987), 'Toward a universal psychological structure of human values', *Journal of Personality and Social Psychology*, **53**, 550–62.

Scitovsky, T. (1976), *The Joyless Economy*, New York: Oxford University Press.

Seligman, M.E.P. (1975), *Helplessness: on Depression, Development, and Death*, San Francisco, CA: Freeman.

Shefrin, H.M. and M. Statman (1985), 'The disposition effect to sell winners too early and ride losers too long: Theory and evidence', *Journal of Finance*, **40**, 777–92.

Snyder, M. and K.G. DeBono (1985), 'Appeals to image and claims about quality: Understanding the psychology of advertising', *Journal of Personality and Social Psychology*, **49**, 586–97.

Solomon, M.R. (1992), *Consumer Behavior*, Boston, MA: Allyn and Bacon.

Storey, C. and C.J. Easingwood (1998), 'The augmented service offering: a conceptualization and study of its impact on new service success', *Journal of Product Innovation Management*, **15**, 335–51.

Stremersch, S. and G.J. Tellis (2002), 'Strategic bundling of products and prices: A new synthesis for marketing', *Journal of Marketing*, **66**(1), 55–72.

Thaler, R. (1980), 'Toward a positive theory of consumer choice', *Journal of Economic Behavior and Organization*, **1**, 39–60.

Thaler, R.H. and H.M. Sheffrin (1981), 'An economic theory of self control', *Journal of Political Economy*, **89**, 392–406.

Treacy, M. and F. Wiersema (1995), *The Discipline of Market Leaders. Choose your Customers, Narrow your Focus, Dominate your Market*, New York: HarperCollins, Perseus Books.

Tversky, A. and D. Kahneman (1974), 'Judgment under uncertainty: Heuristics and biases', *Science*, **185**, 1124–31.

Uusitalo, L. (1979), *Consumption Style and Way of Life*, Helsinki, Finland: Helsinki School of Economics (dissertation).

Van Asseldonk, T.G.M. (1998), *Mass-Individualisation*, Tilburg, The Netherlands: Tilburg University (dissertation).

Van der Zwan, A. (1965), 'Het bezit van duurzame consumptiegoederen',

Economisch-Statistische Berichten, **50**, 644–7.

Van Lun, E. (2005), *Van Massamerk naar Mensmerk*, Heerhugowaard, The Netherlands: F&G Publishing.

Van Praag, B.M.S. (1971), 'The welfare function of income in Belgium: An empirical investigation', *European Economic Review*, **4**, 33–62.

Van Praag, B.M.S., A. Kapteijn and F.G. Van Herwaarden (1979), 'The definition and measurement of social reference spaces', *The Netherlands Journal of Sociology*, **15**, 13–25.

Van Raaij, E.M. (2001), *The Implementation of a Market Orientation*, Enschede, The Netherlands: Twente University Press (dissertation).

Van Raaij, W.F. (1998), 'Interactive communication. Consumer power and initiative', *Journal of Marketing Communications*, **4**(1), 1–8.

Van Raaij, W.F. (2000), *Economische Psychologie in de 21ste Eeuw*, Tilburg, The Netherlands: Tilburg University (inaugural address).

Van Raaij, W.F. and A.Th.H. Pruyn (1998), 'Customer control and evaluation of service validity and reliability', *Psychology & Marketing,* **15**, 811–32.

Van Raaij, W.F. and W.M. Schoonderbeek (1993), 'Meaning structure of brand names and extensions', *European Advances in Consumer Research*, **1**, 479–84.

Van Raaij, W.F. and T.M.M. Verhallen (1994), 'Domain-specific market segmentation', *European Journal of Marketing*, **28**(10), 49–66.

Vargo, S.L. and R.T. Lusch (2004), 'Evolving to a new dominant logic for marketing', *Journal of Marketing*, **68**(1), 1–17.

Wąsowicz-Kiryło, G. (2000), *Financial and Behavioral Resources Budgeting. Toward the Resource Cross-elasticity in Acquisition Behavior*, Warsaw, Poland: University of Warsaw (dissertation).

Wegner, D.M. (2002), *The Illusion of Conscious Will*, Cambridge, MA: MIT Press.

Wright, P (1974), 'The harassed decision maker: time pressure, distractions, and the use of evidence', *Journal of Applied Psychology*, **59**, 555–61.

Zeleny, M. (1996), 'Customer-specific value chain: beyond mass customization', *Human Systems Management*, **15**, 93–7.

Index